Art and Architecture
of the World's Religions

Art and Architecture of the World's Religions

Volume 2

LESLIE ROSS

GREENWOOD PRESS
An Imprint of ABC-CLIO, LLC

A B C ☰ C L I O

Santa Barbara, California • Denver, Colorado • Oxford, England

Library of Congress Cataloging-in-Publication Data

Ross, Leslie, 1956–
   Art and architecture of the world's religions / Leslie Ross.
       p. cm.
   Includes bibliographical references and index.
   ISBN 978-0-313-34286-8 (hard copy set : alk. paper) — ISBN 978-0-313-34288-2 (hard copy v. 1 : alk. paper) — ISBN 978-0-313-34290-5 (hard copy v. 2 : alk. paper) — ISBN 978-0-313-34287-5 (ebook set) — ISBN 978-0-313-34289-9 (ebook v. 1) — ISBN 978-0-313-34291-2 (ebook v. 2)
   1. Art and religion.   2. Architecture and religion.   3. Religions.   I. Title.
N7790.R67   2009
203'.7—dc22   2009014590

13 12 11 10 09 1 2 3 4 5

This book is also available on the World Wide Web as an eBook.
Visit www.abc-clio.com for details.

ABC-CLIO, LLC
130 Cremona Drive, P.O. Box 1911
Santa Barbara, California 93116-1911

This book is printed on acid-free paper ∞

Manufactured in the United States of America

Contents

Volume 1

Volume 2

Contents

Introduction

A friendly study of the world's religions is a sacred duty.
— Mahatma Gandhi, *Young India*, September 2, 1926

SCOPE AND PURPOSE

This book is designed to provide an introduction to the major religions of the world, with special focus on the art and architectural forms associated with these belief systems. The study is divided into two volumes with a total of 16 chapters. Each chapter concentrates on a major world religion and includes sections on: (1) the origins and development of the religion, (2) the principal beliefs and key practices, (3) the traditional art and architectural forms, and (4) selected and illustrated examples of art and architecture.

The religions covered in these volumes include belief systems of very ancient origin as well as religions whose development is, relatively speaking, more modern. Some of the ancient religions discussed in these volumes are not currently practiced today in their original form. The evidence for these ancient belief systems is primarily archaeological, art historical, or textual. The reader will thus find information on prehistoric belief systems, ancient Mesopotamian, Egyptian, and classical Greek and Roman religions in volume 1. Religions that continue to be practiced today in various forms, such as Judaism, Christianity, Islam, Hinduism, and Buddhism are covered primarily in volume 2. The reader will also find chapters on the indigenous belief systems of Africa, Oceania, Australia, and the Native Americas in volume 1, and discussions of Shintoism, Taoism, and Confucianism in volume 2.

World map.

Of necessity, even given the scope of these volumes, readers will doubtless find that several world religions as well as several regions of the world are not included in this study. A full and completely comprehensive coverage of all of the world's religions and the religious art and architectural forms associated with all geographic regions of the globe would require a far greater number of volumes. Such comprehensive coverage is not the goal of this present study. These two volumes are simply designed to present an introduction to the richness, vastness, and diversity of this material, with the hope that readers will be encouraged and inspired to delve further. It is assumed that readers will recognize that the materials presented in these volumes represent carefully selected examples of the religious art and architecture traditionally associated with a diversity of faith traditions and practices. Readers are encouraged to understand that any gaps they may perceive in the coverage of world religions or world regions in these volumes are not intended to either maximize or diminish the status and importance of any world religions or regions.

Further details and suggestions about how to use this book most effectively are found at the end of this introduction. In the interim, some definitions will usefully serve to explain the goals and parameters of this study. Before proceeding further, it will be helpful to define what we mean by "religion" and what we mean by "religious art and architecture."

WHAT IS RELIGION?

Religion can be (and has been) defined in many different ways. Religion can be seen as the inherent human impulse to seek meaning in life and death, to develop and maintain a relationship with the transcendent, to explain or justify why certain things happen in life, to connect or communicate with higher and nonhuman forces, to receive guidance on correct attitudes and ethical behaviors, and to provide and promote community among cultural groups. All of these factors have played significant roles, to a greater or lesser extent, in the development, promulgation, rise, and transformation of the world's religions. The questions traditionally posed by humans, and diversely answered by the world's religions, address the same issues and concerns.

> Is there something "greater than us" that we identify as deity? If there is, who or what is this divine entity? . . . What is the nature of the world and the heavens? Did they emanate from the divine, were they created by the divine, or are they unrelated to anything divine? . . . What is humanity's place both within the world and in relation to the divine? . . . What does the divine expect or demand of us? What actions are good, and what actions are bad? Is there life beyond death? If there is, how is it gained or received? What will it be like? Where will it happen? How shall we get there?[1]

These are some of the fundamental questions that are addressed by the world's religions and to which these religions have responded in diverse ways. Of course, it should be noted that many scholarly and popular studies have been devoted to the question-asking process itself—why, where, when, and in what circumstances do religious beliefs arise? Are religions invented by humans simply to provide meaning in life, to understand and control their circumstances? Or, are religious beliefs firmly based on the awareness or revelation of divine, cosmic, suprahuman forces? Much intriguing—and often contentious—discussion about the origins of religion has been undertaken by many writers.[2] Although these topics are certainly touched on in these present volumes, this study is less concerned with the meanings, purposes, and origins of religion overall but is instead focused on the visible manifestations of diverse beliefs via the evidence in art and architectural forms. In other words, this study assumes (1) that religious beliefs have played a central role in the lives of humans through history and (2) that this fact is exceedingly well demonstrated in humanity's attention to the creation of religious art and architecture, past and present.

WHAT IS RELIGIOUS ART?

For purposes of this study, religious art is defined as any and all visible manifestations of belief. Such a broad definition is necessary because, throughout history and across the world, religious beliefs and practices have been, and continue to be, visually manifested in a great diversity of forms. These forms, of course, include the tangible and traditionally enduring monuments of architecture, sculpture, and painting, customarily studied by art historians. Readers will thus find much coverage devoted to these generally familiar categories of art, albeit in culturally diverse varieties. The forms of religious architecture discussed in these volumes include temples, shrines, synagogues, mosques, churches, and other worship environments constructed by humans. Numerous works of painting and sculpture are also discussed, such as stained glass windows, icons, statues of holy figures, pictorial narrative scenes, and so on. Many of these examples of painting and sculpture are closely associated with religious architectural structures, while other examples are less closely tied to specific architectural contexts.

However, our broad definition of religious art—as any and all visible manifestations of belief—also extends to forms of art that do not necessarily fit neatly into the traditional art historical categories of architecture, painting, and sculpture. Religious art is also performative; it involves actions and attitudes. Much attention in these volumes is thus devoted to the context and usage of religious art—not simply its appearance. Dance, music, song, ceremony, ritual actions, prayer, and the performance of individual or collective worship are all integral aspects of the religious nature of religious art. This study thus delves into areas of investigation most often associated with the disciplinary fields of archaeology, anthropology, and ethnographic studies. What the creators and users of religious art do and say (or do not say) about their beliefs and practices are critical factors in any efforts to understand the visual culture of past and present societies.[3] The ongoing dialogues between art historians, anthropologists, archaeologists, and scholars of visual and popular culture are reflective of a broader approach to the study and definition of religious art, from which this own work has benefited.

Indeed, it can be said that religious art not only reflects, but also creates, the primary symbols of meaning for humans and societies. In this sense, the diverse forms of religious art (from small to large scale, monumental to ephemeral, sophisticatedly crafted to more rustic) all function as activating agents as well as reverberations of humankind's ultimate concerns. A respectful approach to the world's religions, and attentive study and analysis of their visible manifestations can be seen as "itself a deeply religious act."[4]

THE IMPORTANCE OF ART IN RELIGIOUS STUDIES

While the specific beliefs and practices associated with the world's religions vary greatly, all religions can be said to share an interest in creating or acknowledging a sense of the sacred in visible or symbolic form. Humans have expressed their religious impulses from prehistory to the present day in visible forms. Whether these forms are simple or elaborate, small or large scale, permanent or temporary, religious art and architecture serves to make beliefs visible and tangible in ways that sacred texts, writings, and scholarly commentaries do not. Indeed, it can be argued, that it is far more likely to be the visual forms of religious expression that impress and resonate most profoundly with believers and nonadherents alike. The visual expression of religious beliefs in art and architectural forms may be seen as the unity in diversity among the world's religions. It is this shared artistic impulse that provides the primary lens for this study of the world's religions.

> Across time, space, and culture, in all of humanity's wrestling with life and its meaning, the issues have been the same. Recognition of this bond with peoples of the past can give rise within us to an empathy capable of transcending our theological and liturgical particularities, an empathy that permits us to value another people's answers, another people's religion.[5]

When one first enters a medieval cathedral filled with the colorful glow of stained glass windows, or when one first stands in front of a Hindu temple replete with complex and elaborate sculptural carvings, the very special power of the visible expression of belief impresses one with extreme directness and tangibility. Whether this sensation is one of awe, or fright, or confusion, or attraction combined with a desire to know more, it can be said that religious art and architecture serves a critical function as the primary visible entrance or doorway into the belief systems of the world.

Entrances and doorways may be actual physical structures. They may also be seen as more symbolic passages into the realms of religious beliefs. In either case, these entrances are often evoked and assisted by their visual forms. On the literal level, the design of religious architecture functions to create and signal sacred space—space that, in various ways, is differentiated, or set apart, from nonsacred space. One may enter a physical structure of faith (whether a temple, a church, a shrine, or a mosque, for example) by passing through a physical doorway. The entrance to the structure represents a transition from the exterior to the interior—from the world outside to the interior world of the sanctified space. The creation of physical and often permanent forms of sacred space can be (and often has been, historically and presently) a massive architectural undertaking. Many of the most visibly impressive architectural structures created by humans through the ages and around the world have been and continue to be designed for religious purposes.

However, sacred space can be (and often has been, historically and presently) created via other means. Sacred spaces can be created by an event, a temporary acknowledgment of the confluence or presence of sacred forces or powers, a performance, a ritual, or a recognition of preexisting sacredness in the world or in specific natural landscape features. Whether sacred space involves an imposing or humble architectural construction, major or minor manipulation of the environment by humans, or simply involves an acknowledged orientation to, or focus on, a ritual action or landscape feature, it can be argued that visuality, in some form, always plays a critical role in serving as an entrance/doorway/passage into belief systems, and also in directing and inspiring belief.

These closely related functions, of directing, promoting, and inspiring belief, are the fundamental grounds for religious art and architecture through the ages. Art plays an especially didactic and faith-directing role in some religious traditions, specifically in serving to teach adherents about the primary tenets of the religion in the form of visual narratives or symbols. It is often the case that these visual images are actually and physically located at the literal entrances to sacred buildings. These images, such as paintings and sculptures, which may show the events and stories from the sacred texts or may visually narrate the lives and deeds of holy figures, are common in many religious traditions. The appearance of these visual images on the exteriors of sacred structures often reinforces the transition from the secular and worldly to the sanctified and holy interior space.

Of course, the function of visual imagery as an entrance or passage into faith traditions is by no means restricted to the form of physical doorways on the exteriors of buildings. Visual imagery very often enriches the interiors of sacred spaces as well, and in this location serves the same function as doorways into the faith. Regardless of scope, location, and portable or nonportable format, visual images can serve as directing doorways into faith traditions by providing information and inspiration.

The inspiring function of religious art and architecture takes on a variety of different forms as well. The directive and edifying presentation of visuals (especially those involving figural imagery) is not demonstrated or shared by all faith traditions. Islamic religious art, for example, maintains an extremely rich visual tradition but one that generally avoids figural, narrative imagery in sacred spaces. Even so, the primary aim of Islamic religious art is to inspire, and to assist adherents in their experience of the faith. One will not, for example, find visual illustrations of the life of Muhammad in a traditional Islamic mosque, whereas in traditional Eastern Orthodox churches one will often be overwhelmed by the abundance of visual imagery on all available surfaces—walls and ceilings—plus the holy icons placed throughout the church and on towering icon screens. Many protestant Christian denominations avoid visual imagery to a greater or lesser extent, whereas Buddhism and Hinduism are, in general, faith traditions that, in their various branches, significantly rely on visual imagery to teach and to inspire.

Whether in abundant and colorful presence or in determined and sparing absence, visual imagery plays a critical role as an entryway into all faith traditions. The creation and usage of sacred space also serves to provide a fundamental and shared passageway into the belief systems of the world. The study of the art and architecture associated with the world's religions is the guiding gateway through which we truly must enter in our goals of understanding and appreciating this unity and diversity.

> What distinguishes sacred art from other varieties is the window it opens onto another world—a world that is vaster, stranger, more real, and more beautiful than the world we normally encounter. . . . What makes art sacred is not what it depicts, but the way it opens onto transcendence and carries the viewer into it.[6]

It is the hope that this current publication will serve to convey and highlight to readers some sense of the brilliant diversity and shared fundamental importance of the visible in the study of the world's religions.

HOW TO USE THIS BOOK

Readers will find that each chapter, in each of the two volumes of this book, has the same structure. Each chapter includes the same four parts (the origins and development of the religion, the principal beliefs and key practices, the traditional art and architectural forms, and selected and illustrated examples). This is deliberate. In visualizing and planning these volumes, the author has taken great care to ensure that each religion (or related sets of religions) discussed in the book is given the same coverage as all of the others, in the sense that each chapter is approximately the same length.

At the same time, this carefully designed structure has created some significant challenges for the author and will doubtless do so for readers as well. Not all materials ever fit neatly into any scholarly structure, as this book also hopes to demonstrate. Although it is quite sensible to begin discussions of many world religions with a section on the origins and development of the belief system, this model works especially well for religions that can be traced to specific historical founders (such as Muhammad for Islam, Jesus for Christianity, and the Buddha for Buddhism). But, more than a great many other religions of the world cannot be traced to specific founders, and the origins of these belief systems cannot be so easily identified using the historical and chronological model, which assumes some type of starting point before which the religion was not revealed, known, developed, or practiced. Indeed, many of the world's belief systems are of unknown origin and reflect very ancient cultural traditions of diverse groups in a variety of different world regions. One can trace the historical origins of the religion of Islam to Muhammad, for example. One can discuss the cultural context in which he lived; one can describe the importance of his received revelations and the differences his message posed to then-current and previously practiced belief systems in the Arabian peninsula. But one cannot do so with religions such as Shinto and Hinduism, for example, nor for a great many other religions whose origins cannot be traced to a specific founder, although developments can often be traced through a series of later influential figures. In these cases, the origins and development chapter sections are far less relevant scholarly constructs, as the text hopes to point out as well.

Discussions of the principal beliefs and key practices of the religions covered in these volumes have also been fraught with a number of challenges. Several of the world's belief systems are quite clear about what their adherents are expected to believe and to do. Many religions have creeds, dogmas, or detailed descriptions of beliefs deemed to be correct. However, even within religious systems that are highly dogmatic, many variations and practices may exist. Not all Catholics attend Mass, and not all Jews adhere to the dietary regulations suggested in the ancient Hebrew scriptures. When Buddhism arrived in Japan in the sixth century CE, many of the ancient Shinto deities were given new names or developed other shared correlations with Buddhist deities. Islam recognizes the Hebrew and Christian traditions of prophetic revelation. Many Hindus regard the Buddha as one of many divine or divinely inspired beings. Some Protestant Christian groups maintain rites and rituals that are very akin to Roman Catholicism, whereas other Protestant Christians are extremely concerned to avoid any forms of worship practice that resemble those of Catholic or Orthodox Christians. Attempts to define the principal beliefs and key practices of a vast diversity of world religions will always run the danger of generalization. It is hoped that the present study manages to avoids this to some extent.

The traditional art and architectural forms associated with various belief systems also vary widely. In many cases, monumental architecture (temples, churches, synagogues, and mosques) are the most obvious examples, and the reader will appropriately find many discussions of these forms of sacred structures in several chapters of these volumes. Apart from these diverse architectural forms, and the arts of painting and sculpture often associated with them, the reader will also find discussions of how the sacred buildings were and continue to be used for the specific purposes of different faiths. How buildings appear—as well as how they function—are both extremely important considerations in any discussion of religious art. However, the creation of permanent architectural structures (of large or smaller scale) does not characterize the arts traditionally associated with all religions or regions of the world. This fact is acknowledged and embraced in this study, so readers can expect to find a great diversity of forms of art described or illustrated in different chapters.

Each chapter includes a number of accompanying illustrations as well as several selected examples that are described in fuller detail. Although approximately the same overall number of illustrations are included in each chapter, readers will find that the number of examples chosen for more detailed discussion varies somewhat per chapter. It is hoped that this slight divergence in format between chapters will be welcomed and understood by readers as reflective of the richness of these materials overall as well as the potential for any one example to inspire additional research and consideration. In some cases, longer discussion of several illustrated examples will be found. In other cases, the number of examples signaled out for more detailed discussion is fewer. In some chapters, several groups of images are discussed together as examples of different forms that share the same general subject matter but that may demonstrate different dates, styles, and interpretations of traditional imagery. In all cases, the more focused discussion of specific examples is designed to complement and expand on the materials explored in each chapter, and in no cases is it designed to maximize the importance of selected monuments or diminish the importance of others not included.

At the conclusion of each chapter, readers will find a section titled "Bibliography and Further Reading." At the end of volume 2, readers will also find a selected bibliography. The chapter bibliographies—although fairly lengthy—in all cases necessarily represent only a sampling of the materials available for study of the art and architecture of specific religions or world regions. These listings are, of course, not comprehensive by any means, but may, at least, alert students to some of the major sources and the names of important scholarly specialists. Much additional scholarship exists, and continues to be avidly created, on any number of aspects of the world's religious art and architecture. Indeed, the bibliography on particular monuments (such as the Parthenon in Athens) would, in itself, at least fill a complete volume. Specialists might find the bibliographic listings in these present volumes rather eclectic in their inclusion of not only magisterial overall studies but also more arcane articles in highly specialized journals. This too is deliberate. It is hoped that the bibliographies and suggestions for further reading include samples of the vast range of works that demonstrate the ongoing and lively discussion into which students are encouraged to delve further.

The visual arts play an extremely important role in how religions and faith adherents self-define as groups and as individuals. In all cases, and in more than many ways, all faith traditions seem to require art (or at least an artful presentation of actions), and it is on this basis that this study rests.

NOTES

1. Byron Shafer, ed., *Religion in Ancient Egypt: Gods, Myths, and Personal Practice* (Ithaca, NY: Cornell University Press, 1991), 4–5

2. For example, Daniel Dennett, *Breaking the Spell: Religion as a Natural Phenomenon* (New York: Viking, 2006); Barbara King, *Evolving God: A Provocative View of the Origins of Religion* (New York: Doubleday, 2007); David Lewis-Williams, *The Mind in the Cave: Consciousness and the Origins of Art* (New York: Thames and Hudson, 2002); Steven Mithen, *The Prehistory of the Mind: A Search for the Origins of Art, Religion, and Science* (London: Thames and Hudson, 1996); John Pfeiffer, *The Creative Explosion: An Inquiry into the Origins of Art and Religion* (Ithaca, NY: Cornell University Press, 1985); and John Super and Briane Turley, *Religion in World History* (New York: Routledge, 2006).

3. "Visual culture" is a relatively recent term as well as academic discipline. It refers to the broad-ranging analysis of many forms of visual evidence and is especially concerned with acknowledging and including materials not covered in traditionalist art historical studies. Visual culture studies argue that all forms of visual evidence, from high to low—from the traditional art historical hierarchy of architecture, sculpture, and painting—to forms such as film, television, advertising, fashion, and popular visual ephemera are all important indicators of the values and concerns of diverse cultures. The applicability of this approach to religious art is obvious, as much religious art comes in forms that reside outside the traditional art historical arenas and styles. For example, see Margaret Dikovitskaya, *Visual Culture: The Study of Visual Culture after the Cultural Turn* (Cambridge, MA: The MIT Press, 2005); James Elkins, *Visual Studies: A Skeptical Introduction* (New York: Routledge, 2003), W.J.T. Mitchell, "What Is Visual Culture?" in *Meaning in the Visual Arts: Views from the Outside*, ed. Irving Lavin (Princeton, NJ: Institute for Advanced Study, 1995), 207–17; and David Morgan, *The Sacred Gaze: Religious Visual Culture in Theory and Practice* (Berkeley: University of California Press, 2005).

4. John Dixon, "Art as the Making of the World: Outline of Method in the Criticism of Religion and Art," *Journal of the American Academy of Religion* 51, no. 1 (1983), 34.

5. Shafer, 4.

6. Huston Smith, *The Illustrated World's Religions* (San Francisco: Harper San Francisco, 1986), 6.

BIBLIOGRAPHY AND FURTHER READING

Adams, Doug, and Diane Apostolos-Cappadona, eds. *Art as Religious Studies*. New York: Crossroad, 1987.

Dennett, Daniel. *Breaking the Spell: Religion as a Natural Phenomenon*. New York: Viking, 2006.

Dikovitskaya, Margaret. *Visual Culture: The Study of Visual Culture after the Cultural Turn*. Cambridge, MA: The MIT Press, 2005.

Dixon, John. "Art as the Making of the World: Outline of Method in the Criticism of Religion and Art." *Journal of the American Academy of Religion* 51, no. 1 (1983): 15–36.

Dixon, John. "What Makes Religious Art Religious?" *Cross Currents* 43, no. 1 (1993): 5–25.

Introduction

Eliade, Mircea. *Symbolism, the Sacred, and the Arts*. Edited by Diane Apostolos-Cappadona. New York: Crossroad, 1985.

Elkins, James. *Visual Studies: A Skeptical Introduction*. New York: Routledge, 2003.

King, Barbara. *Evolving God: A Provocative View of the Origins of Religion*. New York: Doubleday, 2007.

Lavin, Irving, ed. *Meaning in the Visual Arts: Views from the Outside*. Princeton, NJ: Institute for Advanced Study, 1995.

Lewis-Williams, David. *The Mind in the Cave: Consciousness and the Origins of Art*. New York: Thames and Hudson, 2002.

Mitchell, W.J.T. "What is Visual Culture?" In *Meaning in the Visual Arts: Views from the Outside*, ed. Irving Lavin, 207–17. Princeton, NJ: Institute for Advanced Study, 1995.

Mithen, Steven. *The Prehistory of the Mind: A Search for the Origins of Art, Religion, and Science*. London: Thames and Hudson, 1996.

Morgan, David. *The Sacred Gaze: Religious Visual Culture in Theory and Practice*. Berkeley: University of California Press, 2005.

Morgan, David. "Visual Religion." *Religion* 30, no. 1 (2000): 41–53.

Pfeiffer, John. *The Creative Explosion: An Inquiry into the Origins of Art and Religion*. Ithaca, NY: Cornell University Press, 1985.

Prown, Jules. *Art as Evidence: Writings on Art and Material Culture*. New Haven, CT: Yale University Press, 2001.

Shafer, Byron, ed. *Religion in Ancient Egypt: Gods, Myths, and Personal Practice*. Ithaca, NY: Cornell University Press, 1991.

Smith, Huston. *The Illustrated World's Religions*. San Francisco: Harper San Francisco, 1986.

Super, John, and Briane Turley. *Religion in World History*. New York: Routledge, 2006.

—9—

Judaism

ORIGINS AND DEVELOPMENT

Judaism is the oldest of the three major monotheistic religions of the world. Both Christianity and Islam later evolved from the foundations of Judaism. Although Judaism today is one of "the smallest of the world religions . . . it has had an influence and a geographical distribution inversely proportional to its size."[1] With a lengthy, often unsettled, and dramatic history of dispersal, assimilation, and persecution, Judaism's survival and tenacity are remarkable evidence of the strength of this ancient faith.

The origins of the Jewish faith are traditionally traced back to the second millennium BCE as recounted in the Hebrew scriptural accounts of the lives and deeds of the great patriarch and prophet Abraham and the eminent prophet Moses. Both of their lives are set in the mid-second millennium BCE. Abraham, who lived in ancient Mesopotamia (present-day Iraq), is considered to be the first to receive direct revelations from the one true God, the creator of the universe. The belief in the primacy of this one God posed a contrast to the contemporary polytheistic practices of the other ancient peoples of Mesopotamia and established Judaism as the world's oldest monotheistic belief system. According to tradition, God entered into a covenant (pact, agreement) with Abraham, whose absolute trust in and loyalty to God would be rewarded by prosperity and a homeland for his descendants. Abraham was originally named Abram, and the covenant with God was symbolized by his taking on the new name, Abraham ("Father of Many Nations"). The peregrinations of Abraham and his wife, Sarah, through the eastern Mediterranean regions, the births of his children and grandchildren, and their eventual move to and enslavement in Egypt form the major narratives of early Jewish history as recorded in the biblical book of Genesis.

Of singular importance for the greater formation and development of the Jewish religion is the figure of the prophet Moses, who was chosen by God to free the Israelites and lead them out of captivity in Egypt during the 13th century (ca. 1240) BCE. This event, known as the Exodus (and described in the biblical book of Exodus), involved many years of traveling in the wildernesses of the Sinai peninsula en route to the promised land of Canaan/Israel. During these years, guided by a series of revelations from God, Moses established the fundamentals of the Jewish faith in the form of laws and commandments regarding ritual practice and ethical conduct. The receipt by Moses, on Mount Sinai, of the Tablets of the Law (including the Ten Commandments) is often seen as the single most important event in the formation and codification of the Jewish faith. These God-given commandments ultimately confirmed the covenant between God and the Israelites and established Judaism as the faith of this distinct community of God's chosen people.

The Israelites ultimately reached the promised land of Canaan under the leadership of Joshua and established a kingdom, ca. 1000 BCE, under a series of important monarchs: Saul, David, and David's son Solomon. The first temple in Jerusalem was constructed under the direction of Solomon in the mid-10th century BCE. This period suggests "a golden age that has remained the focus of Jewish aspirations ever since."[2]

Subsequent tumultuous centuries, however, involved periods of territorial loss and Jewish exile (notably as a result of the Babylonian invasion in the early sixth century BCE), the return of many Jews to Israel, first the Greek and then the Roman occupation of the territory in the first century BCE, the Jewish revolt against the Romans, the final destruction of the Temple in Jerusalem in the first century CE, and the eventual diaspora or dispersal of Jews around the world.

With the evolution and eventual dominance of Christianity in the Mediterranean (and ultimately European) world and the later growth and spread of Islam, Jews came to regarded by many as an inferior, heretical, and dangerous group, especially in Christian-dominated western Europe. Jewish history "in Christendom is one of nearly constant persecution. Massacres, expulsions, and forced conversions were common. . . . [Jews were] excluded from most professions . . . restricted in their choice of domicile . . . [and] sequestered in special town quarters."[3]

Anti-Jewish attitudes, or "anti-Semitism" (a term that properly refers to the racial/ethnic/language group of ancient Semitic peoples, including Arabs, but in standard usage refers only to Jews), has a lengthy history. Jews, like Christians in the Roman world, were persecuted for their refusal to worship the Roman gods and emperors and for their perceived subversive activities. Both Jews and Muslims were persecuted under Christian dominance in medieval and Renaissance Europe.

A notable period of exception to the social and religious antagonism between the three related faiths of Judaism, Christianity, and Islam is represented by Muslim-dominated Spain in the 10th through 12th centuries. Often referred to as a medieval "Golden Age" for Jews, or a period of "convivencia" (coexistence, toleration),[4] the Muslim dynasties of medieval Spain, with some exceptions, allowed Jews to flourish "in a manner unthinkable under Christian rule."[5] Although recent critical scholarship has questioned this "myth of an interfaith utopia"[6] in medieval Islamic Spain, this period is traditionally regarded as a time during which the virulent anti-Jewish attitudes of earlier and later periods were held, to some extent, in check.

Sephardic Jews (from the term *Sephardim*, "Spaniards") trace their heritage primarily to medieval Spain, whereas Ashkenazi Jews (from the term *Ashkenazim*, "Germans") trace their heritage primarily to medieval German lands. All Jews who refused to convert to Christianity were expelled from Spain in the late 15th century, and pressures in Christian-dominated northwestern Europe led to the departure of many Jews to eastern Europe. Jewish communities also developed among those who remained in the Middle East as well as in many other world regions: China, India, Ethiopia, the Ottoman Empire, and the Americas.

"The situation of Jews as the outcasts of Christian European society seemed to take a turn for the better"[7] during the 18th century "with the gradual emancipation of the Jews in western Europe and the Americas from their second-class status, as a result of Enlightenment ideals."[8] However, in the late 19th century, anti-Jewish movements again arose, based on racial supremacist concepts. According to these theories, Jews were racially inferior, and they were again subjected to persecution and revilement. The ultimate outcome of this modern anti-Semitism took place in the mid-20th century under the auspices of Nazi Germany and Adolf Hitler (1889–1945), whose attempt to rid the world of the "racially inferior" resulted in the massacre of approximately two-thirds of the Jews in Europe during the Holocaust (1941–45). This unspeakable tragedy for the Jewish people also resulted in further mass migrations of Jews (especially to North America) and, ultimately, the founding of the modern State of Israel in 1948, designed to bring "an end to nearly 1900 years of Jewish disenfranchisement."[9]

PRINCIPAL BELIEFS AND KEY PRACTICES

"As a religion, Judaism has three essential elements: God, Torah, and Israel."[10] For Judaism, there is only one God, the creator of the universe, the transcendent ultimate reality "who is inherently beyond the capacity of words to describe."[11] The God of Judaism is, however, considered to be present and active in the world, and biblical narratives especially detail God's communications in various forms to humans. Judaism can be described as ethical monotheism, in that the belief in one God requires adherence to a set of codes of moral conduct—especially as contained in the Torah.

The Torah ("law," "teaching," "instruction") is the fundamental religious material for Judaism. Although the term can refer to the entire Hebrew Bible, in the strictest sense the Torah consists of the first five books of the Bible (also known as the "Pentateuch" or the "Five Books of Moses," that is Genesis, Exodus, Leviticus, Numbers, and Deuteronomy). These books contain the narratives of the creation of the world, stories of the early patriarchs and prophets, the enslavement and liberation (exodus) of the Israelites from Egypt, Moses receiving God's commandments on Mount Sinai, and the journeys of the Israelites to the promised land of Israel.

"The term 'Israel' denotes a historic political entity, a people, a nation, a belief system, a social group, a culture."[12] The original covenant, described in the book of Genesis, between God and the patriarch Abraham, involved God's promise of prosperity and territory, a homeland, for his faithful followers—the chosen people of Israel. This specific region, previously ruled over by Levantine powers and peopled by the Canaanites, was captured by the Israelites, according to the biblical narratives, after the death of Moses under the direction of the leader Joshua (approximately 1200 BCE). The kingdom, established shortly thereafter, eventually split into two territories after the death of King Solomon in the late 10th century BCE: the southern kingdom of Judah (from which the terms Judaism and Jew derive) and the northern kingdom of Israel (the name given by God to the patriarch Jacob). Ultimately, both territories were controlled by a series of invading empires (Assyrian, Babylonian), displacing substantial population to other parts of the general area and "setting a precedent for Judaism as an exilic faith during centuries of dispersal."[13] Although many Jews returned to Israel in the late sixth century BCE and lived under Persian, Greek, and ultimately Roman rule, the destruction of the Temple in Jerusalem in 70 CE by the Romans and the dispersal of Jews worldwide resulted in the fact that "Jewish national aspirations were effectively shattered until the twentieth century."[14] Nevertheless, the land of Israel (in both actual and symbolic fashion) remained a source of hope and longing for Jews throughout the medieval and early modern periods. Salvation from oppression, linked with hopes of a messiah ("anointed one") who would lead the Jews to freedom, also coincided in the late 19th and early 20th centuries with the movement of Zionism, which sought a return of the Jews to their homeland (Zion is another name for Jerusalem). In 1917 the Balfour Declaration recognized the Jewish homeland in Palestine, and many Jews resettled there under British governance. In 1948 the modern State of Israel was declared, "conceived as a haven for all Jews."[15]

Judaism's ethical monotheism, the importance of the Torah, and the significance of the land and people of Israel provide the primary foundations of the Jewish belief system. Through its lengthy history, Judaism has also grown and developed in culturally diverse contexts and has responded to the challenges posed for an ancient faith in historical evolution. In the modern period, Judaism exists in a number of different branches, primarily the Reform, Conservative,

Reconstructionist, and Orthodox variations. These defined movements arose largely in the 19th century and represent different interpretations of traditions, customs, and obligations. The "key practices" of Judaism vary widely in time and space, from strictly traditional to more liberal ways of practicing.

The interpretation of Judaism's traditions and customs has an extremely lengthy history. Although the Torah remains the fundamental set of scriptures for Judaism, several other texts (originally compilations of oral traditions) are also of signal importance. The Misnah (first compiled in the third century CE) as well as the Talmuds (sixth century CE) represent detailed studies of legal matters and ritual obligations ultimately based on the 613 commandments (including the Ten Commandments) revealed to Moses and contained in the written Torah. Ultra Orthodox Jews may perceive all of these obligations as inviolable, whereas others find them to be historically based and less applicable to modern life. How Jews observe the Torah will thus vary widely. For example, the system of dietary laws (*kashrut*), as noted in the Torah and detailed in rabbinic literature, involves highly specific instructions on foods that are permitted and foods that are forbidden, as well as details on the proper means of slaughtering animals and preparing food. Strict observers of these rules—in other words, those who keep "kosher" in their consumption of only ritually pure food (*kasher*)—will maintain different kitchen tools and implements for the separate preparation of meat and dairy products. Other Jews, who are less actively involved with religious traditions and customs, do not observe all or even any of these dietary restrictions.

Similarly, the observance of religious holidays, whether in synagogue or home contexts, varies widely. Strictly observant Jews attend synagogue for communal prayers and readings from the Torah several times per week and perform daily prayers at home as well. Others observe the weekly holy day or Sabbath (Shabbat—Friday evening through Saturday) in home rituals and/or by attending synagogue services. The Jewish religious calendar has a yearly cycle of major and minor festivals including the High Holy Days in the autumn, which celebrate the Beginning of the Year (Rosh Hashanah), Day of Atonement (Yom Kippur), and Feast of Tabernacles (Sukkot—the tabernacles or booths refer to the temporary structures used by the Israelites in their journeys to the promised land); the late fall/winter celebration of Lights (Hanukkah) commemorating the rededication of the Temple in the second century BCE; the spring festival of Lots (Purim), commemorating the deliverance of the Israelites from destruction in Persia; and the spring festival of Passover (Pesach), which celebrates God's delivery of the Israelites from Egypt.

Special meals, prayers, symbols, ritual objects, and scriptural readings are associated with all of these holidays, although, again, practices vary somewhat according to the historical context and views of the congregation. The maintenance, evolution, and reinterpretation of Jewish customs and traditions through the centuries—in a variety of geographic locations and cultural contexts—provides witness to the living faith of Judaism, ultimately based on God, Torah, and Israel.

TRADITIONAL ART AND ARCHITECTURAL FORMS

The tribulations and tragedies of Jewish history from ancient times to the modern period have resulted in the destruction and dispersal of innumerable structures and objects of art. Literary references and some archaeological evidence, however, make it clear that from the very earliest periods of Jewish history, the production of liturgical art and the creation of an appropriate architectural structure to serve as a focal point for worship were paramount concerns. Indeed, as recorded in the book of Exodus (chapters 25–31), God gave Moses highly detailed instructions about the construction of the Ark of the Covenant—a portable carrying case for the Tablets of the Law upon which were inscribed the Ten Commandments. This gilded chest of acacia wood, with rings in the ends into which poles could be inserted for transportation purposes, was also eventually enriched with a pair of carved and gilded angels (or cherubim) on top. This precious object was carried by the Israelites through their decades of travels from Egypt until they reached their promised homeland of Israel.

The book of Exodus also contains highly detailed directions, from God, about the construction of a portable sanctuary (or "tabernacle"—from the later Latin translation of *tabernaculum*—or "tent") to serve as a moveable and temporary resting place for the Ark. Constructed partially of cloth and partially of wood, the tabernacle was divided into two sections: the "Holy of Holies"—a smaller interior space where the Ark was placed—and a larger "holy place" containing an altar, and area for bread offerings and incense, and a seven-branched candlestick, or lamp stand, made of gold. Further textual details specify the other objects for use in ritual offerings and sacrifices that took place in the exterior enclosed courtyard of the tabernacle. It should be noted, however, that "the costly materials, not to mention the skills in weaving, embossing, and the like, which were necessary to produce the appurtenances described in Exodus are, of course, completely out of keeping with a semi-nomadic existence."[16] Thus, "many Bible scholars have concluded . . . that these appurtenances to the Tent did not exist in the desert, but were inserted into the account at a later time by the final redactors,"[17] possibly based on later worship arrangements.

Nevertheless, whatever its original form or degree of decoration, the Ark of the Covenant contained the Tablets of the Law, and among the Ten Commandments, the Second Commandment speaks specifically against idol worship in the form of "graven" or "sculptured" images. "You shall not make for yourself an idol, whether in the form of anything that is in heaven above, or that is the earth beneath, or that is in the water under the earth. You shall not bow down to them or worship them" (Exodus 20:4–5). Although it has sometimes been assumed that this commandment (and its many later reiterations in the Hebrew biblical chronicles and prophetic writings) represents an anti-art or iconoclastic prohibition on the creation of images of any sort, it is also clear that "there has been no opposition in Judaism to art per se—only opposition to art which could be used for idolatrous purposes."[18] The following should also be noted:

> A religious text like the Second Commandment must be viewed against the historical backdrop or context which gave rise to its distinctive expression . . . Much confusion has been engendered by writers on the subject of the Second Commandment since—assuming it to be unchanging phenomenon, a monolithic concept— they usually discuss it outside its historical context. Such literal interpretations are based on an assumption which entirely overlooks the fact that within the Bible itself, different and varying attitudes are expressed toward images.[19]

This is a complex issue that has had a significant impact on Christianity and Islam as well—similarly, "religions of the book"—which stem from Jewish heritage. The acknowledgment or worship of any deities other than the one true God of these monotheistic belief systems is forbidden because "idols are useless in a universe controlled by a single omnipotent god of all creation."[20] Hence, for Judaism and Islam especially, any representation of the supreme being is impossible. "God is beyond sexuality, bodily forms and the visible world; he is creator of all things and therefore not to be identified with any one of them. . . . God (Yahweh, Allah) may not be represented in visual images."[21] At the same time, it is clear from the biblical narratives concerning the Ark of the Covenant, the ancient tabernacle, and the Temple in Jerusalem that the creation of "functional ritual objects which also served as visible religious symbols for inspiration and spiritual elevation"[22] was sanctioned and permitted from the earliest periods of Jewish history.[23]

The Temple and the Synagogue

After years of traveling, and after the capture of the city of Jerusalem by King David in the 10th century BCE, the Ark of the Covenant was ultimately enshrined in what was intended to be a permanent location: the Temple in Jerusalem[24] (see Figure 9.1). This impressive structure was created in the mid-10th century BCE under the direction of David's son, King Solomon, and is also described in great detail in the Hebrew scriptures (1 Kings, chapters 6–8.) The basic form and layout of the Temple followed the model of the earlier portable tabernacle, but in much more magnificent and durable form. Solomon's Temple was constructed of stone covered with aromatic boards of cedar wood. There were two tall bronze columns set at the entrance. With a longitudinal plan oriented on an east–west axis (the entrance was at the east end), the interior was divided into the two sanctuaries, with access to these areas restricted to priests. The Ark (perhaps raised up on a platform) was kept in

Figure 9.1 The Temple of Solomon, illustrated page from a Haggadah, Moravia, 1729. Scala / Art Resource, NY.

the inner room (the Holy of Holies), and the outer sanctum contained an incense altar, a table for bread offerings, 10 lamp stands, and other objects. The outer courtyard contained a large altar for sacrificial offerings (of animals and birds), 10 bronze basins on wheeled stands, and a larger bronze sea, or basin, supported by sculptures of 12 oxen. The Temple was referred to as the House of God—or the place where God's name was found—and the Ark and its contents represented and symbolized the special covenant between God and his chosen people, the Israelites.

Solomon's Temple was destroyed in 586 BCE when the Babylonians, under the direction of King Nebuchadnezzar, invaded and sacked the city. The Israelites were taken into captivity in Babylon, and at some point during this traumatic process, the Ark of the Covenant and its contents were lost, destroyed, or removed.[25] The Israelites were later allowed to return to their homeland under the Persian king Cyrus, and the Temple was rebuilt on a smaller scale in the late sixth century BCE. Centuries later, this temple was refurbished and enlarged under the direction of the Roman-appointed ruler of Judea, King Herod the Great (37–4 BCE), but the structure was again completely destroyed by the Romans in 70 CE, during the Jewish uprising against Roman rule. Nothing remains of this temple apart from sections of the great masonry platform upon which it stood, notably the western wall (also known as the "Wailing Wall"), which is considered to be the holiest site in Judaism and a major goal of Jewish pilgrimage to the present day. The structures on the Temple Mount today are later Islamic buildings: the Dome of the Rock and the al-Aqsa mosque.

Although the Temple in Jerusalem was the major focal point for Jewish worship for many centuries, due to its destruction, loss of ritual objects, and ultimate obliteration, "it can be argued that the Temple became superfluous to the continuing existence of Judaism."[26] Indeed, it seems clear that alternative forms of Jewish worship, in addition to those rituals purely associated with the Temple, evolved as early as the sixth century BCE during the time of the Babylonian exile (following the destruction of Solomon's Temple). In exile, and deprived of their Temple, the Israelites gathered in small community groups or assemblies, known as synagogues. The word "synagogue" is a

Greek term meaning "assembly" and is derived from the Hebrew *bet keneset* or "gathering place." Although there is little archaeological evidence of the construction of specific buildings to serve as synagogues until close to the end of the Second Temple period, it is clear that even "while the Second Temple was still standing, the synagogue already existed as an identifiable and separate institution."[27] Ultimately, the synagogue replaced the Temple as the primary worship venue for Judaism. "After the destruction of the Temple in 70 CE, the synagogue shifted from being the secondary congregational space in Judaism to the central religious institution in the life of the people of Israel."[28]

Considerable scholarship has been devoted to the origins, early forms, and functions of the synagogue.[29] The term itself did not, at first, refer to a specific building or a particular type of building, but rather to a gathering of people for prayer and study. A quorum (or *minyan*) of 10 men was the minimal requirement, and communal prayer led by laymen (assembly members and educated experts in Jewish scripture and law—rabbis—or "teachers") replaced the priest-led sacrificial rituals associated with the Temple. The earliest datable synagogue structures, in the sense of single-purpose buildings specifically constructed for Jewish worship, show a variety of plans and regional variations based on the materials and building styles of the late Roman world. Some are of a "basilican" plan with a longitudinal axis; some have an "apsidal" format with a semicircular niche or apse at one end; others, of a "broadhouse" plan, have a squarer format or a horizontal axis.

Fragments of sculptural decoration and mosaic floor pavements from early synagogues often depict important symbols, ritual objects, and some narrative scenes as well. For example, the mosaic floor of the early sixth-century synagogue at Maon in southwest Israel features a menorah flanked by lions (symbols of the kingdom of Judah), a *shofar* (or horn, sounded on holy days), *lulav* (palm fronds), and *ethrog* (citron, involved with festal celebrations), plus grapes, birds, and—rather unexpectedly—a pair of elephants (see Figure 9.2). These animals and objects are enclosed in a composition of 55 medallions created by tendrils issuing from a vase. The overall style of this mosaic pavement is similar to contemporary examples of Christian Byzantine mosaics. A sculptural relief fragment from the early synagogue at Gadara in Israel (first or second century CE) also shows a menorah, *shofar*, and palm fronds (see Figure 9.3).

Through the lengthy history of synagogue construction from ancient times to the present, the buildings show a great diversity of architectural styles and decoration depending on their geographic location, the historical period, and the architectural vocabulary of different eras. Certainly, this "reflects the circumstance that Jewish history . . . developed and evolved primarily within multiple societies, cultures, and civilizations."[30]

For example, the 13th-century synagogue of Santa Maria la Blanca (so named after it was converted into a Christian church in the early 15th cen-

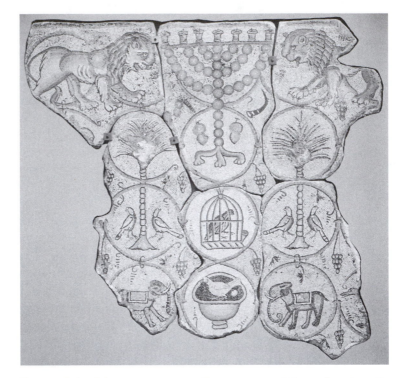

Figure 9.2 Mosaic pavement, Synagogue at Maon, Israel, early sixth century CE. Snark / Art Resource, NY.

Figure 9.3 Sculptural fragment, Synagogue at Gadara, Israel, first to second century CE. Paris: Louvre. Réunion des Musées Nationaux / Art Resource, NY.

tury) in Toledo, Spain, shows Islamic-style, horseshoe-shaped arches in its five-aisled interior (see Figure 9.4). The deeply carved capitals and sculptural decoration on the spandrels and upper levels of the inner aisles show complex foliage, scrolls, and geometric interlacing patterns. The architectural and decorative vocabulary used here might be described as fundamentally Islamic, reflective of the fact that the Iberian Peninsula was under Muslim rule for a number of centuries during the Middle Ages. Although the synagogue was constructed after the Christian conquest of the city in the late 11th century, it is an excellent example of the "complex interrelationships between cultures that resulted when Christian rulers presided over an artistic tradition that had been developed under Islamic rule."[31] The mid-13th century Altneuschul "Old New" synagogue in Prague (Czech Republic), often described as the oldest synagogue in Europe, shows Gothic-style pointed arches and rib vaulting (see Figure 9.5), whereas the late 18th-century synagogue at Cavaillon in southern France is a small gem of the decorative Rococo style, complete with silver and gold leaf details of shells, fruit baskets, and graceful foliage festoons in a wood-paneled pink and white interior (see Figure 9.6).

Figure 9.4 Synagogue of Santa Maria la Blanca, interior, Toledo, Spain, 13th century. Vanni / Art Resource, NY.

Regardless of this stylistic diversity, there are, however, some specific architectural and liturgical features generally found in all synagogues, the chief of which is the container for the Torah scroll or scrolls. Reading from the Torah is an integral aspect of synagogue services, and the scrolls are the most precious possession of the community. A cabinet, box, or niche with doors, known as the "Ark" (recalling the Ark of the Covenant and the Holy of Holies in the ancient Temple), is provided for the safe storage of the Torah scrolls when they are not in use (see Figure 9.7). Generally this is located on the wall faced by the congregation, so that the Ark forms the visual as well as the liturgical focus in synagogues. Customarily, a hanging lamp with a perpetual light burning in it (the *ner tamid*—or eternal light) will be found near or in front of the Ark. This symbolizes the light of God and is also a reminder of the oil lamp that burned perpetually in the ancient Temple. The doors of the Ark are often concealed behind curtains, again reminiscent of the hangings in the inner sanctuaries of the ancient Temple.

The Torah scrolls often have special textile coverings or mantles, metal shields or "breastplates," and metal or wooden finials (*rimmonim*) (see Figure 9.8).

Figure 9.5 Altneuschul Synagogue, interior, Prague, Czech Republic, mid-13th century. Erich Lessing / Art Resource, NY.

Figure 9.6 Synagogue at Cavaillon, interior, France, late 18th century. Erich Lessing / Art Resource, NY.

Figure 9.7 Torah Ark, from Modena, Italy, 1472. Paris: Musée National du Moyen Age—Thermes de Cluny. Réunion des Musées Nationaux / Art Resource, NY.

The care in handling these precious objects also may require use of a *yad* or pointer that allows readers to follow the text without actually touching it with hands or fingers. The term *yad* literally means "a hand" (see Figure 9.9). A raised platform or podium (known as a *bema* or *bimah*), from which scriptural readings are done, is also a common feature in synagogues (see Figure 9.10).

Depending on the historical or geographic context and the specific observances of the community, separate seating areas for men and women may be denoted; for example, an upper gallery area may be set aside for women. A number of other liturgical objects are associated with the daily and weekly activities traditional in synagogues, as well as specific articles used in annual festivals or days of special observance. These may include textiles, metal work objects, and manuscripts.

Traditionally, the scrolls of the Torah are never illustrated with narrative imagery or decorated with images of any sort. However, illuminated manuscripts of other formats were widely produced, especially during the medieval and Renaissance periods, and represent one of the most significant forms of Jewish art. The earliest surviving examples come from Egypt and Palestine and date to the 9th and 10th century. Hebrew manuscripts were produced in great numbers during the 13th through 15th centuries in western Europe, in 15th-century Yemen, and in 17th-century Persia. As is the case with synagogue architecture, the styles and forms of these manuscripts "reveal the stylistic trends prevailing in such Muslim countries as Palestine, Egypt, Yemen, and Persia under such rulers as the Fatimids, Mamluks, and Safavids. Similarly, in Christian Europe, the Hebrew miniatures from Spain, Portugal, Germany, France, and Italy evince the Romanesque, Gothic, Mudéjar, International, and Renaissance styles."[32] Among the religious manuscripts most often illuminated are Bibles, Psalters, legal works pertaining to Jewish law and custom, liturgical manuals, and especially manuscripts of the Haggadah (or "narration"—the text used for the celebration of Passover). These manuscripts, as a whole, also represent a lively tradition of figural narrative imagery in Jewish art, which, in spite of destruction and dispersal, can be traced back for centuries to some of the earliest surviving synagogues with mosaic floors and wall paintings and extends further to the modern period where Jewish art and architecture continue to flourish.[33]

Figure 9.8 Torah cases and finials. Ferrara, Italy: synagogue. DeA Picture Library / Art Resource, NY.

Figure 9.9 Torah Pointers, Prague, Czech Republic. Scala / Art Resource, NY.

בעל הבית נגב ביתך שאומרים היהודיך

Figure 9.10 Manuscript illustration of a synagogue, from the "Sister Haggadah," ca. 1350, Northern Spain. London: British Library Ms Or 2284, f. 17v. HIP / Art Resource, NY.

EXAMPLES

Dura Europos Synagogue, Interior, Fresco Paintings, ca. 250 CE

Dating to the middle of the third century CE, the synagogue at Dura Europos (present-day Syria) represents one of the most renowned and well-studied examples of early Jewish art[34] (see Plate 17). Of special note are the extensive fresco paintings with biblical narrative scenes located on the interior walls of the main assembly hall. This rectangular-shaped hall/sanctuary was equipped with benches lining all four walls, and a niche (or *aedicula*) in the western wall served as a Torah shrine. The frescoes (done in the *secco*, or dry, fresco technique) are arranged in horizontal registers and represent an extensive array of narrative scenes.

When the synagogue was first excavated in the late 1920s and 1930s, scholars were absolutely astounded by the extent of the paintings and the many scenes and symbols represented.

> If there were any doubts beforehand as to whether or not such an art once existed in antiquity, then Dura put them to rest. To date, however, nothing even remotely comparable has been recovered elsewhere. Thus, while the euphoria over the first revelations of Dura has dimmed somewhat in the . . . years that have passed since the original discovery, these finds clearly indicate that a wider Jewish artistic tradition must have existed, one which will come to light sooner or later.[35]

The synagogue at Dura was one of several religious structures in the city. In addition to the synagogue, the city also contained a number of temples dedicated to Greco-Roman and Near Eastern deities, as well as an early Christian structure.[36] These buildings are of various dates and reflect the history and political-cultural transformation of the city beginning from its Hellenistic foundation in the late fourth century BCE by a successor of Alexander the Great. The city was under the control of the Parthian Empire from the second century BCE to the second century CE, when it was captured by the Romans in 165 CE. The synagogue dates to the period of Roman occupation of the city, which came to an end following attack by the Sasanians in 256–57 CE, after which the city was ultimately abandoned. During the siege of the city, a number of residential buildings and other structures close to the western surrounding walls, including the Christian building and the synagogue, were filled in to expand the defensive walls. Thus, although many structures were demolished, the series of archeological excavations of the early 20th century uncovered relatively undisturbed, buried evidence of well-preserved religious and domestic buildings.[37]

"No single site provides more material evidence about the diversity of religious expression in late Antiquity than does Dura Europos."[38] It might also be said that no single site from late Antiquity has provided more fodder for scholarly dispute and criticism of archeological and interpretive methods than has Dura.[39] The fresco paintings of the synagogue have been extensively studied since they were first uncovered, and the bibliography on these materials is vast. Even so, there is a great deal of scholarly disagreement about the identification of some of the individual subjects depicted, as well as the relationship of the individual scenes to any overall, unifying narrative program (if one presumes such to have been intended).

> Most of the copious scholarly literature on this synagogue has been devoted to the meaning of these scenes. All agree that they represent, in one form or another, high points in biblical history, when the hand of God was evident in guiding the destiny of the Jewish people. Nevertheless, the question arises as to the basis of the selection of these particular events, and the extent to which there is a central idea pervading all the scenes. Were these scenes selected at random, or is there a fundamental organizing principle underlying the choice?[40]

About 40 percent of the paintings on the wall surfaces are destroyed; only fragments remain on the east wall, and significant portions of the upper and middle registers on the south and north walls are also missing. The best preserved is the western wall, in which the Torah shrine is located. This wall was oriented in the direction of Jerusalem, and the paintings on this wall include several depictions of the Temple in Jerusalem, the Ark of the Covenant, the ancient tabernacle, and ritual objects associated with the Temple. These visual references to Jerusalem and the Temple may be seen as creating a sense of "memorialized Temple space"[41] within the architectural form of the synagogue structure, with its focus on the Torah shrine. Other scenes on the western wall include episodes from the lives of Moses, Solomon, and David, whereas scenes on the north and south walls feature episodes from the lives of the prophets Ezechiel and Elijah.

The synagogue at Dura was an enlargement of a smaller building on the site that dated to the mid-second century CE. The assembly hall in the first synagogue held about 60 to 65 participants, whereas more than 120 people could gather in the expanded assembly hall of the enlarged synagogue. This interior space may have been the largest public room at Dura, which perhaps indicates significant growth of the Jewish community during this era. Indeed, it appears that the city of Dura, generally, was a venue in which practitioners of a variety of different religions coexisted in some form during the late Antique period. All of the religious structures at Dura were designed for specific groups (a growing Christian community, a flourishing Jewish community, the Roman military and administrative community with temples dedicated to traditional Roman deities as well as a Mithraeum—for worship of the god Mithras—popular with the Roman military). These structures were generally all enriched with either sculptural or painted decoration with appropriate imagery or narratives. The pictorial program within the synagogue was among the most extensive and continues to provide a focus for scholarly discussion of the possible sources, style, and meaning of this unique cycle of early Jewish narrative art.

Two Hebrew Manuscripts from the 14th Century

Hebrew manuscripts were produced in great numbers in Europe during the Middle Ages. The surviving examples exhibit a diverse range of formats and styles depending on where and when they were created. Some of these manuscripts are richly decorated with figural narrative imagery in styles similar to contemporary Christian illuminated manuscripts, while also demonstrating specific Jewish iconography and pictorial interpretations.[42] Other manuscripts, especially those produced in some areas of Spain, tend to use a purely decorative vocabulary akin to Islamic art forms. Yet other examples show the distinctive use of miniature (micrographic) writing for texts and pictures. The 14th-century Bible from Germany, illustrated in Figure 9.11, is a fine example of Hebrew micrography, and the 14th-century "Golden Haggadah," produced in northern Spain, is an excellent example of a Hebrew manuscript with an extensive cycle of illustrations in an essentially European Gothic style (see Plate 18).

Although the practice of micrographic writing can be found in non-Jewish cultures also, some scholars have argued that micrography is an essentially and distinctively Jewish art form.[43]

Other scribal traditions also use writing in order to form pictures, but their method usually is to adjust the length of lines in order to create an object which can then, if required, be indicated additionally in outline. Jewish scribes did this too, but their unique contribution was to make designs by writing continuously in tiny script, often weaving the most intricate patterns. This can be seen very well in German Bibles.[44]

The German Bible, produced ca. 1343, shows the opening page of the Book of Genesis with the enlarged Hebrew letters spelling *Bereshit* ("In the beginning"). The text continues in columns below, and the page is otherwise elaborated with micrographic writing forming geometric designs, an arch, medallions, and panels containing animals and other motifs. These micrographic texts are sections of commentary or "notes called the *masorah*, which surrounds the Biblical texts and contains guidance as to the writing of specific words and their pronunciation, notes on the frequency of rarer words, remarks on different scribal traditions and so on."[45] These

Figure 9.11 Hebrew Bible, ca. 1343, Erfurt, Germany. Berlin: Staatsbibliothek Ms Or fol 1210, f. 1b. Bildarchiv Preussischer Kulturbesitz / Art Resource, NY.

scholarly notes were originally composed during the sixth through ninth centuries CE, and "it is the *masorah* which is frequently used in Hebrew manuscripts for micrographic designs."[46]

Generally speaking, the patterns and animal forms in such examples bear no actual or obvious relationship to either the biblical or the masoretic texts, although certain forms, such as the prominent lions of Judah in this case, may function in a symbolic fashion as well. The architectural niche-like form surmounting the main letters on this page may also have symbolic meaning, for example indicating that the Bible is the "holy sanctuary"[47] for Judaism. Other manuscripts show examples of micrography in the shape of menorah or candelabra forms, but in general, no direct relationship can be seen between the texts and the designs created with them. This fact has long puzzled and intrigued scholarly specialists who are generally rather reluctant to ascribe the popularity of this form (which is, after all, found in the sacred context of Judaism's holy scriptures) purely to expressions of scribal whimsy or flights of creative fantasy to relieve the tedium involved with this painstaking and "not particularly exciting occupation"[48] of detailed text copying. Because "particular love and care were lavished on the copying of manuscripts of the Bible, the most sacred possession of the Jewish people,"[49] several scholars believe that the decorative and figural designs of the micrographic masorah texts are a reflection, ultimately, of the long reverence for the written word in Judaism generally as well as the growth, in medieval Europe, of mystical schools of thought that endowed letters and words with highly complex spiritual meanings.[50] Hence, far from being a purely decorative form of art, micrography may be seen as "a means of suggesting all the potentialities of creation inherent in the letter. Inasmuch as all of creation preexisted in the letter and its combinations in the Torah, the word and the letter became the only and natural form for expressing all of the creative possibilities of the Word."[51]

This may also explain why narrative illustrations are relatively uncommon in Hebrew Bibles per se, whereas biblical narrative scenes are frequently found in other types of medieval manuscripts, most especially those of the Haggadah. "Although the text of the Haggadah was already fixed in its essentials during the second century [CE] . . . other passages were added later up to the 13th century,"[52] and it was during the medieval period that "the illustrated Passover Haggadah emerged in Europe as a new type of book around 1300."[53] Some of the most richly illustrated medieval Hebrew manuscripts are examples of this text, which is customarily read in traditional Jewish homes during Passover (*seder*) celebrations in the spring. The Haggadah texts include "a collection of biblical and homiletical verses, poems, and religious customs and songs, focusing essentially on the Exodus of the ancient Hebrews, their attainment of freedom from Egyptian bondage, and their ultimate hope of redemption with the coming of Elijah, the messianic herald."[54] The lavish "Golden Haggadah," produced in northern Spain ca. 1320, is among the most noted and well-studied examples of medieval Hebrew illuminated manuscripts[55] (see Plate 18).

In addition to in-text decorations and illustrations, the "Golden Haggadah" includes a notable cycle of 14 prefatory full-page illustrations, each divided into four framed scenes. The name of the manuscript reflects the extensive use of gold leaf backgrounds enriched with stamped diamond patterns in these scenes. The illustrations primarily cover selected sequential narrative episodes in the biblical books of Genesis and Exodus; the scenes are visually read from left to right and from top to bottom of each page. Scholars have identified the hands of two different (anonymous) artists responsible for the narrative illustrations in the manuscript, both of whom were clearly conversant with the figure style, iconography, and page layout formats of contemporary French and Italian luxury manuscript production. It is unknown for whom the manuscript was originally created, although "in the thirteenth and fourteenth centuries noble Jewish patrons at the European royal courts were keen to have the Haggadah illuminated in the book painting style of the time."[56] It was probably produced in a Catalan workshop in Barcelona during the early 14th century, during which period "the Jewish community of Barcelona was . . . one of the most prominent and affluent in Spain."[57] It is one of the earliest surviving Spanish illustrated manuscripts of the Haggadah.

The two facing pages shown here include scenes from the lives of Abraham, Isaac, Jacob, and Joseph and are based on biblical passages as well as rabbinic commentaries. The scenes include the following: Lot's wide turned into a pillar of salt, the sacrifice (or "binding") of Isaac, Isaac blessing Jacob, Jacob's dream of the heavenly ladder, Jacob wrestling with the angel, Joseph's dream, Joseph relating his dreams, and the appearance of an angel to Joseph. The figural style, facial types, drapery patterns, gestures, color schemes, landscape features, and architectural elements all reveal an expressiveness and elegance typical of High Gothic illumination of the time and compare well with contemporary French and Italian examples especially.

> The patrons who commissioned the sumptuous Spanish illuminated Haggadoth [plural of Haggadah] must have been Jews with not only the financial resources to pay for such luxurious manuscripts, but also the taste, discernment and interest in the visual arts necessary to enjoy them. It is profoundly unfortunate that, following the ravages of time and of deliberate destruction, so few glorious illuminated Sephardi Haggadoth have survived to bear witness to the refined taste of their patrons.[58]

Marc Chagall, *Moses Receives the Tablets of the Law,* 1960–1966

What is "Jewish art"? Similar questions arise in defining the arts of other world religions. Is a work of art "Christian" or "Islamic" because it was produced by or for adherents to those faiths? Must a work of art contain spiritual content or have been designed for pious purposes in order to be classified as "religious"? "The question of what is Jewish art and who is a Jewish artist is nowhere more problematic than in the fine arts . . . perhaps the most justifiable criterion for considering a work to be Jewish art is the issue of identity, perceived or real."[59] The renowned modern artist Marc Chagall (1887–1985) has been quoted as saying, "If I were not a Jew (with the content that I put into that word), I would not have been an artist, or I would be a different artist altogether."[60]

Chagall's lengthy and extremely prolific career spans the most tumultuous and disastrous decades for Jews in the 20th century. Born in Vitebsk (Belarus/Russia), Chagall's Jewish roots and experiences provided a consistent current throughout his career, both in his choice of subject matter and in his overall approach to his art. Although his subject matter ranged widely throughout his career, biblical subjects and images of Jewish life and spirituality were themes to which he consistently returned. The "Jewish world permeated the consciousness, the painterly and fictional worlds of Chagall"[61] in an intensely mystical and deeply spiritual manner, from his earliest images of his Russian homeland to his later stained glass window designs, such as for the synagogue of the Hadassah-Hebrew University Medical Center near Jerusalem.[62]

Chagall said that he had always been captivated by the Bible, ever since his early childhood, and that the Bible always seemed to him to be "the greatest source of poetry of all time."[63] Apart from single works illustrating or including biblical subjects,[64] at several points in his career Chagall was inspired to create larger series of biblical illustrations, interpreting the sacred texts in his own unique style. *Moses Receives the Tablets of the Law* is one in a series of large-scale oil paintings of biblical subjects that Chagall began in the 1950s (see Figure 9.12). The composition is dominated by the figure of Moses, who, in a dramatic diagonal movement, reaches upwards to reverentially receive the tablets proffered by the hands of the otherwise unseen God, whose presence is indicated in a gleaming cloudlike form at the upper right. The majesty and significance of the moment is shown by the overall radiance of the scene and the rays of light gleaming through the composition and glowing from the prophet's head. A complementary diagonal indicates the landscape setting of Mount Sinai where crowds of small figures gather in awe. The idol of the Golden Calf that the Israelites worshiped in Moses's absence can be glimpsed in the distance. Additional small figures appear elsewhere in the composition; these include an angel bearing Torah scrolls and a priest holding a menorah. Sketchily rendered architectural elements can be seen as well. Altogether, this work typifies Chagall's uniquely poetic and lyrical style as well as his ability to render extremely powerful messages from his beloved biblical sources. Chagall gave his Biblical Message series (an extensive group of large oil paintings, prints, watercolors, and sculptures) as a gift to the people of France in the late 1960s, and these works are housed in a museum which was especially constructed for them in Nice: the Musée National Message Biblique Marc Chagall.

Figure 9.12   Mark Chagall, *Moses Receives the Tablets of the Law,* 1960–66. Nice, France: Musée National Message Biblique Marc Chagall. Réunion des Musées Nationaux / Art Resource, NY.

NOTES

1. Carl Ehrlich, "Judaism," in *The Illustrated Guide to World Religions,* ed. Michael Coogan (Oxford: Oxford University Press, 2003), 16.

2. Ehrlich, 18.

3. Ehrlich, 24.

4. Vivian Mann, Thomas Glick, and Jerrilynn Dodds, eds. *Convivenica: Jews, Muslims and Christians in Medieval Spain* (New York: George Braziller, 1992).

5. Ehrlich, 25.

6. Mark Cohen, *Under Crescent and Cross: The Jews in the Middle Ages* (Princeton, NJ: Princeton University Press, 1994), 3–14.

7. Ehrlich, 25.

8. Ehrlich, 48.

9. Ehrlich, 25.

10. Ehrlich, 16.

11. Ehrlich, 26.

12. Ehrlich, 16.

13. Ehrlich, 21.

14. Ehrlich, 22.

15. Ehrlich, 51.

16. Joseph Gutmann, "The 'Second Commandment' and the Image in Judaism," in *No Graven Images: Studies in Art and the Hebrew Bible*, ed. Joseph Gutmann (New York: KTAV Publishing House, 1971), 5.

17. Gutmann, "The 'Second Commandment,'" 4.

18. Michael Kaniel, *Judaism* (Poole, England: Blandford Press, 1979), 5.

19. Joseph Gutmann, ed., *No Graven Images: Studies in Art and the Hebrew Bible* (New York: KTAV Publishing House, 1971), xiv–xv.

20. Albert Moore, *Iconography of Religions: An Introduction* (Philadelphia: Fortress Press, 1977), 207.

21. Moore, 205.

22. Kaniel, 7.

23. For further discussion, see Kalman Bland, *The Artless Jew: Medieval and Modern Affirmation and Denials of the Visual* (Princeton, NJ: Princeton University Press, 2000) and Vivian Mann, *Jewish Texts on the Visual Arts* (Cambridge: Cambridge University Press, 2000).

24. Simon Goldhill, *The Temple of Jerusalem* (Cambridge, MA: Harvard University Press, 2005).

25. According to some Ethiopian traditions, however, the Ark of the Covenant was much earlier removed from Jerusalem by Menelek (the son of Solomon and Makeda, the Queen of Sheba) and carried to safe-keeping at the ancient Ethiopian capital of Aksum, where it remains enshrined (and hidden from view) to the present day, in a sanctuary chapel next to the cathedral of Our Lady Mary of Zion. See Roderick Grierson, *African Zion: The Sacred Art of Ethiopia* (New Haven, CT: Yale University Press, 1993), 5–17.

26. Ehrlich, 42.

27. Ehrlich, 42.

28. Joan Branham, "Sacred Space under Erasure in Ancient Synagogues and Early Churches," *The Art Bulletin* 74, no. 3 (1992): 383.

29. Lee Levine, *The Ancient Synagogue: The First Thousand Years* (New Haven, CT: Yale University Press, 2000); and Leslie Hoppe, *The Synagogues and Churches of Ancient Palestine* (Collegeville, MI: The Liturgical Press, 1994).

30. Joseph Gutmann, *Hebrew Manuscript Painting* (New York: George Braziller, 1978), 12–13.

31. Jerrilynn Dodds, "Mudejar Tradition and the Synagogues of Medieval Spain: Cultural Identity and Cultural Hegemony," in *Convivenica: Jews, Muslims and Christians in Medieval Spain*, ed. Vivian Mann, Thomas Glick, and Jerrilynn Dodds (New York: George Braziller, 1992), 113.

32. Gutmann, 13.

33. Grace Cohen Grossman, *Jewish Art* (New York: Hugh Lauter Levin Associates, 1995); and Grace Cohen Grossman, *New Beginnings: The Skirball Museum Collections and Inaugural Exhibition* (Los Angeles: Skirball Cultural Center, 1996).

34. Kurt Weitzmann and Herbert Kessler, *The Frescoes of the Dura Synagogue and Christian Art* (Washington, DC: Dumbarton Oaks, 1990).

35. Levine, *The Ancient Synagogue*, 238.

36. Susan Matheson, *Dura Europos: The Ancient City and the Yale Collection* (New Haven, CT: Yale University Art Gallery, 1982).

37. For a detailed discussion of the excavation campaigns at Dura, see Clark Hopkins, *The Discovery of Dura Europos* (New Haven, CT: Yale University Press, 1979).

38. Annabel Wharton, "Good and Bad Images from the Synagogue of Dura Europos: Contexts, Subtexts, Intertexts," *Art History* 17, no. 1 (1994): 1.

39. Annabel Wharton, *Refiguring the Post Classical City: Dura Europos, Jerash, Jerusalem and Ravenna* (Cambridge: Cambridge University Press, 1995).

40. Lee Levine, ed., *Ancient Synagogues Revealed* (Jerusalem: Israel Exploration Society, 1981), 176.

41. Branham, 387.

42. For a detailed discussion of the relationship of Christian and Jewish iconography in medieval manuscripts, see Katrin Kogman-Appel, "Coping with Christian Pictorial Sources: What Did Jewish Miniaturists Not Paint?" *Speculum* 74, no. 4 (2000): 816–58.

43. See, for example, Leila Avrin, "Hebrew Micrography: One Thousand Years of Art in Script," *Visible Language* 28, no. 1 (1984): 87–95; Leila Avrin, "Micrography as Art," in *La Lettre Hébraïque et sa Signification*, ed. Colette Sirat (Paris: Editions du Centre National de la Recherche Scientifique, 1981), 43–50; and Stanley Ferber, "Micrography: A Jewish Art Form," *Journal of Jewish Art* 3/4 (1977): 12–24.

44. David Goldstein, *Hebrew Manuscript Painting* (London: The British Library, 1985), 4.

45. Goldstein, 4.

46. Goldstein, 4.

47. Avrin, "Micrography as Art," 46.

48. Avrin, 46.

49. Goldstein, 3.

50. Johanna Drucker, *The Alphabetic Labyrinth: The Letters in History and Imagination* (London: Thames and Hudson, 1995), especially 129–58.

51. Ferber, 21.

52. Bezalel Narkiss, *The Golden Haggadah* (London: The British Library, 1997), 8.

53. Katrin Kogman-Appel, "Hebrew Manuscript Painting in Late Medieval Spain: Signs of a Culture in Transition," *The Art Bulletin* 84, no. 2 (2002): 246.

54. Gutmann, *Hebrew Manuscript Painting*, 19.

55. Narkiss, *Golden Haggadah*.

56. Ingo Walther and Norbert Wolf, *Codices Illustres: The World's Most Famous Illuminated Manuscripts 400 to 1600* (Köln: Taschen, 2001), 204.

57. Narkiss, *Golden Haggadah*, 64.

58. Narkiss, *Golden Haggadah*, 64.

59. Grossman, *Jewish Art*, 273.

60. Benjamin Harshav, *Marc Chagall and the Lost Jewish World* (New York: Rizzoli, 2006), 11.

61. Harshav, 121.

62. Jean Leymarie, *Marc Chagall: The Jerusalem Windows* (New York: George Braziller, 1967); and Alfred Werner, "Chagall's Jerusalem Windows," *Art Journal* 21, no. 4 (1962): 224–32.

63. Quoted in Jacob Baal-Teshuva, ed., *Marc Chagall: A Retrospective* (New York: Hugh Lauter Levin Associates, 1995), 295.

64. For example, see Mira Friedman, "Marc Chagall's Portrayal of the Prophet Jeremiah," *Zeitschrift für Kunstgeschicte* 47, no. 3 (1984): 374–91.

BIBLIOGRAPHY AND FURTHER READING

Avrin, Leila. "Hebrew Micrography: One Thousand Years of Art in Script." *Visible Language* 28, no. 1 (1984): 87–95.

Avrin, Leila. "Micrography as Art." In *La Lettre Hébraïque et sa Signification*, ed. Colette Sirat, 43–80. Paris: Editions du Centre National de la Recherche Scientifique, 1981.

Baal-Teshuva, Jacob, ed. *Marc Chagall: A Retrospective*. New York: Hugh Lauter Levin Associates, 1995.

Baal-Teshuva, Jacob. *Marc Chagall 1887–1985*. Köln: Taschen, 1998.

Berger, Maurice, and Joan Rosenbaum. *Masterworks of the Jewish Museum*. New Haven, CT: Yale University Press, 2004.

Bland, Kalman. *The Artless Jew: Medieval and Modern Affirmation and Denials of the Visual*. Princeton, NJ: Princeton University Press, 2000.

Blatter, Janet, and Sybil Milton. *Art of the Holocaust*. New York: Rutledge, 1981.

Branham, Joan. "Sacred Space under Erasure in Ancient Synagogues and Early Churches." *The Art Bulletin* 74, no. 3 (1992): 375–94.

Cassou, Jean. *Chagall*. New York: Praeger, 1965.

Cohen, Mark. *Under Crescent and Cross: The Jews in the Middle Ages*. Princeton, NJ: Princeton University Press, 1994.

Cohn-Sherbok, Dan. *Atlas of Jewish History*. London: Routledge, 1994.

Cohn-Sherbok, Dan. *A Dictionary of Judaism and Christianity*. Philadelphia: Trinity Press, 1991.

Coogan, Michael, ed. *The Illustrated Guide to World Religions*. Oxford: Oxford University Press, 2003.

Dodds, Jerrilynn. "Mudejar Tradition and the Synagogues of Medieval Spain: Cultural Identity and Cultural Hegemony." In *Convivenica: Jews, Muslims and Christians in Medieval Spain*, ed. Vivian Mann, Thomas Glick, and Jerrilynn Dodds, 113–31. New York: George Braziller, 1992.

Drucker, Johanna. *The Alphabetic Labyrinth: The Letters in History and Imagination*. London: Thames and Hudson, 1995.

Ehrlich, Carl. "Judaism." In *The Illustrated Guide to World Religions*, ed. Michael Coogan, 14–81. Oxford: Oxford University Press, 2003.

Einstein, Stephan, and Lydia Kukoff. *Every Person's Guide to Judaism*. New York: UAHC Press, 1989.

Ferber, Stanley. "Micrography: A Jewish Art Form." *Journal of Jewish Art* 3/4 (1977): 12–24.

Folberg, Neil. *And I Shall Dwell among Them: Historic Synagogues of the World*. New York: Aperture, 1995.

Foray, Jean-Michel. *Marc Chagall*. New York: Harry N. Abrams, 2003.

Friedman, Mira. "Marc Chagall's Portrayal of the Prophet Jeremiah." *Zeitschrift für Kunstgeschicte* 47, no. 3 (1984): 374–91.

Furman, Jacobo. *Treasures of Jewish Art from the Jacobo and Asea Furman Collection of Judaica*. New York: Hugh Lauter Levin Associates, 1997.

Goldhill, Simon. *The Temple of Jerusalem*. Cambridge, MA: Harvard University Press, 2005.

Goldstein, David. *Hebrew Manuscript Painting*. London: The British Library, 1985.

Grierson, Roderick, ed. *African Zion: The Sacred Art of Ethiopia*. New Haven, CT: Yale University Press, 1993.

Grossman, Grace Cohen. *Jewish Art*. New York: Hugh Lauter Levin Associates, 1995.

Grossman, Grace Cohen. *New Beginnings: The Skirball Museum Collections and Inaugural Exhibition*. Los Angeles: Skirball Cultural Center, 1996.

Gutmann, Joseph. *Hebrew Manuscript Painting*. New York: George Braziller, 1978.

Gutmann, Joseph, ed. *No Graven Images: Studies in Art and the Hebrew Bible*. New York: KTAV Publishing House, 1971.

Gutmann, Joseph. "The 'Second Commandment' and the Image in Judaism." In *No Graven Images: Studies in Art and the Hebrew Bible*, ed. Joseph Gutmann, 3–14. New York: KTAV Publishing House, 1971.

Haftman, Werner. *Chagall*. New York: Harry N. Abrams, 1984.

Harshav, Benjamin. *Marc Chagall and the Lost Jewish World*. New York: Rizzoli, 2006.

Hopkins, Clark. *The Discovery of Dura Europos*. New Haven, CT: Yale University Press, 1979.

Hoppe, Leslie. *The Synagogues and Churches of Ancient Palestine*. Collegeville, MI: The Liturgical Press, 1994.

Kagan, Andrew. *Marc Chagall*. New York: Abbeville Press, 1989.

Kaniel, Michael. *Judaism*. Poole, England: Blandford Press, 1979.

Keen, Michael. *Jewish Ritual Art in the Victoria and Albert Museum*. London: HMSO, 1991.

Keller, Sharon R. *The Jews: A Treasury of Art and Literature*. New York: Hugh Lauter Levin Associates, 1992.

Kogman-Appel, Katrin. "Coping with Christian Pictorial Sources: What Did Jewish Miniaturists Not Paint?" *Speculum* 74, no. 4 (2000): 816–58.

Kogman-Appel, Katrin. "Hebrew Manuscript Painting in Late Medieval Spain: Signs of a Culture in Transition." *The Art Bulletin* 84, no. 2 (2002): 246–72.

Krinsky, Carol. *Synagogues of Europe*. New York: The Architectural History Foundation and Cambridge, MA: MIT Press, 1985.

Levine, Lee. *The Ancient Synagogue: The First Thousand Years*. New Haven, CT: Yale University Press, 2000.

Levine, Lee, ed. *Ancient Synagogues Revealed*. Jerusalem: Israel Exploration Society, 1981.

Leymarie, Jean. *Marc Chagall: The Jerusalem Windows*. New York: George Braziller, 1967.

Lipton, Sara. *Images of Intolerance: The Representation of Jews and Judaism in the Bible Moralisée*. Berkeley: University of California Press, 1999.

Mann, Vivian, ed. *Jewish Texts on the Visual Arts*. Cambridge: Cambridge University Press, 2000.

Mann, Vivian, Thomas Glick, and Jerrilynn Dodds, eds. *Convivenica: Jews, Muslims and Christians in Medieval Spain*. New York: George Braziller, 1992.

Matheson, Susan. *Dura Europos: The Ancient City and the Yale Collection*. New Haven, CT: Yale University Art Gallery, 1982.

Meek, Harold Alan. *The Synagogue*. London: Phaidon, 1995.

Moore, Albert. *Iconography of Religions: An Introduction*. Philadelphia: Fortress Press, 1977.

Narkiss, Bezalel. *The Golden Haggadah*. London: The British Library, 1997.

Narkiss, Bezalel. *Hebrew Illuminated Manuscripts*. Jerusalem: Keter Publishing House, 1969.

Schwartzman, Arnold. *Graven Images: Graphic Motifs of the Jewish Gravestone*. New York: Harry N. Abrams, 1993.

Sed-Rajna, Gabrielle. *The Hebrew Bible in Medieval Illuminated Manuscripts*. New York: Rizzoli, 1987.

Sed-Rajna, Gabrielle. "Hebrew Illuminated Manuscripts from the Iberian Peninsula." In *Convivenica: Jews, Muslims and Christians in Medieval Spain*, ed. Vivian Mann, Thomas Glick, and Jerrilynn Dodds, 133–55. New York: George Braziller, 1992.

Sirat, Colette, ed. *La Lettre Hébraïque et sa Signification*. Paris: Editions du Centre National de la Recherche Scientifique, 1981.

Smith, Huston. *The Illustrated World's Religions*. San Francisco: Harper San Francisco, 1986.

Walther, Ingo, and Norbert Wolf. *Codices Illustres: The World's Most Famous Illuminated Manuscripts 400 to 1600*. Köln: Taschen, 2001.

Weinstein, Jay. *A Collector's Guide to Judaica*. New York: Thames and Hudson, 1985.

Weitzmann, Kurt, and Herbert Kessler. *The Frescoes of the Dura Synagogue and Christian Art*. Washington, DC: Dumbarton Oaks, 1990.

Werner, Alfred. "Chagall's Jerusalem Windows." *Art Journal* 21, no. 4 (1962): 224–32.

West, Shearer. *Chagall*. London: PRC, 1994.

Wharton, Annabel. "Good and Bad Images from the Synagogue of Dura Europos: Contexts, Subtexts, Intertexts." *Art History* 17, no. 1 (1994): 1–25.

Wharton, Annabel. *Refiguring the Post Classical City: Dura Europos, Jerash, Jerusalem and Ravenna*. Cambridge: Cambridge University Press, 1995.

Wigoder, Geoffrey, ed. *Jewish Art and Civilization*. Secaucus, NJ: Chartwell, 1972.

Wolfson, Elliot. *Through a Speculum that Shines: Vision and Imagination in Medieval Jewish Mysticism*. Princeton, NJ: Princeton University Press, 1994.

− 10 −

Christianity

ORIGINS AND DEVELOPMENT

Christianity, along with Judaism and Islam, is one of the three major monotheistic religions of the world. It has a very lengthy history of change and transformation, is presently the largest of the world's religions, and is represented today by an enormous variety of different groups, branches, and denominations found in all areas of the world. The three main branches of Christianity today are Roman Catholic, Eastern Orthodox, and Protestant (which itself comprises hundreds of different denominations). All Christians, regardless of branch or denomination, accept the teachings of Jesus as central, even normative.

The religion of Christianity was begun by Jesus (Yeshu'a) of Nazareth, a Jew of humble origin who lived in the region of Galilee in what is now modern-day Israel. He is traditionally believed to have been born in the city of Bethlehem (ca. 4 BCE), to have been raised in the city of Nazareth by pious Jewish parents named Mary (Miryam) and Joseph (Yosef), and to have died in Jerusalem (ca. 30 CE). During his time, this area of the world was part of the vast Roman Empire, and the territory of Judea/Palestine where Jesus lived and taught was administered both directly and by Roman-appointed Jewish kings.

Jesus is briefly mentioned by several later Roman historians (in the early second century CE) and by Josephus (a first-century Jewish historian), but the principal sources of information about the life and teachings of Jesus are contained in the first four books of the Christian scriptures (or "New Testament"). These texts, known as the Four Gospels (authored by or associated with the names of Matthew, Mark, Luke, and John) include various accounts of his career, words, and actions.[1] Written several decades after his death to promote the then-growing religion, the Gospels present Jesus as a teacher, healer, and miracle worker whose apocalyptic message of the coming of the kingdom of God challenged both Jewish and Roman authorities. His public career began when he was about age 30, after his baptism (or "washing of repentance") in the Jordan River by the Jewish prophet known as "John the Baptist." Jesus then traveled for a time through the rural regions of Galilee gathering followers who believed in his teachings and who saw him in some way as the promised messiah or savior of the Jewish people. He offered hope to all social classes, criticized some aspects of the rituals, practices, and hieratic structure of the Judaism of his time, and asserted principles of ethical behavior based on the fundamental Ten Commandments of Judaism but expanded via the "Beatitudes" (right behavior as a result of blessings), which he offered during his "Sermon on the Mount" (recounted in the Gospel of Matthew). This "new ethical system [extended] the Mosaic law in a way that became central to the formation of a distinctly Christian morality."[2] Jesus was a social and religious reformer whose sphere of influence was originally restricted to a relatively small group of Jewish followers and whose career was cut dramatically short by his execution by the Roman authorities, but his enormous impact has been of lasting and worldwide significance.

Although the deeds and teachings of Jesus during his lifetime provide the critical foundation for the Christian religion, his death and subsequent return to life (resurrection) are of absolutely signal importance in the Christian belief system. At the end of his life, Jesus

> was betrayed by one of his followers and arrested:[After] cross-examination by the Jewish authorities, Jesus was sent before the Roman governor, Pontius Pilate, [was charged] and found guilty of claiming to be the king of the Jews, a claim that was blasphemous under Jewish law and treason to the Romans. Jesus was sentenced to death by crucifixion, a normal Roman punishment for criminals, and died on the cross.[3]

The Gospels, however, tell that Jesus was raised to life several days after this, and some of his followers had experiences that inspired them to believe that he had been resurrected by God. This further convinced them of his status as the Messiah, the redeemer, the Christ (from the Greek *Christos*, a translation of the Hebrew term *mashiach*—messiah—the "anointed one of God"). The term "Christ" was originally a title given to Jesus to signify his role as the Messiah, and it then became used as a name: Jesus Christ. Thus, "Christians" are the followers of Jesus (the) Christ.

The news of Jesus's death, resurrection, and ultimate ascension to heaven spread rapidly among Jews and Gentiles (non-Jews) alike. The missionary work of Saul of Tarsus (Saint Paul, ca. 3–65 CE) was especially instrumental in the spread of Christianity through the wider Roman world during the early growth of the religion. Not among the original disciples or initial 12 apostles of Jesus (from the Greek *apostolos*, "messenger" or "delegate" of Christ), Paul, originally an avid anti-Christian, experienced a dramatic conversion, and became one of the most active and ardent supporters and spreaders of the faith, especially to Gentiles. A well-educated Greek-speaking Jew with Roman citizenship, "Paul was one of the first to articulate a Christian theology distinct from Jewish practice and law."[4] He journeyed widely through Italy, Greece, and Asia Minor promoting the new faith, and his writings (letters, or "epistles") to the growing Christian communities in these regions form the major section of the Christian New Testament.

Up through the early fourth century, Christianity continued to grow within the late Roman empire in spite of opposition. The spread and popularity of the religion and the perceived potential political threats to the authority of the Roman state resulted in periodic and at times extremely severe persecutions of Christians through the early centuries. These persecutions came to an end formally under the auspices of the Emperor Constantine (ca. 280–337) whose Edict of Milan in 313 declared "toleration" of Christianity—the religion to which he himself is said to have ultimately converted. The state support for Christianity represented by Constantine's toleration and conversion paved the way for Christianity to ultimately be declared the official religion of the Roman Empire, via edict of the Emperor Theodosius I (ca. 346–395) in 392. From this period onward, the history of Christianity became especially connected with the politics and events that took place in the late Roman world—the re-division of the Roman Empire into two jurisdictions: the Eastern Roman empire (or "Byzantine" empire—based in the city of Constantinople, the ancient Greek city of Byzantium) and the Western Roman empire (centered on the city of Rome).

The first through eighth centuries of Christianity are often called the "Patristic era" (from the Latin *Patres Ecclesiae*, "Fathers of the Church"). During this time, the Christian Church developed systems of administrative hierarchy and jurisdiction, based on Roman government models, and defined the basic and authorized tenets of the faith in a series of Church Councils, such as the Council of Nicea, convened by Constantine in 325, and the Council of Chalcedon, convened by the emperor Marcian in 451. The meetings served to clarify basic doctrines of the Christian faith. Various disputes and disagreements had arisen about such matters as the exact identity of Jesus, the role and position of Mary, and the definition of the Holy Trinity (defining Jesus's relationship to God). Many influential theologians discussed these issues in their writings. Heretical (incorrect) beliefs were identified and discarded as the early Church sought to codify the essential and correct (orthodox) fundamentals of the faith.

Many significant figures among the early Church Fathers include Saint Augustine (354–430, the bishop of Hippo), Saint Ambrose (ca. 339–97, the bishop of Milan), Saint Basil (ca. 329–79, the bishop of Caesarea), and Saint Jerome (342–420) who, at the direction of Pope Damascus, translated the Hebrew and Greek scriptures of the "Old" and "New" Testaments into

Latin. Jerome's translation is known as the "Vulgate" Bible, from the Latin *Versio Vulgata*, "Common Translation." The vast body of patristic literature was greatly expanded during the medieval period, often called the "Scholastic" era of Christianity. Major authors such as Saint Thomas Aquinas (1225–74), whose writings represent highly intellectual and philosophical approaches to theological issues, are especially important for the history of Christianity.

During the earlier medieval period, an event of monumental significance took place for the Christian church, known as the "East-West Schism." In 1054, as a result of complex and long-standing cultural and doctrinal differences, the Eastern (Orthodox) and Western (Roman) churches formally split. A number of factors contributed to this, but it was most notably a result of the insistence of the Western Church on the ultimate authority of the Pope (bishop of Rome) over all Christians and all church matters. To the present day, the Orthodox and Catholic churches remain divided. The Catholic Church accepts the supreme authority of the Pope in Rome, whereas the Eastern churches are less centrally organized and are made up of several different and autonomous branches (such as the Greek Orthodox and the Russian Orthodox) governed by bishops and patriarchs (senior priests) and guided by councils.

The authority of the Roman Pope as well as other practices of the Catholic Church were again questioned definitively in the early 16th century, during what is known as the Protestant Reformation. The movement was begun by leaders such as Martin Luther (1483–1546), Ulrich Zwingli (1484–1531), and John Calvin (1509–64), who criticized the hierarchical structure of the Church and complained against many practices that they deemed corrupt. The Protestant reforming movements, in general, can be said to have been seeking a return to the foundations of the Christian faith, the fundamental teachings of Jesus, and the authority of the Bible, not mediated through any scholastic philosophy or religious institution (the Catholic Church in particular).

The history of Protestant Christianity from the 16th century to the present day is extremely complex and involves the growth of literally hundreds of different variations or denominations. Among the oldest Protestant groups, founded in the 16th through 18th centuries, are the Lutheran, Presbyterian, Anglican (or Episcopal), Methodist, Congregationalist, and Baptist churches, all of which exist in numerous branches. The Seventh-Day Adventists, Christian Scientists, and Jehovah's Witnesses were all founded in the 19th century, and the Pentecostal movement dates to the early 20th century. Other groups, such as the Unitarians (18th century) and Mormons (or Church of Jesus Christ of Latter-day Saints, founded in the 19th century), diverge significantly from other groups in their understanding and interpretations of the nature and role of Jesus.

In the wake of the challenges posed by the initial Protestant reformers of the 16th century, the Catholic Church responded via a period of internal reflection, renewal, and public outreach. Often called the "Catholic Reformation" or "Counter Reformation," this period was characterized by a reaffirmation of the Catholic faith, a modification of some of the practices deemed objectionable by the Protestant reformers, a great flourishing of the arts, and the formation of new orders such as the Society of Jesus (Jesuits) under the leadership of Saint Ignatius of Loyola (1491–1556).

> As Christianity moved into the modern period, powerful rationalist and skeptical influences were exerted on the faith by the eighteenth-century Enlightenment, the Industrial Revolution and the emergence of industrial capitalism, and advances in science from the seventeenth century to the present. Urbanization and secularization, particularly in the West, were among the factors that changed traditional roles and functions performed by the church and its community in earlier historical periods.[5]

In addition to the further development and growth of Protestant denominations in the early modern period, and intensive missionary work by Catholics as well as Protestant groups, the mid-20th century was especially marked by several events and new trends in Christianity. The Second Vatican Council, convened by Pope John XXIII in 1962, inspired significant changes in Catholic beliefs and practices. These included a simplification of the liturgy and use of local languages (rather than Latin) in church services. The decisions of Vatican II were designed to update and energize the Catholic Church. They also reflect the growing spirit of ecumenism—the acceptance of differences, if not actual conciliation, between the various branches of Christianity—as well as the hope for mutually beneficial dialogue with other world religions.

PRINCIPAL BELIEFS AND KEY PRACTICES

Christian beliefs and practices have gone through many centuries of evolution and interpretation since the time of Jesus.

> Like any living religious tradition, the vitality of the Christian faith is evidenced in a continual process of reform and internal pluralism. Today, over four hundred denominations all identify themselves as Christian. Many regard this worldwide religious diversity as one of the greatest challenges facing Christianity in the modern world.[6]

The great diversity of Christian practices may also present some enormous challenges in any attempts to define what is foundational or most fundamental about the Christian religion. Catholic Christians diverge from Orthodox Christians in some significant ways; they follow different church calendars and, in some cases, celebrate different holy days. The major holy days in the Christian Church are Christmas (celebrating the birth of Jesus) and Easter (commemorating his resurrection.) Numerous other holy days are observed by different Christian groups.

The many denominations of Protestant Christianity, though largely sharing the distinction of being "non-Catholic" and "non-Eastern-Orthodox," have different approaches to what they believe are the most important matters for Christians. Certain liturgical practices (which have themselves evolved and changed) have characterized Catholic worship services through history. Orthodox churches also have their unique rites, many of which would not be recognized at all or understood in either Catholic or Protestant churches of vastly different types. Nevertheless, there is unity in this diversity.

The Christian religion is monotheistic. Christians believe that there is one God alone and that this God is a supreme and transcendent being. This God-force is also an active principle in human lives and has communicated directly with humans through the ages. This God (sharing some continuity with the God of the Jews/Israelites) has offered and continues to require specific ethical behaviors of his followers. As an ethical monotheism, the religion of Christianity shares much with its Jewish ancestors and Islamic heirs. The focus of Christianity is, however, on the figure of Jesus Christ. The majority of Christians believe that Jesus was not simply an inspired teacher, or a social reformer, or an incarnation of any one of a number of divine beings, but that Jesus was and is the only Son of the One God who was sent to earth by God to fulfill God's promise of salvation for all humankind.

The concept of salvation—although fundamental for Christianity—has involved a number of different iterations and related precepts throughout Christian history. Diverse branches of Christianity have, in different eras, emphasized specific aspects of salvation, ranging from the rewards anticipated in a glorious afterlife in heaven (versus punishments for sinners in hell[7]) to the liberation from socially or personally oppressive situations.

> Salvation, the term for the state of redemption and reconciliation with God, is a primary spiritual goal of Christians. Aside from the Calvinist notion of predestination, which holds that only an elect body of worshippers is saved, in most Protestant communities salvation is guaranteed solely by the worshipper's faith, the acceptance of Jesus Christ. For Roman Catholicism and Eastern Orthodoxy, salvation is also dependent upon faith in the mysteries of the church, and on the fulfillment of sacraments. Interpretations of the path to salvation vary, but the belief that humans have an immortal soul is generally accepted in Christianity.[8]

Some Christian groups, notably Roman Catholic and Eastern Orthodox, place great emphasis on the acknowledgment and veneration of saints. These holy figures range from the martyrs of the early Church through a progression of historical examples up to the present day. The process by which saintly figures are officially deemed worthy of veneration is known as canonization. This is especially developed in the Roman Catholic Church. Protestant groups tend to place far less emphasis on the mediating role of saints (including Mary), focusing primary attention on the figure of Jesus.

Regardless of group or denomination, Jesus provides the central focus for all Christians as the humanly embodied revelation of God. Belief in the divinity of Jesus and adherence to his ethical teachings brings reconciliation with God. God's continued and abiding presence in human life is acknowledged by all Christians.

TRADITIONAL ART AND ARCHITECTURAL FORMS

Given the diversity of Christian denominations, the lengthy history, and the worldwide spread of the religion, it is no surprise to see that an enormous variety of art and architectural forms are characteristic of Christianity at various periods in history and in different regions of the world. The function and purposes of Christian religious structures, and the use of and attitude toward visual imagery, have diverged as well.

The religion originally developed within the late antique Greco-Roman world, where artistic traditions in painting, sculpture, and architecture had long flourished. The production of art by and for Christians in the first several centuries was, however, somewhat restricted because of the uneasy position and often persecuted status of the new religion. Examples of the very earliest Christian art, such as the fresco paintings in the Roman catacombs (underground cemeteries), often make use of a symbolic visual vocabulary closely akin to works produced for non-Christian patrons. Sub-

jects such as the "Good Shepherd," an image presumably understood by Christians to represent Jesus Christ in his role as savior of humankind, can ultimately be seen as based on the developed and popular pre-Christian Roman traditions of pastoral landscape scenes inhabited by sheep, shepherds, and other bucolic elements (see Figure 10.1). As with many other subjects and symbols found within the funerary context of the catacombs, there are problems with "knowing precisely what these early images meant to Christians—how far the memory of pre-Christian meanings survived and what changes were wrought by successive Christian interpretations."[9] A number of specific biblical (especially Old Testament) subjects appear in early Christian art, in catacomb frescoes, on carved sarcophagi, and on other small-scale objects. It has often been said that the selection of these particular scenes, many of which focus on God's miraculous interventions to save deserving humans from destruction (Daniel in the Lion's Den, Jonah and the Whale, Noah's Ark, and so on), appears to reflect the fears and

Figure 10.1 *The Good Shepherd*, catacomb painting, first through third century. Rome: Catacomb of Priscilla. Scala / Art Resource, NY.

hopes of Christians during these early centuries of oppression. These subjects, as well, may indicate a rich heritage of Jewish pictorial sources from which early Christians also drew.

After the Constantinian Edict of Milan in 313, the now-tolerated and soon-to-be-official religion of the Roman Empire entered an important phase of art and architectural activity. Swiftly growing Christian communities, with a rapidly expanding administrative structure as well, were in need of specifically designed churches for liturgical assemblies. Before the fourth century, Christian gatherings took place in private homes, in rented halls, or in open spaces such as markets.[10] There appears to be no literary or solid archaeological evidence for any structures being intentionally and exclusively designed for Christian worship before the fourth century, although some very early churches may rest on the foundations or sites of private homes previously used for Christian assemblies.

The architectural form used for the earliest actual Christian churches was adopted from the model of the Roman basilica (from the Greek *basilike*, "royal"). Basilicas were ubiquitous public structures in Roman towns and cities and were used for many purposes, such as audience halls, meeting halls, and law courts. The basilican model suited Christian purposes very well because it provided adequate interior space for communal gatherings. The horizontal, longitudinal layout of the Christian church-basilica customarily involved placement of the altar at the east end with the entrance on the west front. Depending on size, the main rectangular hall (nave) of the basilica might be subdivided by rows, piers, or columns, creating aisles. Traditionally, the east end terminated in a semi-circular shape called the apse. A transept with projecting arms, running perpendicular to the nave and creating a Latin cross plan for the overall building, also became a common feature. Many basilicas have an enclosed entry porch (narthex) at the west end, and several are preceded by an open-air courtyard (atrium). Old Saint Peter's in Rome, begun during the time of Constantine, provided the fundamental model of the early Christian basilica. "By the fifth century, every major city in Christendom possessed at least one church on the basilican plan, providing ample room for growing congregations"[11] (see Figure 10.2).

Centrally planned churches (of various layouts: circular, polygonal, and equal-armed cruciform—or "Greek cross" shape), topped by domes, also developed in the early Christian period. Variations on this style became especially characteristic of Byzantine and later Eastern Orthodox forms. An important early Byzantine example is the famous church of the Hagia Sophia (Holy Wisdom) constructed in the early sixth century in the city of Constantinople (present-day Istanbul) under the direction of the emperor Justinian (527–65) (see Figure 10.3). This massive and complex structure, crowned by an impressive dome, provided inspiration for many later Byzantine structures as well as Islamic mosques, especially in the Ottoman Empire. The minarets (tall slender towers) were added after the mid-15th century when the Hagia Sophia was converted into a mosque.

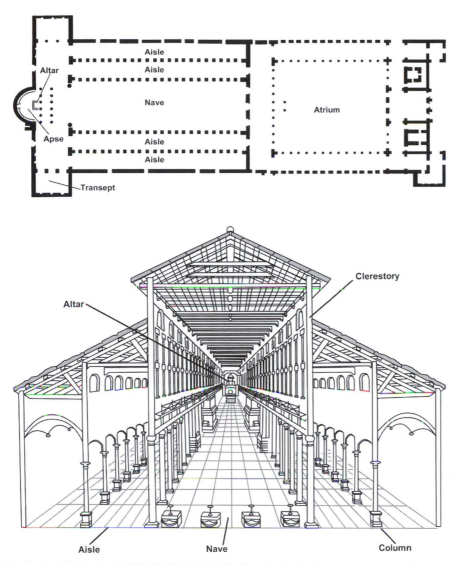

Figure 10.2 Floorplan (above) and diagram (below) of Old Saint Peters, Rome, Italy, early fourth century. Courtesy of Ricochet Productions.

The early Christian basilican form has served as the basic model for many Western Christian churches up to the present day. In Western Europe, during the Middle Ages, many of the still-standing and most impressive monuments of Christian art were created. These Romanesque and Gothic buildings, constructed primarily during the 11th, 12th, and 13th centuries, are traditionally regarded as the epitomes of medieval Christian art and devotion—and the forms that have influenced and colored Christian art modes in the modern world as well. During the Gothic era, the use of architectural forms such as

Figure 10.3 Hagia Sophia, Istanbul, Turkey, early sixth century. Mediamix-photo / Dreamstime.com.

pointed arches, rib vaults, and exterior building supports in the form of flying buttresses resulted in the creation of tall and light-filled buildings that are extremely impressive on both the interior and the exterior for their enormous size and loftiness. The Cathedral of Notre Dame of Chartres, France, is one of the most celebrated examples (see Figure 10.4). The art of stained glass developed greatly during the Gothic period, and religious structures were often enhanced with many impressive examples of narrative and symbolic windows of colored glass (see Plate 19). Although the production and use of glass (for vessels and small-scale objects) has a very lengthy history, and the technology of glass production dates back to ancient Egypt, the use of colored glass for large-scale windows is especially characteristic of the Gothic period, when architectural advances allowed for the creation of larger windows.

Whether of round-arched Romanesque or rib-vaulted Gothic style during the medieval era, classically inspired Renaissance of the 15th and 16th centuries, dramatic 17th-century Baroque, or decorative 18th-century Rococo, Christian church architecture reflects a very wide range of historical and regional styles (see Figure 10.5). Simple wooden construction is typical of many American vernacular examples, and quaint, white-painted churches are a common sight in the American landscape. Numerous other examples of Christian church architecture, in unique and revolutionary forms, have been created by some

Figure 10.4 Notre Dame Cathedral, Chartres, France, 12th to 13th century. Courtesy of Shutterstock.

of the most notable modern architects, such as the pilgrimage church of Notre Dame du Haut, in Ronchamp, France, designed by Le Corbusier (1887–1965) in the mid-20th century (see Figure 10.6).

What take places within Christian churches, and their degree of interior and exterior decoration, varies widely throughout history and between different branches of the religion. From the earliest periods of Christianity to the present day, much discussion and debate has taken place about the proper role and function of art in the Christian religious context. As heirs to the Old Testament commandments conveyed by God to the ancient Israelites, Christians (as well as Jews and Muslims) have been deeply concerned with God's direction against creating or worshiping "graven images" or "idols." The fear of committing idolatry via the creation of any forms of religious imagery has been an underlying theme throughout the history of Christian art. Many Christian theologians have argued eloquently for the usefulness of art in providing inspiration and in serving didactic purposes in conveying biblical narratives and messages in visual and appealing form. Pope Gregory I ("the Great," 590–604) was an early advocate of the educational possibilities of the visual arts, stating, "To adore images is one thing; to teach with their help what should be adored is another. What Scripture is to the educated, images are to the ignorant, who see through them what they must accept; they read in them what they cannot read in books."[12]

Figure 10.5 Vierzehnheiligen Church, Germany, 1742–44. Erich Lessing / Art Resource, NY.

Numerous other Christian authors, however, have been equally eloquent in describing the perilous sinfulness of image creation. This debate was especially heated in the Byzantine world during the eighth- and ninth-century "Iconoclastic Controversy." During this time period—of complex political dimensions too—religious imagery was banned. Images were destroyed, and the creation of holy images was prohibited. Pro- and counter-arguments were avidly presented.[13] Ultimately, the iconodules (supporters of images) triumphed. After the reaffirmation of images in the Byzantine world (celebrated by the Eastern Church in the Feast of Orthodoxy), the prominent role of icons (from the Greek *eikon*, "image," and more specifically, "holy image") in the liturgy and in private devotions in the Byzantine world continued to be a matter of divergence with the Western Roman Church and ultimately may be seen as one of the several factors contributing to the East–West Schism of 1054.

In the 12th century West, the writings of Saint Bernard of Clairvaux (ca. 1090–1153) again represent a type of iconoclastic stance, and the Cistercian monastic order that he revived was known for great austerity and minimal decorative art.[14] His contemporary Abbot Suger of Saint-Denis (1081–1151) was, however, one of the greatest art patrons of the time. Suger was responsible for the magnificent renovation and expansion of the Parisian abbey of Saint-Denis in the new Gothic style and produced glowingly written praises of the abilities of the religious arts to raise human spirituality to the highest realms.[15]

The Protestant reformers of the 16th century and later, in stances against the Roman Catholic Church and all associated with it, generally also represent a strongly iconoclastic tendency, eschewing the use of visual art as potentially idolatrous and misguided. There is thus a great variety of religious artistic expression in the history of Christianity. Early Christian churches were often enriched with fresco paintings and mosaics; elaborate interior and exterior sculptural programs characterize the medieval Romanesque and Gothic styles; stained glass windows play a prominent role in the Gothic era; statues and paintings are generally typical of Roman Catholic churches; icons (often in multi-tiered presentation on an iconostasis—icon screen) abound in Orthodox churches; and minimal and often austere decorations (sometimes only a plain

Figure 10.6 Notre Dame du Haut, Ronchamp, France, 1955. Courtesy of Shutterstock.

cross—lacking the figure of Jesus) may characterize the art associated with specific Protestant denominations.

Just as the forms of art vary widely, so do the forms of worship services that take place within Christian churches. Some branches of Christianity have very elaborate and traditional rites involving the enactment of highly structured rituals that may be performed only by specially trained and authorized figures. Although most all Christian liturgy (from the Greek *leitourgia,* "work of the people") is communal and congregational, the roles of the public congregants and the appointed leaders who preside at these rituals vary widely. This is well reflected by the variety of interior furnishings that may be found in Christian churches.

The Roman Catholic and Eastern Orthodox liturgies, for example, focus on the sacrament of Communion and the miraculous "transubstantiation" of the bread and wine into the actual body and blood of Christ. These sacred mysteries are celebrated at the church altar, led by those trained and authorized to do so, and the congregants are then invited to come forward and partake of these blessings in an orderly and pious fashion. In many Eastern Orthodox churches, the high altar itself is hidden from public view (customarily by a large screen of icons—separating the "most holy" space of the altar from the "holy" space of the church itself), and the congregants do not themselves witness the sacred rites in which they may later be invited to partake via Communion. Protestant Christian groups in general tend to regard the rites of Communion as extremely significant also, but primarily in their purely symbolic and faith-affirming nature as remembrances of the life, death, and resurrection of Jesus. Thus, the interior spaces of Protestant churches may place far less emphasis on a prominently positioned church altar and rather more emphasis on a pulpit or podium from which scriptural readings and sermons may be delivered. The importance of the rite of adult baptism (by partial or full immersion) is reflected by the interior accouterments of many Baptist churches, and the importance of personal faith and healing testimonials is reflected in Christian Science churches often by the arrangement of prominent and dual podiums from which church leaders may encourage speakers to describe their healing experiences.

EXAMPLES

Religious imagery plays a prominent role in the history of Christianity. Images of holy figures (such as Jesus, Mary, the apostles, and saintly martyrs) and scenes depicting episodes from their lives have been created through the centuries in a variety of styles and cultural contexts. Nevertheless, the production of visual and figurative imagery in the service of the Christian religion (for teaching or devotional purposes) has been a source of intense discussion up to the present day. Some Protestant branches of Christianity eschew the use of visual/narrative imagery altogether, whereas the Catholic and Orthodox traditions have traditionally made maximal use of figural art for worship-directed practices. The following selections have been chosen to demonstrate the richness and diversity of Christian imagery as well as the changes in style and interpretation represented by different time periods. With literally thousands of examples to choose from, the following selections are simply a small sample focusing on depictions of the key figures and events in the Christian religion.

Three Images of Mary and Jesus

These three images represent quite different interpretations of the same subject matter: Mary and the infant Jesus. They are vastly different in style, format, and technique. Their differences not only reflect their art historical contexts but also can be seen as significant reflections of important theological issues concerning the role and position of Mary and her relationship to Jesus.

The earliest image is a Byzantine icon that was produced, probably in the city of Constantinople, in the late sixth century (see Figure 10.7). This particular icon is one of the rare survivals from the early Byzantine period; it was produced before the Iconoclastic Controversy. It was created in encaustic (colored wax pigments) on a wooden panel. The second example (the *Madonna of Vladimir*) is also a Byzantine icon (see Figure 10.8). It was created in Constantinople in the late 11th or early 12th century. This later image was produced long after the period of Iconoclastic Controversy in the Byzantine world. It was created with egg tempera paint on a wooden panel.[16]

Figure 10.7 *Virgin and Child with Saints,* late sixth century. Mount Sinai, Egypt: Monastery of Saint Catherine. Erich Lessing / Art Resource, NY.

Figure 10.8 *Madonna of Vladimir,* early 12th century. Moscow: Tretyakov Gallery. Scala / Art Resource, NY.

The third example was also painted with egg tempera on a wooden panel. It was created ca. 1465–67 during the Italian Renaissance period by the artist Fra Filippo Lippi (1406–69) (see Figure 10.9).

Comparing these three similar images is extremely useful in tracking the changes in, and diversity represented by, Christian art forms from different historical and style periods. Although all of the works primarily focus the viewer's attention on the holy figures themselves, there are many notable differences between the three images. The early icon depicts Mary seated on a chair, facing forward, holding the infant Jesus on her lap. Mary and Jesus are flanked by two saintly figures on either side, and two heavenward-looking angels appear behind them. The composition is extremely symmetrical and formal in appearance. The infant Jesus and the two saints (traditionally identified as Saints Theodore and George—both later saints who lived long after the time of Mary and Jesus) all stare straight out at the viewer. Mary gazes slightly off to the right. All of the figures appear solemn and serious. The viewer thus sees that this is a significant and formal work of art, whose intention was to convey the theological importance of these sacred figures. Mary, at the center of the composition, is shown

Figure 10.9 Fra Filippo Lippi, *Madonna with Child and Two Angels*, ca. 1465–67. Florence: Uffizi Gallery. Scala / Art Resource, NY.

as the holy person who miraculously gave birth to the Son of God. She is the "God-bearer" (or *Theotokos*)—a title that she formally received in the preceding century at the Council of Ephesus in 431. Jesus is the God-being seated on her lap whom she presents to the viewer but with whom she otherwise demonstrates little interaction or motherly affection.

The later Byzantine icon (the *Madonna of Vladimir*) shows a quite different level of interaction between Mary and Jesus. In contrast to the frontal formality of the earlier image, this later icon depicts the infant Jesus snuggling up to his mother's cheek while she tenderly supports him on her arm. This icon has been frequently restored and over-painted so that only the faces of Mary and Jesus are close to their original appearance. The disproportionate body of the infant Jesus and the dramatic gold highlighting on his garment are largely the result of later additions. This panel was given as a gift by the Patriarch of Constantinople to the Grand Duke of Kiev in Russia in the early 12th century and ultimately was taken to the city of Vladimir (hence its name). Believed to be a wonder-working image, it was taken to Moscow in the late 14th century and, according to tradition, protected the city of Moscow from Mongol invasions of the time. The image was employed in such a capacity at several later periods in Russian history as well. The *Theotokos* (Mary) is seen as the holy protectress of Russia.

This icon presents a much more maternal and loving relationship between the two holy figures than the earlier pre-iconoclastic version. This type, known in Greek as the *Eleousa* and in Russian as *Umoleniye* ("merciful" or "loving kindness"), developed in the post-iconoclastic period as a reflection of continued theological discussions about the position of Mary and the divine/human nature of Jesus. A comparison between the two panels also indicates significant changes in art style; the works "were surely made in worlds with different expectations regarding what a representation was and what effect it was expected to create."[17]

The desire to represent the visible nature of Christ resulted in the emphasis on his human aspect, and the representation of the human nature is necessarily tied to the miracle of the incarnation through the Virgin Mary. Her human qualities rather than her utility as a source of doctrine had to be brought out directly, and emphasizing her motherhood was the most obvious means of achieving this.[18]

In images of this later type (and numerous variations exist in Byzantine and Russian art on the overall theme of Mary and the infant Jesus[19]), the emphasis is on the emotional relationship between the two figures. Warmth, tenderness, mercy, and sorrow combine in Mary's expression of motherly care and compassion for her son and his ultimate sacrificial and redemptive role. Although intense emotion and powerful spiritual messages are conveyed in images of this sort, all icons generally adhere to strict guidelines and traditions of image and presentation format. The figures are meant to be seen as holy and sacred, existing in a spiritual rather than earthly realm.[20]

This poses a great contrast to the depiction of the *Madonna with Child and Two Angels* created by the Italian Renaissance artist Fra Filippo Lippi, in the mid-15th century. In contrast to the frontal formality and expressive stylization of the Byzantine icons, Lippi's image shows a very worldly Madonna, elegantly dressed in the finest Florentine fashion of the day. She is seated on an elaborate chair in front of a window through which a detailed landscape can be seen. The infant Jesus is presented here as a plump child who reaches out to touch his mother's shoulder. He is supported by a mischievous-looking angel who smiles out at the viewer. Another angel can be glimpsed behind the main figures. Although some traditional religious symbolism can be seen in this work—Mary and Jesus both have thin golden haloes over their heads (indicating their holiness), and the prominent pearl on Mary's headdress as well as the coastline and water in the far distance may refer to theological commentaries describing Jesus as the "pearl of great price" (Matthew 13:46) and Mary as the "star of the sea"—the overall impression of this work bespeaks the artist's "enthusiasm for the beauties of light and atmosphere, rocks and fruitful plains, cities and soft cloud masses, lovely young women and healthy babies, tasteful garments and splendid furnishings."[21] Indeed, the holy figures here appear to have specific portrait-like qualities, as if they are representations of actual people known by the artist, painted from life. This may in fact be the case.[22]

In any event, Lippi's Madonna typifies, in many ways, the humanization of sacred subject matter and the interest in earthly realism characteristic of the Renaissance period in Western art. "Renaissance" means "re-birth" and is used to describe the interests of post-medieval writers and artists in the works of literature, philosophy, and art from ancient Greece and Rome. At the same time, the continued dominance of the Christian religion inspired artists and writers of the Renaissance period to create works that convey and reinforce Christian themes in a classically styled manner. Lippi's work certainly exemplifies these trends and is worlds apart from the earlier examples—although the artistic subject is the same.

Three Images of the Crucifixion of Jesus

Although the death and resurrection of Jesus is a fundamental aspect of the Christian belief system, images of the crucifixion of Jesus have varied greatly through the ages. The death of Jesus on the cross, his subsequent return to life, and the importance this holds for all Christian believers have been interpreted and depicted variously through the centuries. Nevertheless, the crucifixion of Jesus was not one of the very first subjects depicted in Christian art. Although crosses are found in early Christian art, the subject of the crucifixion itself appears to have been avoided at first. A number of scholars have speculated that this may have been because early Christians preferred to focus on Jesus's victory over death rather than on his torture and disgraceful public execution as a criminal in the Roman Empire. When crucifixion was outlawed in the Roman Empire under the emperor Constantine, the image of Jesus's death on the cross gradually entered the pictorial vocabulary of Christian imagery and has evolved with different emphases ever since.

The early fifth-century ivory plaque illustrated shows one of the very earliest images of the crucifixion[23] (see Figure 10.10). It was probably made in Rome and is a small work measuring about three by four inches. It is one of four panels (now separated) that originally must have formed the sides of a small box, or "casket." The exact function of these small decorated caskets is unknown; perhaps they were used to hold relics or other holy objects. Each of the four plaques contains one or two narrative scenes carved in relief. These include

Figure 10.10 Ivory plaque with the Crucifixion, ca. 420–430. London: The Trustees of The British Museum / Art Resource, NY.

Pilate washing his hands, Jesus carrying the cross, the Marys and angel at the empty tomb, and doubting Thomas. The scene of the suicide of Judas and the crucifixion of Jesus appear together on one panel. The other figures represented as present at the crucifixion are Mary and Saint John (to the left) and Longinus (the Roman soldier who pierced the body of Jesus with his spear). The inscription above the head of Jesus reads REX IUD (AEORUM), meaning "King of the Jews."

Taken as a whole, the subjects shown on the casket provide a succinct pictorial narrative of the events in the final days of the life of Jesus, his death, and his resurrection. His death, however, is definitely de-emphasized. Although the figure of Judas is clearly shown dead—with closed eyes and lifeless body hanging from the tree—Jesus is depicted as vigorous, muscular, and alert. His eyes are open, and he seems to be standing upright on or in front of the cross, rather than hanging from it. His pose, outstretched arms, and facial expression give no indication of pain or suffering. Jesus is depicted as triumphant over death, a message that is repeated in the vignette of the mother bird feeding her chicks in a nest—found in the tree branch bending toward the body of Jesus. "The first Christians wished to emphasize that Christ was risen, that is, he had overcome death and conquered evil. He would come again to judge the living and the dead. This was what mattered to them."[24] This early depiction of the crucifixion and the related scenes on the other ivory panels certainly well emphasize these themes.

A vastly different image of the crucifixion was created many centuries later by the German painter Matthias Grünewald (ca. 1475/80–1528) (see Plate 20). The central panel of his complex and multifaceted work, *The Isenheim Altarpiece* (ca. 1510–15), depicts a scene of extreme horror. The physical suffering of Jesus on the cross is conveyed in detail. His body is covered with sores; blood pours from his side and from the wounds of the nails in his twisted feet and hands. His arms pull from their sockets with the weight of his slumping body, which also pulls down the top bar of the cross. His face falls forward; his mouth is open, and his eyes are closed. The dead Jesus, placed in the center of the composition against a dark landscape background, is accompanied by the mourning figures of Saint John and Mary (who is shown collapsing with grief), the kneeling figure of Mary Magdalene convulsed in anguish at the foot of the cross, and the figure of Saint John the Baptist holding a book and pointing at Jesus. The Latin inscription next to John reads, "He must increase but I must decrease" (John 3:30). John the Baptist had announced the coming of Jesus as the Messiah, the sacrificial Lamb of God, which theme is also amplified by the small cross-bearing lamb bleeding into a chalice at John's feet.

Much has transpired in Christian imagery and history since the early ivory plaque was created, reflective of continued theological discussion regarding the human and divine aspects of Jesus. Images of the crucifixion that show Jesus clearly dead or dying began to appear during the early medieval period and became more common and accepted by the 10th and 11th centuries in both Western Europe and the Eastern Byzantine realms. Also during the Middle Ages, a number of new artistic themes developed, many based on a growing body of mystical and visionary literature. Images such as the *Pietà* (Pity, Mary holding the dead body of Jesus), the *Man of Sorrows* (Jesus wounded and suffering), the *Arma Christi* (Instruments of the Passion), and other devotional images designed to inspire a deeply emotional response from viewers became highly popular, especially in northern Europe.[25]

Grünewald's well-studied work needs to be understood within this overall context as well as within the particular circumstances for which it was created.[26] Commissioned by the monastic order of Saint Anthony in Isenheim, the altarpiece was designed to be placed in a chapel connected to the hospital run by the Antonines. Among the sick cared for were

> particularly those afflicted with St. Anthony's fire or ergotism, a disease causing horrific lesions and eruptions of the skin. A new patient was brought first before the altarpiece in the chapel in the hope of a cure through direct divine intervention. If such a miracle did not occur, the patient at least had the consolation of knowing that Christ's sufferings were like his.[27]

The side panels on the front of the altarpiece depict two other figures who suffered greatly but who ultimately triumphed: Saint Sebastian (an early Christian martyr who was tortured by being shot full of arrows—often invoked against the plague and other diseases) and Saint Anthony himself (the patron of the order—whose torments by demons are vividly recounted in stories of his life and graphically depicted on an inner panel of the altarpiece). The altarpiece is a polyptych with multiple hinged panels. Grünewald's work continues on successive openings with scenes including the Annunciation, the Madonna and Child, episodes in the lives of Saints Anthony and Paul the Hermit, and a brilliant image of the resurrection that shows Jesus rising from his tomb with a fully healed and glowing body. It is a highly complex work, an excellent example of the evolution and changes in Christian imagery as well as a special testimony to the needs and concerns of its time.

The crucifixion, one of the most frequent images in Christian art, has been depicted in all centuries and continues to provide a powerful motif for modern and contemporary artists. In the 20th century, the French painter Georges Rouault (1871–1958) produced several versions of the subject (see Figure 10.11). He became a devout Catholic, and his early training as a stained glass artist may be reflected in his unique style characterized by dark black outlines and glowing patches of color. Rouault's style is akin to, but also diverges from, the early 20th-century art movements with which he is sometimes associated, such as Fauvism and Expressionism. Like many of his contemporaries, Rouault worked in an abstract style while maintaining an interest in the representation of recognizable imagery. He was a highly prolific artist whose subjects ranged widely; however, religious imagery was always extremely important to him. He once said, "Art, the art that I aspire to, will be the most profound, the most complete, the most moving expression of what man feels when he finds himself face to face with himself and his humanity. Art should be a . . . passionate confession, the translation of the inner life."[28]

In his *Christ on the Cross* (1939), the traditional elements of the subject are present. The enlarged figure of Jesus on the cross dominates the center of the composition; the accompanying figures of Mary and John appear to the right side of the cross, and Mary Magdalene kneels to the left. Minimal landscape details are indicated, and the figures are quite simplified, consisting of carefully rendered color patches encased in Rouault's typically broad black outlines. Although he has followed the traditional iconography of the crucifixion, Rouault's rendition is a highly personal expression as well. We sense that the artist's own feelings inspired this work. "This is not just a painting for public art, to be viewed from afar. It is the artist's deeply felt personal response to the Crucifixion which in turn seems to require a personal response from the viewer."[29]

Figure 10.11 Georges Rouault, *Christ on the Cross*, 1939. Paris: Musée National d'Art Moderne. CNAC/MNAM/Dist. Réunion des Musées Nationaux / Art Resource, NY.

This brief selection of crucifixion imagery—from the early Christian period, through the northern Renaissance, and to the 20th century—indicates how this most-important event for Christianity has been continually reinterpreted by visual artists through the ages. It remains, regardless of style, format, and artistic interpretation, one of the most recognizable and distinctive of Christian images.

NOTES

1. The "synoptic gospels" (Matthew, Mark, and Luke) present similar versions of Jesus's life, through they are organized somewhat differently. The Gospel of John focuses less on the biography of Jesus and devotes more attention to theological issues and Jesus's position as the Son of God. In addition to the four canonical gospels, many other early writings, collectively known as the New Testament Apocrypha (from the Greek *apokryphos*—hidden), were composed during the early centuries of Christianity. "Although the New Testament canon was established in the late fourth century, subject matter from apocryphal writings, frequent in early Christian art, continued to play an important role in Christian iconography and literature . . . A great many subjects which

were extremely popular in medieval [and later] art are based on apocryphal writings and later literary and hagiographic elaborations of these tales." Leslie Ross, *Medieval Art: A Topical Dictionary* (Westport, CT: Greenwood Press, 1996), 20.

2. Rosemary Drage Hale, "Christianity," in *The Illustrated Guide to World Religions*, ed. Michael Coogan (Oxford: Oxford University Press, 2003), 75.

3. Hale, 59.

4. Hale, 60.

5. Hale, 63.

6. Hale, 63.

7. Alan Bernstein, *The Formation of Hell: Death and Retribution in the Ancient and Early Christian World* (Ithaca, NY: Cornell University Press, 1993).

8. Hale, 84.

9. Albert Moore, *Iconography of Religions: An Introduction* (Philadelphia: Fortress Press, 1977), 231–32.

10. Graydon Snyder, *Ante Pacem: Archaeological Evidence of Church Life Before Constantine* (Macon, GA: Mercer University Press, 1985).

11. Hale, 77.

12. Caecilia Davis-Weyer, *Early Medieval Art 300–1150: Sources and Documents* (Englewood Cliffs, NJ: Prentice-Hall, 1971), 48.

13. For an extensive selection of texts, see Cyril Mango, *The Art of the Byzantine Empire 312–1453: Sources and Documents* (Englewood Cliffs, NJ: Prentice Hall, 1972), especially 149–77.

14. Conrad Rudolph, *The "Things of Greater Importance:" Bernard of Clairvaux's Apologia and the Medieval Attitude Toward Art* (Philadelphia: University of Pennsylvania Press, 1990).

15. Leslie Ross, *Artists of the Middle Ages* (Westport, CT: Greenwood Press, 2003), 81–92.

16. For an excellent introduction to the materials and techniques of icon painting, see Guillem Ramos-Poqui, *The Technique of Icon Painting* (Tunbridge Wells, England: Search Press/Burns and Oates, 1990). For the use of icons in the Orthodox liturgy, see Nancy Sevcenko, "Icons in the Liturgy," *Dumbarton Oaks Papers* 45 (1991): 45–57.

17. Jeffrey Anderson, "The Byzantine Panel Portrait Before and After Iconoclasm," in *The Sacred Image: East and West*, ed. Robert Ousterhout and Leslie Brubaker (Chicago: University of Illinois Press, 1995), 30.

18. Ioli Kalavrezou, "Images of the Mother: When the Virgin Mary Became 'Meter Theou,'" *Dumbarton Oaks Papers* 44 (1990), 169.

19. Leonid Ouspensky and Vladimir Lossky, *The Meaning of Icons* (Crestwood, NY: Saint Vladimir's Seminary Press, 1983), and Kurt Weitzmann, *The Icon: Holy Images—Sixth to Fourteenth Century* (New York: George Braziller, 1978).

20. Ross, *Artists of the Middle Ages*, 123–37.

21. Frederick Hartt, *History of Italian Renaissance Art* (New York: Harry N. Abrams, 1994), 224.

22. Megan Holmes, *Fra Filippo Lippi: The Carmelite Painter* (New Haven, CT: Yale University Press, 1999), 9–13, 150.

23. This work is traditionally described as *the* earliest extant image of the crucifixion, dating to ca. 420–30. The carved wooden doors of the church of Santa Sabina in Rome (dating ca. 432) also contain a very early image of the crucifixion.

24. Richard Harries, *The Passion in Art* (Aldershot, England: Ashgate, 2004), 13.

25. Henk van Os, *The Art of Devotion: 1300–1500* (London: Merrell Holberton, 1994).

26. Andrée Hayum, *The Isenheim Altarpiece: God's Medicine and the Painter's Vision* (Princeton, NJ: Princeton University Press, 1989), and Ruth Mellinkoff, *The Devil at Isenheim: Reflections of Popular Belief in Grünewald's Altarpiece* (Berkeley: University of California Press, 1988).

27. Harries, 94.

28. Harries, 115.

29. Harries, 117.

BIBLIOGRAPHY AND FURTHER READING

Anderson, Jeffrey. "The Byzantine Panel Portrait Before and After Iconoclasm." In *The Sacred Image: East and West*, ed. Robert Ousterhout and Leslie Brubaker, 25–44. Chicago: University of Illinois Press, 1995.

Belting, Hans. *The Image and Its Public in the Middle Ages: Form and Function of Early Paintings of the Passion.* New Rochelle, NY: A. D. Caratzas, 1990.

Bernstein, Alan. *The Formation of Hell: Death and Retribution in the Ancient and Early Christian Worlds.* Ithaca, NY: Cornell University Press, 1993.

Brown, Frank. *Good Taste, Bad Taste, and Christian Taste: Aesthetics in Religious Life.* Oxford: Oxford University Press, 2000.

Buecher, Frederick. *The Faces of Jesus.* New York: Simon and Schuster, 1974.

Cavarnos, Constantine. *Orthodox Iconography.* Belmont, MA: Institute for Byzantine and Modern Greek Studies, 1977.

Christian Iconography. http://www.aug.edu/augusta/iconography/.

Christus Rex. http://www.christusrex.org/.

Coogan, Michael, ed. *The Illustrated Guide to World Religions.* Oxford: Oxford University Press, 2003.

Cormack, Robin. *Byzantine Art.* Oxford: Oxford University Press, 2000.

Courthion, Pierre. *Rouault.* New York: Harry N. Abrams, 1961.

Davis-Weyer, Caecilia. *Early Medieval Art 300–1150: Sources and Documents.* Englewood Cliffs, NJ: Prentice-Hall, 1971.

Drury, John. *Painting the Word: Christian Pictures and their Meanings.* New Haven, CT: Yale University Press, 1999.

Finaldi, Gabriele. *The Image of Christ.* London: National Gallery, 2000.

Frisch, Teresa. *Gothic Art 1140–c1450: Sources and Documents.* Englewood Cliffs, NJ: Prentice-Hall, 1971.

Grubb, Nancy. *Revelations: Art of the Apocalypse.* New York: Abbeville Press, 1997.

Hale, Rosemary Drage. "Christianity." In *The Illustrated Guide to World Religions*, ed. Michael Coogan, 52–87. Oxford: Oxford University Press, 2003.

Harries, Richard. *The Passion in Art.* Aldershot, England: Ashgate, 2004.

Hartt, Frederick. *History of Italian Renaissance Art.* New York: Harry N. Abrams, 1994.

Hayum, Andrée. *The Isenheim Altarpiece: God's Medicine and the Painter's Vision.* Princeton, NJ: Princeton University Press, 1989.

Holmes, Megan. *Fra Filippo Lippi: The Carmelite Painter.* New Haven, CT: Yale University Press, 1999.

Howe, Jeffery. *Houses of Worship: An Identification Guide to the History and Styles of American Religious Architecture*. San Diego, CA: Thunder Bay Press, 2003.

Hutter, Irmgard. *Early Christian and Byzantine Art*. New York: Universe, 1971.

Huysmans, J. K. *Grünewald*. Oxford: Phaidon, 1976.

Kalavrezou, Ioli. "Images of the Mother: When the Virgin Mary Became 'Meter Theou.'" *Dumbarton Oaks Papers* 44 (1990): 165–72.

Lowden, John. *Early Christian and Byzantine Art*. London: Phaidon, 1997.

Maguire, Henry. *The Icons of Their Bodies: Saints and Their Images in Byzantium*. Princeton, NJ: Princeton University Press, 1996.

Mango, Cyril. *The Art of the Byzantine Empire 312–1453: Sources and Documents*. Englewood Cliffs, NJ: Prentice Hall, 1972.

Martin, F. David. "What Is a Christian Painting?" *Leonardo* 10, no. 1 (1977): 23–29.

Mellinkoff, Ruth. *The Devil at Isenheim: Reflections of Popular Belief in Grünewald's Altarpiece*. Berkeley: University of California Press, 1988.

Moore, Albert. *Iconography of Religions: An Introduction*. Philadelphia: Fortress Press, 1977.

Morgan, David. *Visual Piety: A History and Theory of Popular Religious Images*. Berkeley: University of California Press, 1998.

Nelson, Robert, and Kristen Collins. *Holy Image, Hallowed Ground: Icons from Sinai*. Los Angeles: J. Paul Getty Museum, 2006.

Ouspensky, Leonid, and Vladimir Lossky. *The Meaning of Icons*. Crestwood, NY: Saint Vladimir's Seminary Press, 1983.

Ousterhout, Robert, and Leslie Brubaker, eds. *The Sacred Image: East and West*. Chicago: University of Illinois Press, 1995.

Panofsky, Irwin. *Abbot Suger on the Abbey Church of Saint-Denis and Its Art Treasures*. Princeton, NJ: Princeton University Press, 1946, 1979.

Pelikan, Jaroslav. *The Illustrated Jesus through the Centuries*. New Haven, CT: Yale University Press, 1997.

Ramos-Poqui, Guillem. *The Technique of Icon Painting*. Tunbridge Wells, England: Search Press/Burns and Oates, 1990.

Ross, Leslie. *Artists of the Middle Ages*. Westport, CT: Greenwood Press, 2003.

Ross, Leslie. *Medieval Art: A Topical Dictionary*. Westport, CT: Greenwood Press, 1996.

Rudolph, Conrad. *The "Things of Greater Importance": Bernard of Clairvaux's Apologia and the Medieval Attitude Toward Art*. Philadelphia: University of Pennsylvania Press, 1990.

Sevcenko, Nancy. "Icons in the Liturgy." *Dumbarton Oaks Papers* 45 (1991): 45–57.

Snyder, Graydon. *Ante Pacem: Archaeological Evidence of Church Life Before Constantine*. Macon, GA: Mercer University Press, 1985.

Van Os, Henk. *The Art of Devotion: 1300–1500*. London: Merrell Holberton, 1994.

Weitzmann, Kurt. *The Icon: Holy Images—Sixth to Fourteenth Century*. New York: George Braziller, 1978.

$-11-$

Islam

ORIGINS AND DEVELOPMENT

The religion of Islam is the youngest of the three major monotheistic religious systems popular in the world today and also the fastest growing of the world religions. Closely related to Judaism and Christianity by sharing a belief in one God, Islam expands on aspects of the earlier two systems by its acceptance of the culminating revelations received by the Prophet Muhammad (570–632 CE). Islam acknowledges the sacred nature of the Hebrew and Christian scriptures and accepts figures such as Moses and Jesus as inspired prophets of God. According to Islam, however, Muhammad was the final prophet whose revelations and teachings complete and supersede all earlier. Muhammad is regarded as the "seal" of the prophets, and his message represents a return to the one, true religion, as originally revealed to the first man, Adam, and the ancient biblical patriarch Abraham (Ibrahim). Muslims trace their heritage to the common "Abrahamic tradition" of Jews and Christians, but believe that Muhammad's message represents the final renewal of this tradition.

Muhammad (Muhammad ibn Abdallah) was born in the city of Mecca in present-day Saudi Arabia. He was a merchant and a member of an important tribe. Circa 610, when he was about 40 years old, he began to have mystical experiences that continued throughout the rest of his life. These divine revelations led him to proclaim that there was one God only (Allah) and that the traditional polytheistic beliefs previously held by the Arabian tribal groups were idolatrous. The religious beliefs of the society into which Muhammad was born involved worship of a number of different major and minor deities. His proclamation of the one God was thus extremely controversial and originally met with great opposition. Nevertheless, the strength of his message impressed many, and he quickly gained followers who accompanied him to the city of Yathrib (later named Medina—Madinat al-Nabi—the City of the Prophet) in 622. This exodus/emigration from Mecca to Medina is known, in Arabic, as the Hegira (or Hijra), and it marks the first year of the Muslim calendar, as well as the formal founding of the Islamic community, or *Umma*. For the next decade, Muhammad continued his teachings and gained many followers. He returned to Mecca with a military force in 630, captured the city, and proclaimed the end of idol worship. By the time of his death in Medina in 632, most of the Arabian peninsula was under his military and religious control, and his successors continued to expand this empire rapidly by political conquest and conversion.

After the death of Muhammad, disputes arose regarding the leadership of the Muslim community, and it is to this early period that the two major divisions still found within Islam today can ultimately be traced. The majority of Muslims in the world today follow the Sunni branch. Sunni refers to *sunna* ("tradition"), and Sunni Muslims are "the people of the tradition." Although the Sunni movement did not formally arise until the 10th century, it can be seen as the ultimate result of doctrinal disputes and political rivalries of the first several decades after the death of Muhammad and, in particular, the claims of the Shi'ite sect to overarching legitimacy and authority.

The Shi'ite movement opposed the election of Abu Bakr al-Asamm (leader from 632 to 634), a close companion of Muhammad, as the first caliph ("deputy" or "successor" of Muhammad) and believed that the Prophet's cousin and son-in-law, Ali ibn Abi Talib (caliph from 656 to 661), should have been chosen instead as the rightful leader and spiritual guide, or *imam*. The term Shi'ite comes from Shi'at Ali, the "partisans" or "followers" of Ali. Although Ali did ultimately become the fourth caliph, the divisions over rightful succession and correct lineage of the leaders resulted in military uprisings and conflicts that continue to occur in the Islamic world today.

In addition, the Shi'ite movement itself divided into two major branches in the eighth and ninth centuries, over similar issues. Ismaili Shi'ism (which itself contains many subsects) arose with the supporters of Ismail as the seventh Imam, and Ismailis "believe in an unbroken line of Imams to the present day."[1] "Twelver" Shi'ism maintains a belief in the return, at the end of time, of a "hidden" twelfth Imam who disappeared in the late ninth century into "a miraculous state of concealment . . . 'occultation.'"[2] In Shi'ite traditions, the Imams are divinely inspired spiritual leaders who must be direct descendants of the Prophet (through Ali and Muhammad's daughter, Fatima). The Imam "is a link in the chain of prophecy stretching back through Muhammad and Jesus to Abraham and Adam. . . . The Imam, therefore, is the only legitimate authority on earth, and obedience to him is required of all humankind. He is held to be infallible, without sin, and in possession of a body of knowledge transmitted by God."[3]

Sunni Muslims, "while thinking of themselves as members of the single worldwide community of Islam . . . recognize internal social and cultural differences born of the encounter between Islamic teaching and local and regional practices."[4] Thus, Sunni Muslims themselves represent a vast diversity of groups in different geographic settings and cultures. Shi'ism, with a greater emphasis on clerical authority and more narrowly defined doctrines, is followed by only 10 percent of Muslims today; the vast majority of Muslims are Sunnis. It was primarily within Sunni traditions that the four major schools of Islamic law (the Sharia) developed in the eighth and ninth centuries, with a series of scholars who devoted attention to codifying rules for proper conduct according to Islamic principles. These different schools of legal study and interpretation are still followed in the Islamic world today.

The initial growth of Islam was primarily among Arabic peoples, but in the centuries following, "Arabs were joined by large numbers of people from other ethnic and religious backgrounds . . . [and] in this way, Islam was transformed from the religion of a relatively small number of Arabs to a universal faith."[5] One can trace this growth through a series of eras associated with different dynasties of rulers: the Umayyads in the Middle East and Spain, the Abbasids in Iraq, the Fatimids in Egypt, the Seljuk Turks in Central Asia and Anatolia, the Mongol Ilkanids in Central Asia and Persia, the Timurids in Persia, the Ottomans based in Anatolia, the Safavids in Persia, and the Moghuls in India. In all cases, the art and architecture associated with these different eras and peoples represent a great cultural diversity. Islam continues to flourish and grow rapidly around the world today. Thus, it is extremely wise to recognize that the historical development and present nature of Islam involve a plethora of Islamic cultures rather than a faith based on one sole religious leader or political authority. All Muslims, however, share some fundamental beliefs and key practices.

PRINCIPAL BELIEFS AND KEY PRACTICES

"There is no God but God and Muhammad is his Prophet." This statement, known as the *shahada* ("confession" or "witnessing"), contains the two fundamental beliefs that provide the foundation for Islam. Islam is an Arabic word that means "submission" or "surrender" to the will of God, and the followers of Islam are called Muslims—those who "submit" or "surrender" to God. "To submit to the divine will . . . is . . . to bring about a harmonious order in the universe. In this sense, Islam refers not only to the act of submission but to its consequence, that is, peace (*salam*.)"[6] Muslims do not worship Muhammad but regard him as the Prophet of God, through whom God spoke.

The sacred scriptures for Islam are known as the Qur'an, or "recitation," and consist of a series of revelations received by Muhammad beginning in ca. 610

when he had the mystical experience of first being visited by the angel Gabriel, who told him to "recite" the words from God. This was followed by many further mystical revelations through the rest of his life. The text of the Qur'an was dictated by Muhammad to several scribes during his lifetime and is also based on slightly later memories of his teachings. The final and authorized version of the Qur'an was created within 20 years of Muhammad's death and remains unchanged today. Because the Qur'an was received and written in the Arabic language, translations into other languages are not considered truly authentic or authoritative. The subsequent importance of the Arabic language and script for Islamic art is discussed later in this chapter.

The Qur'an is a complex and poetic text (about the same length as the New Testament/Christian scriptures) filled with narratives, metaphors, mystical expressions, and directions for specific duties and moral obligations. Chief among these latter are the "Five Pillars" of Islam. These are (1) confession of faith in the one God, Allah, and Muhammad's role as Prophet, (2) prayer five times daily, (3) charity to the poor in terms of specific tithes/taxes, (4) fasting from sunrise to sunset during the holy month of Ramadan, and (5) making a pilgrimage (or Hajj) to Mecca at least once during one's life, if one is able (and preferably at the designated period for this). The focal point of the pilgrimage to Mecca is the visit to the Ka'ba. This is an ancient sacred structure in the form of a cube-shaped building—presently about 43 feet tall. Tradition holds that the Ka'ba was first constructed by Adam, rebuilt by Abraham, and purified by Muhammad when he rid Mecca of idol worship.[7]

In addition to the Qur'an, the other sacred scriptures of Islam are known as the Hadith. This is a vast compendium of material that includes sayings of the Prophet as well as information and anecdotes about his life and deeds. The Hadith, originally transmitted purely orally, were primarily collected and compiled in the late eighth and ninth centuries. They trace their transmission back to authoritative sources such as close companions and family members of the Prophet, but in some cases may also be seen as reflecting later interpretations of doctrine.

The Qur'an and the Hadith are the foundational and most revered texts of Islam, and these works provide the basis for the Sharia (the "Islamic way")—codes of contact, social, and legal obligations. Reflections on these foundational works by Islamic writers through the eras have also resulted in a vast body of theological and mystical literature, which may be categorized under the general term of Sufism. "The term may perhaps derive from the Arabic *suf* ('wool'), and thus is perhaps a reference to the rough, simple garb worn by ascetics in the formative period of Islam."[8] Although Sufism is often described as the "mystical branch" of Islam, in many ways, Sufism "should be seen as an integral dimension of Islamic life rather than as something pursued apart from the mainstream practices and doctrines of the tradition."[9] Through the centuries and in different Islamic cultures, Sufi teachers and movements have been responsible for remarkable works of devotional literature and art.

TRADITIONAL ART AND ARCHITECTURAL FORMS

Definitions and Dilemmas

The focus of this study is on Islamic religious art and not on the vast and multifaceted field of Islamic art in general.[10] However, the terms Islamic art, Islamic religious art, and even religious art are, as a whole, all extremely problematic. Because Islam itself represents many coexisting variants, and because the extent and influence of Islam covers "not just one period and one country but fourteen centuries in nearly forty countries,"[11] it is wise to acknowledge the dangers and difficulties inherent in a "religiously based classification"[12] for this vastness and diversity of material.

Indeed, much scholarship has been devoted to the complex issues of defining what is Islamic about Islamic art or to posing questions such as this: "What is one meant to attend to in Islamic art?"[13] It can be said that many of the copious studies of Islamic art include works of art that are, arguably, not specifically religious in nature. Many works of a secular nature—objects and architecture designed for nonreligious, domestic purposes—are often included in studies of Islamic art. Are works of art Islamic simply because they were produced for Muslim patrons, or in regions of the world where Islam was, or is, the dominant faith? Is it the case that "the art of Islam is Islamic art not only because it was created by Muslims but because it issues forth from the Islamic revelation"?[14]

There are no simple answers to these questions, and the definition of Islamic art remains an intriguing matter of intense scholarly debate. This dilemma also brings up "a key issue of contemporary thought: whether it is valid to apply the same investigative methods to the art of all cultures, or whether the very nature of artistic experience requires methods created by the culture itself."[15] Again, opinions on this diverge widely. Whereas some scholars have claimed that Islamic art requires "specific rules in order to be understood,"[16] others have argued that this attitude creates a dangerous "mystification"[17] of the topic.

In addition, one of the issues that needs to be addressed immediately in any discussion of Islamic religious art (or Islamic art in general) regards the attitude of Islam to the arts, the figurative arts in particular. Many religions place great emphasis on narrative imagery and make use of two- and three-dimensional images for didactic and inspirational purposes. Deities are often pictured in human or human-like forms in many religious art traditions. Stories from the lives and deeds of saintly figures feature prominently in some traditions, and images may function and be understood as containers or sacred receptacles for divine presences. In some religious traditions, holy images are housed within shrines or temples, and these images are objects of intense veneration in the form of prayers, ceremonies, and offerings. The images may be taken out and processed in special religious festival contexts and otherwise may not only serve as reminders of divine presence but may also be understood *as* divine presences.

The worship of a multitude of different deities, and the use of imagery to visualize and embody a number of deities, was characteristic of some of the religious practices of pre-Islamic Arabia before the time of Muhammad. By his lifetime in the sixth century, of course, the traditions of Christian art and iconography had significantly developed, and Jewish art forms had continued to evolve. Figural and narrative scenes involving representations of humans and animals had played a greater or lesser role in both Jewish and Christian art for centuries by the time of Muhammad. Muhammad's message of the oneness of God (Allah) posed a sharp contrast to any polytheistic beliefs and practices and reconfirmed the monotheistic message of both Judaism and Christianity. The belief in one single all-powerful God required that the worship practices and imagery associated with polytheism be rejected in favor of submission to the one, true God. The creation, use, and worship of images of deities was seen as indicative of the misguided polytheism of pre-Islamic times, which was supplanted by the message and revelations of Muhammad.

There are, however, no specific strictures against art in general in the Qur'an itself, although the text does emphasize and reassert the evilness of idol worship following the Hebrew and Christian scriptures on this matter. The blasphemy represented by the worship of false gods and idols was dramatically signaled by Muhammad's reported actions when he overtook the city of Mecca in 630. According to several accounts, one of his first actions upon his return to Mecca was to order the destruction of all idols in the city, many of which were housed near or inside the Ka'ba—"the most important ritual site of the nomadic tribes that inhabited Arabia, [originally] built at God's express command by Abraham and Ismael, according to Islam."[18] By the time of Muhammad,

> there were said to be 360 different deities including Awf, the great bird, Hubal, the Nabatean god, the three celestial goddesses, Manal, Al-Uzza and al-Lat, and statues of Mary and Jesus. The most important of all these deities was called Allah ('god'). This deity was worshiped throughout southern Syria and northern Arabia, and was the only deity not represented by an idol in the ka'ba.[19]

All the pagan idols were destroyed, "with the notable exception of the statues of Mary and Jesus . . . Thus, by gaining both religious and political control over Mecca, Muhammad was able to redefine the sacred territory and restore Abrahamic order to it."[20]

Although it is certainly possible to interpret this act of idol-smashing as an act of iconoclasm—and iconoclastic tendencies certainly do exist and have repeatedly surfaced in the history of Islam (as in Christianity, Judaism, and other world religions as well)—the destruction of the idols was most primarily a reflection of Muhammad's wish to rid the city of pagan religions and have his followers turn to the one true God: Allah.

Other more specific statements concerning art can be found among the Hadith traditions (the sayings of Muhammad as later recorded or remembered by his companions), and several of these statements have been interpreted as representing a negative attitude toward figural art in general. For example, several Hadiths say that those who attempt to imitate what God has created, or those who attempt to imitate God by creating representations of living beings, will be punished on the day of judgment. However, it seems clear that, even from the very earliest era, the target of concern was not art per se but rather idolatrous art created for the worship of false gods.

This is borne out by the fact that figural and narrative imagery *are* found in Islamic art and even in art of an intensely religious nature. Although it has been convenient for many who have written about Islamic art in the past to draw a distinction between "secular" art (where it is clear that figural images appear from the very earliest periods) and "religious" art (where "prohibitions" upon or at least avoidance of figural imagery appear to have been in place from the earliest periods), the situation is not as simple and clear cut as this implies. "Figural representation has always been a part of secular art in the Islamic world,"[21] and in some cases—notably later Persian manuscripts illustrated with images of the Prophet and scenes from his life—figural imagery also plays an important role in reflecting the political and religious aims of different eras.[22] It is certainly a mistake to characterize Islamic art as anti-figural or to regard figurative art, when it does appear, "as an aberration within a strictly aniconic culture."[23] Nevertheless, there is no doubt at all that Islamic art, in general, makes highly sophisticated use of patterns—geometric, vegetal, and calligraphic—and these patterns play a dominant role in both the religious and the secular arts characteristic of a diversity of periods and Islamic cultures.

The Mosque

In terms of religious architecture, the mosque is the fundamental form of gathering space designed to suit the specific needs of Muslim worship. "As a type, the mosque is ubiquitous, and at once old and very new. It is a culture-bound place of worship, representing local and regional traditions, and a trans- or supra-regional expression of . . . a pan-Islamic worldwide character."[24] The principal function of mosques is to accommodate groups of believers who may gather in prayer at the five specified times daily. The term mosque (or *masjid*) derives from the Arabic word meaning "to prostrate oneself." Thus, a mosque is a "place or worship" and specifically a "place of prostration." Muslims may perform their daily prayers alone and in whatever areas or spaces are convenient for them, but the communal gathering in a mosque is especially important in some Islamic cultures—and especially on Friday (the Islamic holy day), Muslims are encouraged to attend communal prayer services and listen to teachings and sermons (*khutba*) at a mosque. Traditionally, men and women are afforded separate spaces for prayer in mosques, although variations exist, especially in current practices.

Depending on the time period and cultural context, the architectural forms and styles of Islamic mosques vary widely. All mosques, however, share specific requirements. Chief among these is orientation. All Islamic mosques worldwide are oriented as closely as possible to the direction of the holy city of Mecca. All Muslims throughout the world pray in the direction of Mecca and perform their prayers (*salat*—by a series of formalized physical movements and gestures, involving standing, kneeling and prostration, plus the recitation of specific phrases) in the direction of the *qibla* (the wall of the mosque that is oriented to Mecca) and the *mihrab* (a niche in the *qibla* wall). A *qibla* and *mihrab* are thus among the requirements for Islamic religious architecture. In addition, most mosques are equipped with a *minbar* (often located next to the *mihrab*), which is an elevated platform or podium from which the prayer leader (*imam*) may deliver a sermon. Large mosques may also include a *dikka* (raised platform) from which the speeches of the *imam* may be re-conveyed to the congregants. Because ritual preparation for prayer requires cleansing and washing of head, feet, and hands, mosques are customarily provided with fountains or other ablution areas for worshipers. Towers (or minarets) are often a customary aspect of mosque architecture, but are by no means a universal feature.[25] They exist in a wide variety of styles, some characteristic of particular regions. The minarets may not only signal the location of the mosque but may also provide the location from which the formalized call to daily prayers (*adhan*) can be conveyed or broadcast by the *muezzin* (a specially trained and appointed person) or—in modern times—often a taped broadcast through loudspeakers).

Within these basic parameters of function and requirements, mosque architecture and style vary widely depending on the historical time period and world region (see Figure 11.1). The form and style of mosques may also depend on their status as smaller community mosques constructed for local audiences or as grander and perhaps royal or state-sponsored mosques with connections to political authority in some manner. Some mosques enclose more space than others, a factor that also depends on climate conditions.

In some case, mosques will show a hypostyle (or multi-columned hall) arrangement preceded by an open-air courtyard or *sahn*. Some of the very ear-

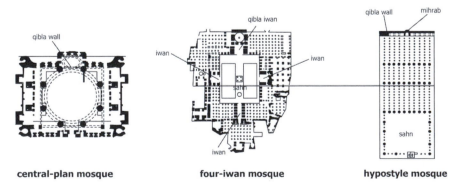

central-plan mosque   **four-iwan mosque**   **hypostyle mosque**

Figure 11.1 Mosque floor plans—general types. Courtesy of Ricochet Productions.

liest mosques are of this type, such as the Great Mosque in Cordoba, Spain, constructed beginning in the late eighth century under the Umayyad rulers (see Figure 11.2). This building was enlarged several times in the 9th and 10th centuries and ultimately became transformed via the insertion of a large Christian chapel in the midst of the former prayer hall in the 16th century. The prayer hall contains multiple rows of columns supporting horseshoe-shaped arches on superimposed levels. Red brick and white stonework add to the visual complexity and "startling originality"[26] of the large hypostyle interior space.

Other mosques are of central-plan format with an emphasis on a vast domed interior space. Courtyards may or may not appear in this type, which is especially characteristic of medieval Ottoman style, such as the "Blue Mosque" in Istanbul, constructed in the early 17th century under the Ottoman sultan Ahmed I (1590–1617). Six tall, slim minarets grace the exterior edges of this mosque complex, and the interior is famous for its thousands of glazed, patterned tiles of dominantly blue tones (see Figures 11.3 and 11.4).

A central courtyard surrounded on all four sides by vaulted halls with wide arched entrances (or *iwans*) is yet another format. The four-*iwan* plan was especially developed in medieval Persia, such as seen with the Royal Mosque (now the Imam Mosque), which was constructed under the patronage of the Safavid ruler Shah Abbas (1571–1629) in the early 17th century. The central courtyard

Figure 11.2   The Great Mosque, Cordoba, Spain, 8th to 10th century, interior. Art Resource, NY.

Figure 11.3 Blue Mosque (Mosque of Sultan Ahmed I), Istanbul, Turkey, 1609–16, exterior. Courtesy of Shutterstock.

contains a large, square pool of water that reflects the multiple small and large arches of the enclosure (see Figure 11.5).

Many contemporary mosques represent variations on these traditional historical formats while also demonstrating materials, elements, and styles of modern and postmodern architectural design. Apart from purely religious functions as centers for communal worship, Islamic mosques have traditionally also functioned as focal points in larger architectural complexes involving schools of Islamic law and theology (*madrasas*) plus hospitals and other facilities for charitable works. The Islamic mosque is often not a stand-alone religious building but incorporates these other functions too.

However, regardless of architectural style, date, and cultural context of Islamic mosques, the interior and exterior decoration of mosques rarely if ever shows any designs that include human figures. Strictly speaking, as mentioned previously, Islamic religious art does not include or permit the representation of human beings. This is a complex issue and has been understood and variously interpreted by different Islamic cultures through the centuries. However, the interior and exterior decoration of mosques is traditionally restricted to non-figural motifs and will primarily include geometric and calligraphic forms.

The Word in Islamic Art

The holy scriptures of Islam (the Qur'an) were received by and recited in the Arabic language to Muhammad, who transmitted the sacred words to his followers, in Arabic. Hence, Arabic is considered to be the holy language of Islam, and the careful transmission of the sacred scriptures, in written form, in the original Arabic, is one of the most important forms of Islamic art and religious devotion. Although it is surely the case that many other world religions regard their sacred texts as divinely inspired, and certainly the care and attention that adherents of other faiths devote to the correct copying and transmission of sacred scriptures can be seen to parallel that of Islam, the written word truly plays a quite distinctive role in Islamic art. Because of the dominant role of the written word in Islam, the art of calligraphy is one of the most stellar and most esteemed forms of Islamic art generally. In strictly religious contexts, such as manuscripts of the Qur'an and the decoration of mosques, where figural and narrative imagery are

Figure 11.4 Blue Mosque (Mosque of Sultan Ahmed I), Istanbul, Turkey, 1609–16, interior. Vanni / Art Resource, NY.

Figure 11.5 Royal Mosque (Imarı Mosque), Isfahan, Iran, 1612–37, interior courtyard. The Art Archive / Gianni Dagli Orti.

avoided, calligraphic inscriptions are certainly paramount in ways unparalleled in the religions arts of other cultures. Moreover, calligraphy appears in all media of Islamic art—it is not simply restricted to the obvious context of text transmission in manuscripts of the Qur'an, but appears in all forms of Islamic art from large to small scale, of both strictly religious and more secular forms.

Much scholarship has been devoted to the topic of the artful word in Islamic cultures and the "love of the written word that turned Islamic calligraphy into an elevated noble art."[27] It is traditionally explained "that calligraphy is so developed because of the absence of a representational tradition in Islamic art, because of theological difficulties in representation and because the Arabic language, and the Qur'an at the heart of it, is so significant in Islam."[28] The artistic evidence certainly demonstrates that artful writing is among the most ubiquitous forms of Islamic art.

The history of Islamic calligraphy and its use *in* art, and *as* art, is a lengthy and fascinating topic. Various styles of script developed in different Islamic cultures and these different styles can be recognized by their degrees of angularity and uprightness (such as the early and traditionally esteemed kufic script—which also has many variant forms) or by their rounded, slanting, and more cursive appearance (such as thuluth, naskhi, muhaqqaq, and numerous other styles of cursive script).[29] Sometimes different styles of script will be found on the same page in a manuscript or in close proximity on an architectural monument. In some periods and regions, the script styles were elaborated to a highly complex degree. Words and letter forms may be elongated, twisted, braided, overlaid, or enhanced with decorative extensions and geometric designs to the extent that textual legibility appears to be of relatively minor concern in favor of overall pattern, ornamental aesthetics, or mystical letter and word symbolism. Sometimes figural forms are created of text as well.

A page from an early 14th-century Qur'an created in Baghdad by the esteemed calligrapher Ahmad ibn-al-Suhrawardi al-Bakri includes sections of both kufic and muhaqqaq script (see Figure 11.6). The more angular kufic script appears in the upper and lower bands (reading, "Baghdad may Allah the Exalted honor it"), and the three lines of elegant cursive muhaqqaq script in the center of the page identify the artist "praising Allah and blessing His Prophet Muhammad."

Figure 11.6 Qur'an Manuscript, 1307–08, from Baghdad; calligraphy by Ahmad ibn al-Suhrawardi al-Bakri. New York: The Metropolitan Museum of Art / Art Resource, NY.

A complex combination of script styles and layouts can be seen in the mosaic tile inscriptions on the dome of the Royal Mosque (Shah Mosque, now Imam Mosque) in Isfahan, Iran (see Figure 11.7). Created for the great art patron Shah Abbas in the early 17th century, cursive bands of thuluth-style script praise the Shah and the Safavid dynasty in the upper section of the dome's base (or drum), whereas lines of elongated ornamental kufic offer praises to Muhammad in the center of the drum, above geometric blocks of square kufic with inscriptions featuring statements such as "God is most mighty" and "Allah is God."

EXAMPLES

The Dome of the Rock, Jerusalem, begun 691

The Dome of the Rock in Jerusalem is certainly one of the most well-known, intensely studied, and frequently reproduced examples of Islamic architecture (see Figure 11.8 and Plate 21). It is one of the very first examples

Figure 11.7   Royal Mosque (Imam Mosque), Isfahan, Iran, 1612–37, dome. Courtesy of Shutterstock.

of Islamic architectural construction, and although it has been much restored through the centuries, it still stands today in a form that fundamentally retains its original appearance. It was constructed in Jerusalem under the patronage of the caliph Abd al-Malik in the late seventh century. A powerful symbol of Islam, the shrine is considered the third of the most holy of Islamic sites (after the Ka'ba in Mecca and the Mosque of the Prophet in Medina). Although it "is often called the first work of Islamic architecture . . . this building so completely follows the traditions of late antique and Byzantine architecture that some people do not even regard it as Islamic at all. The people who built it, however, undoubtedly meant it to serve an 'Islamic' function."[30] Understanding the function, history, and symbolism of this unique structure in particular is a critical element in any discussion of Islamic religious art.

The city of Jerusalem has played an extremely important, if at times somewhat variable, role in the history of Islam since the foundation of the faith in the early seventh century and to the present day. A holy city for Jews and Christians alike (it is the site of the ancient Jewish Temple and the site of the death and resurrection of Jesus), the city of Jerusalem came under Islamic control in the early seventh century (around 636–38) just a few years after the death of Muhammad. During his lifetime, and up until 622 when he proclaimed

Figure 11.8   The Dome of the Rock, Jerusalem, Israel, begun 691, exterior. Courtesy of Shutterstock.

that the proper direction for prayer was Mecca, early Muslim prayers were originally directed to the city of Jerusalem, reflecting the sanctity of this holy city in Judeo-Christian tradition as well. "Although the Qur'an does not explicitly say so, the original direction for prayer was Jerusalem."[31]

Jerusalem is also intimately connected with Muhammad via the account of his mystical "Night Journey" (or *isra'*), which is briefly mentioned in sura (chapter) 17 of the Qur'an. According to tradition, the angel Gabriel appeared to Muhammad one night and gave him a mystical winged creature called *al-Buraq* (or "Lightning"). This celestial steed had the face of a woman and the tail of a peacock and transported the Prophet through the night skies to the city of Jerusalem. Alighting at the site of the Temple of Solomon and on the sacred rock of the Temple Mount, Muhammad met and prayed with Abraham, Moses, Jesus, and other prophets before climbing a ladder of light up through the heavens to meet with Allah. This ascension to and return from heaven is known as the *mi'raj*. This Night Journey and Ascension, Muhammad's "real and physical or spiritual and mystical journey to cosmic boundaries . . . was a major part of the collective memory shared by the faithful."[32] The tangible evidence of this is said to be marked by the footprint of the Prophet visible in the sacred rock in Jerusalem. In the same night, Muhammad returned down the heavenly ladder of light to Jerusalem, and his mystical steed transported him back to Mecca.

In Muslim tradition (mirroring Christian and Jewish traditions), the site is also associated with the last days and the final judgment, at which time "the angel of death, Isra'fil, will stand on the Rock and sound the end of time with his trumpet."[33] Thus, the building has a multitude of meanings. It "has become a commemorative monument for the Prophet's mystical journey into the heavens, but it was built . . . for the very ideological local purposes of sanctifying the old Jewish Temple according to the new Revelation and of demonstrating to the Christian population of the city that Islam was the victorious faith."[34]

The sacred oblong rock (approximately 56 by 42 feet) that is enshrined in the Dome of the Rock is enclosed within an octagonal structure with four doors facing the cardinal directions. The architectural form with its centralized plan closely resembles slightly earlier Byzantine models of shrines and *martyria* (saintly tombs). The exterior is richly decorated with brilliant tile work of geometric patterns and largely Qur'anic inscriptions, which primarily date from the early to mid-16th century under the patronage of the Ottoman sultan Suleyman the Magnificent (1494–1566). Similar tile work appears on the drum that supports the impressive golden dome. The present gold-colored aluminum of the dome dates to the 20th century, but the shape and color of the dome today mirror the original lead-sheathed and gilded original.

The interior space is divided by columns and piers into two ambulatories encircling the Rock itself. This arrangement allows for the ritual circumambulation (*tawaf*) undertaken by pilgrims to the shrine. The interior dome rises 70 feet above the floor and is covered with gilt plaster in intricate patterns and calligraphic verses. Windows of colored glass in the walls and drum bathe the interior and extensive mosaics in a soft light. Pilgrims proceed around the rock and gaze upwards at the glowing dome, as Muhammad himself was transported to and returned from the heavens.

"It is important to recall that, in addition to its continued forceful presence, the Dome of the Rock was the first monument sponsored by a Muslim ruler that was conceived as a work of art, a monument deliberately transcending its function by the quality of its forms and expression."[35] The balance, symmetry, and brilliant decoration of the monument also reflect its religious and political significance. Situated on the Temple Mount (known to Muslims as the *Haram al-Sharif* or Noble Sanctuary), on the site of the ancient Jewish Temple, in a city long sacred to Christians also, the lengthy history of the Dome of the Rock continues, in many ways, to symbolize the relatedness as well as the tensions between the faiths of Judaism, Christianity, and Islam and the supreme significance of the city of Jerusalem for all of these faiths.

Two Persian Manuscripts with Narrative Illustrations

Exquisitely illuminated manuscripts—enriched with complex, jewel-like paintings—typify the arts produced for royal patrons of the Timurid and Safavid dynasties in late medieval Persia. Both of these examples are illustrated pages from manuscripts produced for courtly patrons. They may serve as exemplars of the richness, delicacy, and detail associated with one of the most flourishing eras in the history of Islamic book production.

The production of manuscripts has a lengthy history in the Islamic world. Unlike their Western counterparts, which were written on parchment (animal skin), most Islamic manuscripts were—from at least the 10th century onward—written and illustrated on paper (knowledge of which had been earlier introduced from China). The paper (a mixture of rag and shreds of flax) was starched and given a glossy sheen by burnishing. The jewel-like pigments were derived from mineral and vegetable materials. Gold leaf and polished gold and silver flecks can also contribute to the glowing details of these lavish pages.

Although manuscripts of the Qur'an with figural and narrative scenes will not be found, many other works were often enriched with illustration programs from the 11th century onward in various regions of the Islamic world. These include historical chronicles, scientific and medicinal treatises, works of philosophy, moral teachings, literature, and poetry. The styles of painting and script vary widely from region to region and often demonstrate various cross-cultural influences as well as distinct local styles.

Both of the examples shown here also demonstrate the interesting and complex paradox of figural imagery in Islamic art. As mentioned earlier, "traditional Islamic civilization is supposed to have spurned images altogether. Specialists . . . have therefore tended to remain extremely wary of trying to account for the undeniable existence of this civilization's plastic and especially figurative arts."[36] Although it has been argued that figural imagery in Islamic art appears primarily in secular contexts, such as literary and historical works produced for lay patrons, in cases such as the examples shown here, the subject matter of the texts and the illustrations is far from purely secular. "Many of these paintings lie embedded in didactic sacral texts with explicitly moral or mystical themes [or texts which] are themselves deeply devout, laced with Koranic inscriptions, and closely styled upon Koranic verbal imagery."[37]

Figure 11.9 Joseph and Zulaykha, manuscript illustration by Bihzad, in a *Bustan* of Sa'di, 1488, Herat. Cairo: National Library Ms Arab Farsi 908, f. 52v. Erich Lessing / Art Resource, NY.

The illustrated manuscript depicting the scene of Joseph and Zulaykha, created by the renowned painter Bihzad (Kamal al-Din Bihzad, 1465–1535), in the court sphere of Herat (present-day Afghanistan) in 1488, is an excellent case in point (see Figure 11.9). The manuscript is a copy of a work titled the *Bustan* (The Orchard)—a collection of moral lessons that were originally composed in the 13th century by the Persian poet Sa'di of Shiraz.

Ever since he composed them in the thirteenth century, Sa'di's *Bustun*, in Persian verse, and its companion volume, the *Gulistan* ("Rose Garden") in mixed Persian verse and prose, were regarded throughout Persianate Eastern Islam as the civilization's twin supreme literary models of the genre known as *andarz*, or 'moral admonishment,' consisting of a collection of pious fables in the first place addressed to princes.[38]

The late 15th-century copy was created for the Timurid ruler of Herat, Sultan Husayn Mirza Bayqara (reigned 1470–1506), under whose patronage Herat became a major center of literature and manuscript production.

Each of the 10 sections of the poem concerns specific moral virtues—as well exemplified by the scene of the attempted seduction of Joseph by Zulaykha. This is one of four full-page illustrations in the manuscript securely attributed to (indeed, signed by) Bihzad, in addition to a frontispiece which, it is generally agreed, includes work by Bihzad and his teacher, Mirak. The story itself ultimately derives from the tale of Joseph and Potiphar's wife from the Hebrew scriptures, in which the wife of the Egyptian minister, Potiphar, attempts to entrap the young Joseph during his captivity in Egypt. Featured also in sura 12 of the Qur'an—and embellished and expanded in later commentaries—for the 13th-century poet Sa'di, the tale primarily served as a "warning to distinguish between God and idols,"[39] to remain steadfast and chaste in one's piety and devotion. This religious reading of the poem had also been greatly expanded by another writer just a few years before the illustrated copy was produced in Herat. "The most eminent literary figure and religious authority in contemporary Herat, the mystic writer Jami,"[40] composed, in 1484, a work titled *Yusef* [Joseph] *and Zulaykha*. Verses from this work, as well as Sa'di's, can be found inscribed in the illustration by Bizhad.

Indeed, the elaborate architectural structure found in Bihzad's illustration derives purely from Jami's description of the magnificent and labyrinthine palace that Zulaykha had constructed in order to entrap Joseph. The structural complexity of the palace is brilliantly conveyed in Bihzad's painting with its flat and angular patterns showing doors, windows, gates, and balconies all extending and overlapping in a claustrophobic and complicated fashion. The palace ultimately symbolizes the material world and its temptations, and the seven rooms (through which Zulaykha led Joseph, locking the doors behind them) represent stages of the soul's journey to God. "The doors, which are so prominently displayed and lead the eye through the composition, are tightly shut and can only be opened by God."[41] At the moment of Joseph's epiphany, when he flees from Zulaykha, all the locked doors miraculously open before him. Joseph is also understood to be a symbol for God, and Zulaykha represents the soul's yearning for God. "The woman completely lost in her love of Joseph is a fine symbol for the enrapturing power of love, expressed by the mystic in the contemplation of divine beauty revealed in human form. . . . Zulaykha has become . . . the symbol of the soul, purified by ceaseless longing in the path of poverty and love."[42]

"Religious imagery in medieval Islam raises a theological problem far more complex than usually allowed, perhaps even realized, by most contemporary writers on the arts of this culture."[43] It appears that "a later owner of this manuscript, in an iconophobic fit, scratched away Joseph's face."[44] The issue of facial features in figural narrative imagery is handled differently in the next example.

An illustration of the *Ascent of Muhammad* comes from another Persian manuscript produced for a royal patron, the Safavid ruler Shah Tahmasp I (1524–76), who established his capital at Tabriz in present-day Iran (see Plate 22). The manuscript dates to ca. 1540 and is a copy of another very popular and often-illustrated literary work: the *Khamsa* (Five Poems or Five Jewels) of Nizami (Nizami Ganjavi, 1141–1209). The *Khamsa* is a lengthy work, composed in the *masnavi* style of rhymed couplets. It contains five major sections, including historical and folk tales, romantic stories, and didactic, philosophical materials dealing with theological matters. The illustrated copy made for Shah Tahmasp in the mid-16th century "is constantly cited . . . as one of the masterpieces of Persian book-painting."[45]

There are 14 paintings in the book that date to the time of Tahmasp. Four additional paintings were added later. The manuscript was not finished during the lifetime of the patron, who appears to have lost interest in the arts of the book around 1545, shortly after this manuscript was started. Among the paintings from the mid-16th century is the illustration of the ascent (or Night Journey) of Muhammad; this painting is attributed to the master artist Sultan-Muhammad. The scene shows the prophet in the center of the composition; he is seated on his mystical steed who transports him through the night sky on his journey between Mecca and Jerusalem. Guided by the archangel Gabriel, attended by a hoard of gift-bearing angels, the prophet is surrounded by golden, radiant flames, indicating the miraculous nature of this event. The brilliant colors, exquisite details, and the energy and animation of the figures are especially remarkable.

One notes that the face of the prophet is hidden behind a veil, so no facial features are shown. But many other *Khamsa* manuscripts (which often include this scene) show the prophet's face.[46] Indeed, the illustration of the Night Journey and Ascension of Muhammad appears frequently in medieval Persian manuscripts, and in fact, there are some manuscripts completely devoted to the details of this miraculous event.[47] Perhaps the emphasis on this subject in Persian art may be "because, from the 11th century, the Ascension played a special role in the mystical imagination of Islam in Iran [or] because the imagination of a quasi-magical vision lends itself more easily to illustration than more common scenes from the Life of Muhammad."[48] Again, it seems clear that at some periods and in some regions, "the proscription against human and animal representation in Qur'ans did not extend to secular manuscripts, and consequently they frequently contain a wealth of figural imagery,"[49] even if the imagery and texts are of a highly religious and clearly non-secular nature. It is also obvious that "attitudes to the use of images clearly differed between periods, between regions and between social classes"[50]—a situation that still exists today.

An Ottoman Prayer Rug, Late 16th Century

When Muslims perform their prayers—which involve physical actions of kneeling and prostration—they often make use of mats or rugs, such as this especially fine example from the late 16th century (see Figure 11.10). Prayer rugs (the term "rug" officially applies to works of a smaller size than carpets) are, most often, distinguishable by designs that indicate a directional emphasis rather than an overall or purely symmetrical pattern. In this case, the directional emphasis is shown via the three-arched architectural motifs with single and paired columns indicating niches. These represent the *qiblah* (direction of prayer to Mecca) and the *mihrab* (niche), traditionally found in Islamic mosques. In this example, a lamp is depicted in the mihrab, suspended from the central arch.

The rich colors, as well as the floral, foliate, and decorative designs on this example, are typical of the luxury arts produced for the Ottoman court sphere of the 16th and 17th centuries. This particular example has

Figure 11.10 Prayer rug, 16th century, Ottoman. New York: The Metropolitan Museum of Art, The James F. Ballard Collection, Gift of James F. Ballard, 1922 (22.100.51) Image © The Metropolitan Museum of Art.

been attributed to a workshop in Bursa or Istanbul and is a very early example of a triple-arched format as well as a rare early survival of an Ottoman court prayer rug.

Rugs such as these are painstakingly hand-knotted on a matrix of vertical (warp) threads stretched on a loom. Horizontal (weft) threads are inserted between the rows of hand-tied knots. The closely cropped knots create the slightly raised pile surface of the rug. Especially detailed patterns, such as seen here, are created with knots of very fine, thread-like yarn, whereas bolder and less detailed patterns are obtained with thicker and denser yarns. In this example, warp and weft threads are of silk, and the knotted pile is of wool and cotton threads. The colors of the yarns are derived from dyes made of various mineral, vegetable, and animal substances, such as plants, insects, and nutshells.

Examples such as this indicate not only the opulence of Ottoman court style but also the continued importance and ubiquitous presence of textiles in the Islamic arts generally. There is a lengthy tradition of fine textile production across the centuries and regions associated with Islamic cultures. The study of textiles is a vast and complex field. Different styles, motifs, colors, and materials are associated with many different centers of textile production from Egypt to Persia to India, and specific style variants typify Safavid, Ottoman, and Mughal productions, for example. Given the perishable nature of the materials however, few examples survive from much earlier than the 12th century, although literary references and depictions of textiles in other media certainly demonstrate the continued prominence of the textile arts.

It has been noted "that textiles in Islamic society fulfilled far more than the functions normally expected of them in other societies . . . [and that this may] account for some of the major characteristics of Islamic art in general."[51] Knotwork, interlace patterns, surface decoration, and textile-derived motifs are pervasive in Islamic ornamentation, and "the terms which naturally and insistently impose themselves refer back to textiles."[52] Any discussion of Islamic religious art (and Islamic art in general) would be dramatically incomplete without at least a brief mention of the textile arts and the critical role of the prayer rug in Islamic worship.

NOTES

1. Matthew Gordon, "Islam," in *The Illustrated World Religions*, ed. Michael Coogan (Oxford: Oxford University Press, 2003), 109.

2. Gordon, 109.

3. Gordon, 108–9.

4. Gordon, 92.

5. Sheila Blair and Jonathan Bloom, *Islam: A Thousand Years of Faith and Power* (New Haven, CT: Yale University Press, 2002), 80.

6. Gordon, 90.

7. Good illustrated sources on Mecca include Abdelaziz Frikha and Ezzedine Guellouz. *Mecca: The Muslim Pilgrimage* (New York: Paddington Press, 1979); and Desmond Stewart, *Mecca* (New York: Newsweek, 1980).

8. Gordon, 101.

9. Gordon, 101.

10. Sheila Blair and Jonathan Bloom, "The Mirage of Islamic Art: Reflections on the Study of an Unwieldy Field," *The Art Bulletin* 85, no. 1 (2003): 152–84.

11. Blair and Bloom, "Mirage," 171.

12. Blair and Bloom, "Mirage," 152.

13. Terry Allen, *Five Essays on Islamic Art* (Sebastopol, CA: Solipsist Press, 1988), 35.

14. Seyyed Nasr, *Islamic Art and Spirituality* (Albany: State University of New York Press, 1987), 7.

15. Oleg Grabar, "The Iconography of Islamic Architecture," in *Content and Context of Visual Arts in the Islamic World*, ed. Priscilla Soucek (University Park: Pennsylvania State University Press, 1988), 53.

16. Oliver Leaman, *Islamic Aesthetics: An Introduction* (Notre Dame, IN: University of Notre Dame Press, 2004), 187.

17. Leaman, 187.

18. Leaman, 4.

19. Leaman, 4–5.

20. Leaman, 5.

21. Allen, 17.

22. Priscilla Soucek, "The Life of the Prophet: Illustrated Versions," in *Content and Context of Visual Arts in the Islamic World*, ed. Priscilla Soucek (University Park: Pennsylvania State University Press, 1988), 193–218.

23. Michael Barry, *Figurative Art in Medieval Islam and the Riddle of Bihzad of Herat (1465–1535)* (Paris: Flammarion, 2004), 49.

24. Renata Holod and Hasan-Uddin Khan, *The Contemporary Mosque: Architects, Clients, and Designs since the 1950s* (New York: Rizzoli, 1997), 10.

25. Jonathan Bloom, *Minaret: Symbol of Islam* (Oxford: Oxford University Press, 1989).

26. Jerrilynn Dodds, ed., *Al-Andalus: The Art of Islamic Spain* (New York: Harry N. Abrams, 1992), 12.

27. Gabriel Mandel Khan, *Arabic Script: Styles, Variants and Calligraphic Adaptations* (New York: Abbeville Press, 2001), 7.

28. Leaman, 48.

29. An especially useful source on this topic is Yasin Safadi, *Islamic Calligraphy* (Boulder, CO: Shambhala, 1979).

30. Sheila Blair and Jonathan Bloom, *Islamic Arts* (London: Phaidon, 1997), 25–28.

31. Oleg Grabar, *The Dome of the Rock* (Cambridge, MA: Belknap/Harvard University Press, 2006), 48.

32. Oleg Grabar, *The Shape of the Holy: Early Islamic Jerusalem* (Princeton, NJ: Princeton University Press, 1996), 48.

33. Grabar, *Dome*, 56.

34. Grabar, "Iconography of Islamic Architecture," 52.

35. Grabar, *Shape of the Holy*, 52.

36. Barry, 39.

37. Barry, 50.

38. Barry, 191.

39. Barry, 199.

40. Barry, 201.

41. Sheila Blair and Jonathan Bloom, *The Art and Architecture of Islam: 1250–1800* (New Haven, CT: Yale University Press, 1994), 64.

42. Annemarie Schimmel, *Mystical Dimensions of Islam* (Chapel Hill: University of North Carolina Press, 1975), 429.

43. Barry, 228.

44. Barry, 197.

45. Blair and Bloom, *Art and Architecture of Islam: 1250–1800*, 324.

46. Richard Ettinghausen and Marilyn Jenkins, *The Arts of Islam: Masterpieces from the Metropolitan Museum of Art* (New York: Harry N. Abrams, 1982), 176.

47. Such manuscripts include the 15th-century *Miraj Nameh* (Paris, Bibliothèque Nationale MS Supplément Turc 190), which contains over 60 illuminations detailing all the visions and stages in this event. See Marie-Rose Seguy, *The Miraculous Journey of Mahomet* (New York: George Braziller, 1977).

48. Oleg Grabar, *Mostly Miniatures: An Introduction to Persian Painting* (Princeton, NJ: Princeton University Press, 2000), 91.

49. Nasser Khalili, *Islamic Art and Culture: A Visual History* (New York: Overlook, 2006), 64.

50. Tim Stanley, *Palace and Mosque: Islamic Art from the Middle East* (London: V & A Publications, 2004), 52.

51. Lisa Golombek, "The Draped Universe of Islam," in *Content and Context of Visual Arts in the Islamic World,* ed. Priscilla Soucek (University Park: Pennsylvania State University Press, 1988), 25.

52. Dominique Clevenot, *Splendors of Islam: Architecture, Decoration, and Design* (New York: Vendome, 2000), 203.

BIBLIOGRAPHY AND FURTHER READING

Allen, Terry. *Five Essays on Islamic Art.* Sebastopol, CA: Solipsist Press, 1988.

Barry, Michael. *Figurative Art in Medieval Islam and the Riddle of Bihzad of Herat (1465–1535).* Paris: Flammarion, 2004.

Blair, Sheila, and Jonathan Bloom. *The Art and Architecture of Islam: 1250–1800.* New Haven, CT: Yale University Press, 1994.

Blair, Sheila, and Jonathan Bloom. *Islam: A Thousand Years of Faith and Power.* New Haven, CT: Yale University Press, 2002.

Blair, Sheila, and Jonathan Bloom. *Islamic Arts.* London: Phaidon, 1997.

Blair, Sheila, and Jonathan Bloom. "The Mirage of Islamic Art: Reflections on the Study of an Unwieldy Field." *The Art Bulletin* 85, no. 1 (2003): 152–84.

Bloom, Jonathan. *Minaret: Symbol of Islam.* Oxford: Oxford University Press, 1989.

Brend, Barbara. *Islamic Art.* Cambridge, MA: Harvard University Press, 1991.

Chebel, Malek. *Symbols of Islam.* Paris: Editions Assouline, 1997.

Clevenot, Dominique. *Splendors of Islam: Architecture, Decoration, and Design.* New York: Vendome, 2000.

Coogan, Michael, ed. *The Illustrated World Religions.* Oxford: Oxford University Press, 2003.

Dodds, Jerrilynn, ed. *Al-Andalus: The Art of Islamic Spain.* New York: Harry N. Abrams, 1992.

Ecker, Heather. *Caliphs and Kings: The Art and Influence of Islamic Spain.* Washington, DC: Smithsonian Institution, 2004.

Esposito, John, ed. *The Oxford History of Islam.* Oxford: Oxford University Press, 1999.

Ettinghausen, Richard, and Oleg Grabar. *The Art and Architecture of Islam: 650–1250.* New Haven, CT: Yale University Press, 1987.

Ettinghausen, Richard, and Marilyn Jenkins. *The Arts of Islam: Masterpieces from the Metropolitan Museum of Art.* New York: Harry N. Abrams, 1982.

Freedberg, David. *The Power of Images: Studies in the History and Theory of Response.* Chicago: University of Chicago Press, 1989.

Frikha, Abdelaziz, and Ezzedine Guellouz. *Mecca: The Muslim Pilgrimage.* New York: Paddington Press, 1979.

Frishman, Martin, and Hasan-Uddin Khan. *The Mosque: History, Architectural Development, and Regional Diversity.* London: Thames and Hudson, 2002.

Golombek, Lisa. "The Draped Universe of Islam." In *Content and Context of Visual Arts in the Islamic World,* ed. Priscilla Soucek, 25–49. University Park: Pennsylvania State University Press, 1988.

Gordon, Matthew. "Islam." In *The Illustrated World Religions*, ed. Michael Coogan, 88–123. Oxford: Oxford University Press, 2003.

Grabar, Oleg. *The Dome of the Rock*. Cambridge, MA: Belknap/Harvard University Press, 2006.

Grabar, Oleg. *The Formation of Islamic Art*. New Haven, CT: Yale University Press, 1973.

Grabar, Oleg. "The Iconography of Islamic Architecture." In *Content and Context of Visual Arts in the Islamic World*, ed. Priscilla Soucek, 51–65. University Park, Pennsylvania State University Press, 1988.

Grabar, Oleg. "The Implications of Collecting Islamic Art." In *Discovering Islamic Art: Scholars, Collectors and Collections, 1850–1950*, ed. Stephen Vernoit, 194–200. London: I. B. Taurus, 2000.

Grabar, Oleg. *Mostly Miniatures: An Introduction to Persian Painting*. Princeton, NJ: Princeton University Press, 2000.

Grabar, Oleg. *The Shape of the Holy: Early Islamic Jerusalem*. Princeton, NJ: Princeton University Press, 1996.

Gray, Basil. *Persian Painting*. New York: Rizzoli, 1977.

Hattstein, Markus, and Peter Delius, eds. *Islam: Art and Architecture*. Cologne: Könemann, 2000.

Hillenbrand, Robert. *Islamic Art and Architecture*. London: Thames and Hudson, 1999.

Hillenbrand, Robert. *Islamic Architecture: Form, Function, and Meaning*. Edinburgh: University of Edinburgh Press, 1994.

Hillenbrand, Robert, ed. *Persian Painting from the Mongols to the Qajars: Studies in Honour of Basil W. Robinson*. London: I.B. Taurus, 2000.

Holod, Renata, and Hasan-Uddin Khan. *The Contemporary Mosque: Architects, Clients, and Designs since the 1950s*. New York: Rizzoli, 1997.

Irwin, Robert. *Islamic Art in Context: Art, Architecture, and the Literary World*. New York: Harry N. Abrams, 1997.

Khalili, Nasser. *Islamic Art and Culture: A Visual History*. New York: Overlook, 2006.

Khan, Gabriel Mandel. *Arabic Script: Styles, Variants and Calligraphic Adaptations*. New York: Abbeville Press, 2001.

Leaman, Oliver. *Islamic Aesthetics: An Introduction*. Notre Dame, IN: University of Notre Dame Press, 2004.

Lewis, Bernard, ed. *The World of Islam: Faith, Culture, People*. London: Thames and Hudson, 1976.

Lowry, Glenn, and Susan Nemazee. *A Jeweler's Eye: Islamic Arts of the Book from the Vever Collection*. Washington, DC: Smithsonian Institution, 1988.

Mahmutcehajic, Rusmir. *The Mosque: The Heart of Submission*. New York: Fordham University Press, 2006.

Michell, George, ed. *Architecture of the Islamic World: Its History and Social Meaning*. London: Thames and Hudson, 1978.

Nasr, Seyyed. *Islam: Religion, History, and Civilization*. San Francisco: Harper San Francisco, 2003.

Nasr, Seyyed. *Islamic Art and Spirituality*. Albany: State University of New York Press, 1987.

O'Kane, Bernard, ed. *The Treasures of Islamic Art in the Museums of Cairo*. Cairo: The American University in Cairo Press, 2006.

Roxburgh, David. *The Persian Album 1400–1600: From Dispersal to Collection*. New Haven, CT: Yale University Press, 2005.

Safadi, Yasin. *Islamic Calligraphy*. Boulder, CO: Shambhala, 1979.

Schimmel, Annemarie. *Deciphering the Signs of God: A Phenomenological Approach to Islam*. Albany: State University of New York Press, 1994.

Schimmel, Annemarie. *Mystical Dimensions of Islam*. Chapel Hill: University of North Carolina Press, 1975.

Seguy, Marie-Rose. *The Miraculous Journey of Mahomet*. New York: George Braziller, 1977.

Soucek, Priscilla, ed. *Content and Context of Visual Arts in the Islamic World*. University Park: Pennsylvania State University Press, 1988.

Soucek, Priscilla. "The Life of the Prophet: Illustrated Versions." In *Content and Context of Visual Arts in the Islamic World*, ed. Priscilla Soucek, 193–218. University Park: Pennsylvania State University Press, 1988.

Stanley, Tim. *Palace and Mosque: Islamic Art from the Middle East*. London: V & A Publications, 2004.

Stewart, Desmond. *Mecca*. New York: Newsweek, 1980.

Vernoit, Stephen, ed. *Discovering Islamic Art: Scholars, Collectors and Collections, 1850–1950*. London: I.B. Taurus, 2000.

Welch, Stuart Cary. *Persian Painting: Five Royal Safavid Manuscripts of the Sixteenth Century*. New York: George Braziller, 1976.

−12−

Hinduism

ORIGINS AND DEVELOPMENT

Hinduism is an ancient, complex, and multifaceted belief system whose early origins can be traced to the end of the prehistoric periods of civilization in the Indus Valley region of India and Pakistan (ca. 2000–1500 BCE). With a long history of vibrant development continuing to the present day, Hinduism might be more correctly termed a "way of life," rather than a "religion" involving a standard creed or consistently shared set of worship practices. Hinduism has no one single founder and has evolved through the centuries to encompass a great variety of beliefs and worship modes, or "traditions which share a family resemblance."[1] Hinduism, in various forms, is the major religion of India today and also has adherents in numerous branches worldwide. Additionally, Hinduism has given rise to two other major belief systems—Buddhism and Jainism—and many variations of Hindu beliefs and practices have evolved in different forms through its long history.

The terms Hindu and Hinduism originally derived from a geographic rather than religious designation. Both words come from *sindhu*, the ancient name for the Indus River. Later usage expanded the term to refer to India generally, but it was not until the 19th century, under British Colonial rule, that the term Hindu was used to refer to the religious practices of Indians who were not Muslims, Christians, or members of any other specifically named religion. However, "even though anachronistic, the term 'Hinduism' remains useful for describing and categorizing the various schools of thought and practice that grew up within a shared Indian society and employed a common religious vocabulary."[2]

The earliest evidences of many foundational Hindu beliefs and practices date to ancient India during the Vedic period—named after the Vedas, the original sacred texts of Hinduism. The term *Vedas* means "knowledge" or "wisdom" in Sanskrit—the language in which these ancient texts were composed and origi-nally orally transmitted. The oldest of the four major Vedic texts (the *Rig Veda*) has been dated to ca. 1500–1200 BCE. The Vedas are collections of hymns and prayers to a variety of gods and goddesses and, along with other early sacred works (such as the *Brahmanas* and *Aranyakas*), include descriptions of and direc-tions for rituals and sacrifices. These ceremonies were carried out by carefully trained priests (or brahmins) and were designed to worship and honor various deities associated with specific natural and cosmological forces or events, such as fire, water, wind, and so on. More philosophical texts that contain didactic and allegorical stories, plus mystical meditations, were composed ca. 600 BCE. These significant later texts are known as the Upanishads and are considered the last of the divinely inspired Vedic writings. The term *Upanishad* means "sit-ting near" or "sitting at the feet" of a teacher. These texts primarily take the form of dialogues or question-and-answer sessions between students seeking spiritual guidance and sages who offer their wisdom. Altogether, the sacred texts of the Vedic period are often categorized as *shruti* (heard or revealed), reflecting the ultimate divine sources of their inspiration and their original oral transmission.

In the post-Vedic period, many other significant sacred texts were created. As a whole, these are often categorized as *smriti* (remembered) literature, reflecting their inspired human authorship, different sources, and formats. Among the massive corpus of these writings are *puranas* (ancient stories about the major deities, especially Vishnu, Shiva, Brahma, and the Goddess), *sutras* (commen-taries), *shastras* (religious law texts), and the great epics of the *Ramayana* and the *Mahabharata*, which are still exceedingly popular today. The *Ramayana* (Story of Rama), the *Mahabharata* (Great Epic of India—often described as the longest poem in the world), and the *Bhagavad Gita* (Song of the Blessed One—an especially significant section of the *Mahabharata*) were created, edited, and expanded between the fourth century BCE and the fourth century CE. These lively and complex stories of adventures, battles, and romance con-tain allegories, critical moral teachings, and spiritual guidance. They provide the foundation for classical Hindu beliefs in multiple manifestations of deities, the importance of devotion to these deities, codes of moral conduct, and the concepts of karma and reincarnation, and they define the traditional social structures in Indian society involving class and status (or caste).

Both Buddhism and Jainism, respectively founded in the sixth century BCE by the historical figures of Siddhartha Gautama (the Buddha, ca. 566–486 BCE) and Vardhamama (called Mahavira the Jina, the Victorious One, ca. 599–527 BCE), represent evolutions from and reactions to some aspects of the Hinduism of their time period, especially the belief in the divinely inspired status of the Vedas, the monolithic authority of the priestly class, and the caste system of social hierarchy as a whole. Concurrently, the expanding body of post-Vedic literature, especially in the form of the great epics and the *puranas*, is also reflective of many dynamic transformations in worship practices, new schools of thought, and growing branches (sects, subcommunities, or denominations) of Hinduism well into the first several centuries CE.

The period from ca. 700 to 1200 CE represents an especially flourishing time for Hinduism when a number of regional dynasties in India adopted worship practices focusing primarily, but not exclusively, on the gods Vishnu and Shiva. Often known as the period of Temple Hinduism, many of the great architectural and sculptural monuments date from this time.

Buddhism, as a separate religious system, was virtually extinct in India by ca. 1200 CE, having migrated widely elsewhere in Asia and having been, to some extent, reintegrated by Hinduism. Both faiths were also dramatically challenged by the arrival of Islam in India via political/military conquest in the 11th and 12th centuries. From about 1200 to 1700 CE, northern India came under the control of Islamic rulers. There were periods of intense conflict during this time, as well as evidences of mutual toleration and intermingled influences, such as the special growth of mystical Islamic Sufism in India. During this period of Muslim rule, following the centuries of Temple Hinduism, "Hindus responded to the presence and political sway of Islam . . . in complex, diverse, and creative ways. . . . What is most apparent in late medieval Hinduism is the vitality of forms of religion that are devotional, esoteric, or syncretic, and a corresponding de-emphasis on the role of religion in constituting the political and social order."[3]

Of particular importance in the continued evolution and widespread appeal of Hinduism have been the various *bhakti*, or devotional movements, which focus on personal and often intense worship of specific deities in ways accessible to all believers. During this late medieval period also, the religion of Sikhism was founded by Guru Nanak (1469–1539), who disagreed with the religious practices and beliefs of both Hindus and Muslims. The term Sikh derives from the Sanskrit word *sisya* (pupil). Sikhism continues to flourish today among a minority of the population in India and elsewhere.

From the late 18th to the mid-20th century, India was under British Colonial rule. Hindu religious response to this situation was varied and notably took the form of several reform movements that sought to modernize Hindu practices or rephrase the beliefs into terms more appealing to Western audiences.

Throughout the colonial period, the British viewed India as a society made up of distinct, identifiable religious communities: Hindus, Muslims, Sikhs, Jains, "tribals," and so on . . . the British use of unequivocal categories to classify a religious reality that was complex and mingled promoted a clarification and hardening of religious distinctions. . . . The outcome of this "communalization" was that, when the English finally quit India in 1947, they felt it necessary to divide their colony along religious lines into two nation-states, Islamic Pakistan and Hindu India. This tragic decision led to terrible violence and suffering amongst Muslims, Hindus, and Sikhs alike during the Partition, and its consequences are still felt powerfully in the politics of modern South Asia.[4]

The diversity of practices characteristic of Hinduism throughout its lengthy history continue to be evident today. Hinduism continues to evolve and develop, retaining and expanding a vibrant and complex set of traditions, practices, and art forms.

PRINCIPAL BELIEFS AND KEY PRACTICES

Because of Hinduism's lengthy history and continued multifaceted evolution to the present day, the diversity of its branches, and its remarkable ability to transform, there is no clear and simple way to succinctly define the principal beliefs and key practices of Hindus. "Hinduism is not a reality that succumbs to this process . . . it is a kind of unity-in-diversity, a continuum forever adapting to new circumstances."[5] It "is a dynamic, living reality (or rather, a macro-reality of organically united micro-realities. . . .) whose strength lies in its ability to adapt to circumstances while it maintains strands of continuity with the past."[6]

Perhaps because Hinduism does not have one single founder, one prophet, or even several divinely inspired seers accepted by all Hindus, and because Hinduism does not have a formal creed or a set of sacred scriptures universally acknowledged as fully authoritative by all Hindus, some fundamental questions arise about the nature of the religion. For example, is Hinduism a polytheistic or a monotheistic religion? It is typical of Hinduism that the answer to this question is both yes and no. It could be said that "philosophically, Hinduism is a monotheistic religion, but in practice it is pluralistic and polytheistic."[7]

In other words, although many gods and goddesses may be and are worshiped by Hindus, the various deities are all understood, by the majority of Hindus, to be manifestations of a single supreme principle: Brahman. This supreme Brahman is infinite and cannot be described or comprehended. It is truth, knowledge, existence, and consciousness, and it encompasses everything known and unknown. This entity is both without attributes (*nirguna*) and with attributes (*saguna*) and in this latter aspect "assumes a form and name to make itself accessible to humankind."[8] Hence, "the statement that 'God is One' does not mean the same thing in India and the West."[9]

The primary deities traditionally recognized by many Hindus as manifestations of the ultimate Brahman are Brahma (the creator of the universe), Vishnu (the preserver of the universe), Shiva (the destroyer of the universe), and Devi (the Goddess/feminine principle). The perpetual creation-maintenance-destruction cycle of regeneration that is overseen and directed by the major deities is enhanced and also complicated by the fact that all three major male deities have various "manifestations" (both male and female) and are paired with female counterparts, and each god or goddess can take many forms. For example, Shiva (the destroyer of the universe) is also considered to be a creative and regenerative force. He is often paired with the goddess Parvati, who represents his female energy. Their son, the elephant-headed god Ganesha, brings good luck and prosperity[10] (see Figure 12.1). Shiva is the Lord

Figure 12.1   Ganesha, stone sculpture, ca. 1141, Hoysalesvara Temple, Halebid, Karnataka (Mysore), India. Art Resource, NY.

of the Dance, setting the universe in motion. He is also a teacher, and he represents the forces of change and destruction as well. The Goddess/feminine principle (Devi) is not only nurturing but also fierce and highly destructive. Additionally, many of the gods and goddesses have various reincarnations, or avatars. For example, the life and deeds of Krishna, the eighth incarnation of the god Vishnu, are featured especially in the *Bhagavad Gita*. Rama (the hero of the *Ramayana*) is also an avatar of Vishnu, and many Hindus consider the Buddha to have been another (and the most recent) avatar of Vishnu.

Other fundamental beliefs characteristic of classical Hinduism include the concepts of *samsara* (rebirth/reincarnation), *karma* (actions and consequences), and *moksha* (liberation from *samsara*). The earliest references to these ideas can be found in the Upanishads (ca. 600 BCE). These three related concepts have provided the foundation for centuries of discussion and interpretation. The belief in reincarnation rests on the concept that the souls of all beings (human and animal) are not confined to purely earthly bodies and that, upon death, souls transmigrate into and animate new beings. Just as the seasons of the year and the hours of the day perpetually cycle from light to dark and from winter to spring, so do souls/life forces undergo a cycle of birth/death/rebirth and continually begin anew. The belief in karma offers an explanation for the diversity of life forms and the relative positions of these lives in the earthly hierarchy—from the lowest, most downtrodden beings to the creatures with higher positions of relative comfort and greater abilities. Karma can be translated as "actions" or "merit," and although souls perpetually transmigrate and begin anew, these new beginnings are directly influenced by past actions and deeds. Good moral conduct and appropriate actions in one life can influence one's next life and one's next lives. Gaining release or liberation from this endless cycle of birth and rebirth may be achieved by souls who attain the highest state of enlightenment and are thus freed from the karmic cycle. Needless to say, the many diverse schools of Hindu thought approach these topics in different ways.

Similarly, different branches of Hinduism have various worship practices. The principal form of worship involves rituals known as *puja*, which are expressions of devotion and the making of offerings to the deities. *Puja* takes place both in temples and in homes.[11] Generally speaking, *puja* is not a congregational event that involves a fixed day per week (as groups of Christians may attend church every Sunday) but is an ongoing and fundamental aspect of the daily lives of devout Hindus. In large temples especially, *puja* is generally performed two or three times a day or more (morning, noon, evening, nighttime) and takes the form of symbolic actions involving offerings of flowers, food, water, adornments, light (candles or lamps—the waving of lamps is known as *arati*), and prayers directed to an image of a deity or an object that symbolizes the deity (see Figures 12.2 and 12.3). Painted images, three-dimensional sculptures, and symbolic forms such as the *linga* (a pillar, representing divine energy, specifically associated with Shiva) and *yoni* (basin surrounding a linga, often said to represent female creative power), are focal points for Hindu worship.[12] Daily temple *puja*, often assisted by priests, can involve more elaborate rituals and objects than *puja* performed in home shrines.

Figure 12.2 *Women Worshiping a Shiva linga*, ca. 1610, manuscript illumination. London: The Trustees of The British Museum / Art Resource, NY.

Temple *puja* is not truly congregational worship, but devotees do attend the ceremony as an audience. Some are present only for a short time: they reverently present their offerings . . . they behold the image of the god, make their requests to him, say mantras, and then leave. Others, however, will sit or stand throughout the ceremony, praying and singing devotional songs at appropriate times.[13]

There are also a number of special events, rites of passage, and other commemorations that call for special *pujas* to be performed. "Whether as a simple act of private devotion or as a multileveled communal performance, *pujas* bring together the human and the divine worlds at specific times and places . . . *Puja* . . . embodies the very reality that it seeks to adore."[14]

There are also an enormous number of religious holidays in the Hindu calendar for which larger communal festivals are held in honor of specific deities. In a sense, every day is an opportunity for worship, and the complexity and diversity of Hindu practices means that nearly all days are set aside for special festivals by various groups. Some of the largest festivals are those held at the fall equinox (the *Durga Puja* or *Navaratri*—nine nights—celebrations in honor of the goddesses Durga, Sarasvati, and Lakshmi), the late winter/spring *Holi* celebrations (commemorating the downfall of the evil female demon Holika, a joyous occasion reveling in the colors of spring when people throw brightly colored powders at each other), and the mid-fall *Dipavali* or *Diwali* festival (Necklace of Lights) marking the triumph

Figure 12.3 *Woman Worshiping the Goddess* (Devi), ca. 1750, painting. New Delhi: National Museum. Giraudon / Art Resource, NY.

of good and light over evil and darkness. *Diwali* is probably the most widely celebrated of Hindu festivals. During this period, homes and temples are decorated with lights, fireworks displays are held, new clothes are worn, presents are exchanged, and special meals are enjoyed. Processions of sacred images, dance, music, and chanting are essential aspects of Hindu worship practices.

Pilgrimage also plays an extremely important role in Hinduism.[15] There are thousands of sacred sites and cities associated with specific deities or divine events. Indeed, it can be said that "the entire land of India is, to the eyes of Hindu pilgrims, a sacred geography."[16] All sacred sites are known as *tirthas* (crossing places or fords) where pilgrims may receive blessings and spiritual assistance in crossing through the realms of *samsara* and *karma*, the oceans of life and death, to achieve ultimate liberation.

Many of the preeminent pilgrimage places in India are located on rivers or near water. The Ganges river is especially venerated, and the ancient city of Varanasi (also known as Benares or Kashi—the City of Light—the abode of the god Shiva), located on the Ganges, is generally regarded as Hinduism's most sacred city (see Figure 12.4). "Bathing in the Ganges, a river said to have fallen from heaven to earth, is the first act of Banaras pilgrims and a daily rite for Banaras residents."[17] Many Hindus believe that bathing in the Ganges provides

Figure 12.4 View of the ghats in Varanasi, India. Courtesy of Shutterstock.

release from the karmic cycle; many come to Benares to die and have their cremated remains placed into the holy river in order to achieve liberation from the cycle of death and rebirth.

TRADITIONAL ART AND ARCHITECTURAL FORMS

Hinduism, with its complex panoply of deities and extensive sacred literature, is no doubt among the most actively "art-friendly" of the major world religions. Although formal congregational worship is, or may be, of relatively minor importance for many devotees, Hinduism is characterized by extremely vibrant art forms: images of gods and goddesses, impressive temple architecture, and home shrines with a high degree of color and decoration.

The richness and complexity of Hindu art may indeed seem quite overwhelming, as is especially well demonstrated in the history of western European writings about and responses to India and Indian art.[18] To eyes unfamiliar with the forms and symbols, the depictions of Hindu deities (with multiple arms and heads, often in half-human, half-animal form) may seem quite bizarre and outlandish. Hindu temples do not really function like Christian churches or Islamic mosques but rather serve as dwelling places for deities who are embodied in the cult images or symbols contained therein. The worship of the Shiva *linga* (a highly phallic form) and the presence of apparently erotic sculptures on the exteriors of numerous Hindu temples have all contributed to a history of Western fascination with, as well as—at times—bafflement about, Hindu art. Much early Western scholarship on "Hindu art tells us a great deal about the dominant values of the West—when other exotic and distant arts [appear to have been] assimilated more easily in Western culture."[19] Another great challenge in studies of Hindu art (and indeed with all religious art in general) is that oftentimes objects designed to be placed and used within specific ritual contexts are now likely to be seen as "art objects" in museums. It is critical to maintain, as far as possible, an awareness of the original context and function of works of religious art.[20]

The Hindu Image

To begin to approach and preliminarily understand the arts of Hinduism, one needs to be aware of several concepts, among the most significant of which is *darsan* (or *darshan*). *Darsan* has been translated in a variety of ways, such as "sacred seeing," seeing and being seen by God, the benefits and blessings pursuant to viewing sacred images, and the power and efficacy involved with and inherent in sacred images. Many world religions rely on sacred images as teaching tools and as focal points for devotional practices. The Hindu concept of *darsan* transcends and expands these meanings of sacred images in significant ways. *Darsan* "is the single most common and significant element of Hindu worship" and bespeaks "the power and importance of 'seeing' in the Hindu religious tradition."[21]

Understanding the concept of *darsan* requires recalling that, in the Hindu worldview, the universe and everything in it are related manifestations of the unbounded energy of the unknowable and supreme Brahman. This force exists *with* and *without* attributes. The energies of nature, the deities, humans, all forms of life, and all earthly and heavenly surroundings are aspects of the divine. "According to traditional Indian belief every creature has its own purpose which it fulfills on earth. The purpose of the artist was to reproduce those Divine forms which in turn lead the spectator to union with the Divine."[22]

Images of the divine thus play a fundamental role in Hindu religious practices. Seeing these images, and in turn *being seen by* the images, is the primary goal. "When Hindus go to a temple, they do not customarily say, 'I am going to worship,' but rather, 'I am going for *darsan*.'"[23] *Darsan* can be achieved in several ways. In general, it implies a worshiper's receptivity to the sacred experience, an opening of oneself to the presence of the divine.

> Most individuals . . . need to approach God through images and with rituals specific to that deity, not so much because the deity requires it but because of the limitations of the devotee . . . humans need something concrete on which to focus in prayer. . . . Images are created as receptacles for spiritual energy; each is an essential link that allows the devotee to experience direct communion with the Gods.[24]

The painted images, sculptures, and symbols of the deities that are found in Hindu temples and home shrines are created, consecrated, and treated with the utmost care and respect because they are believed to be inhabited with divine energy. The processes involved with image creation and consecration are governed by specific rules and procedures and must be carried out with appropriate attitudes. The images themselves are believed to be enlivened with the divine, and if damaged or treated with disrespect, they will lose their divine presence. "The divine image is both means (*upaya*) and end (*upeya*.) It leads the devotee toward God, and it also *is* God, the devotee's object of enjoyment. . . . As an instantiation of the god-head, the image is ultimately the message."[25]

The power of the divinity resident in images, and the possibility of divine reanimation of images that have been removed from their original liturgical settings, was well demonstrated quite recently in a 1988 court case in London involving a 12th-century bronze sculpture of Shiva. Discovered (carefully buried) in the ruins of an Indian temple, the object eventually appeared on the black market, was identified, and was ultimately returned to India after a trial in the British court during which "the god Shiva himself appeared as a plaintiff . . . acting as a 'juristic person' to sue for the recovery of his image."[26]

The Hindu Temple

Hindu temples have been constructed in India and elsewhere for many centuries, and they appear in a great variety of forms and styles. Scholarly writing about Hindu temples has also taken on many different forms and styles through the ages.[27] The long history, diversity, and widespread nature of Hinduism have created challenges for writers wishing to describe and catalogue the myriad architectural examples. Some scholars have focused on chronology, dividing the study of Hindu temples into distinct period units with the goal of seeing an overall stylistic progression. Other writers have focused on matters such as the patronage of specific regional rulers in India, attributing certain styles of architecture to the aims and tastes of these dynasties. Still other writers have concentrated on the symbolism of the Hindu temple, focusing on meanings and messages. Some writers have concentrated on the ritual use of temples. Others have described temple architecture while barely mentioning the sculptural programs; others have focused on temple sculpture while barely mentioning the architectural context. The material, in other words, is vast. All architecture can convey many meanings: the prestige and ambitions of the patrons, the skill and creativity of the artists involved, the original purposes, alterations over time, and present status or usage.

Archaeological and literary evidence suggests that in the ancient Vedic period in India, ritual attention was focused on practices of making offerings and sacrifices to the major Vedic deities. Open-air altars as well as roofed enclosures were constructed for these rituals. As Vedic sacrificial practices gradually declined, the housing and worship of images of deities in shrine structures became more common. The creation of image-shrines for Hindu deities may have begun during the fourth century BCE, a period when Buddhist and Jain art forms were simultaneously developing too, often in close association with each other. The histories of Hindu, Buddhist, and Jain religious art are closely intertwined.

Ultimately, the primary function of the Hindu temple is to serve as an image-shrine, to serve as a sanctuary and shelter for the deity, and to provide a setting where devotees may offer their prayers. The impressive rock-cut cave-temples on the island of Elephanta, off the coast near Mumbai, demonstrate this well. Dating from the sixth century CE, the large cave-temple dedicated to Shiva contains several sculptured panels depicting different aspects of the deity. Deep within the main cave chamber is a triple-headed bust of Eternal Shiva (*Sadashiva*) in multiple guises (see Figure 12.5). The central head is calm and meditative, the head on the left represents a fierce masculine aspect, and the head on the right depicts a peaceful feminine aspect.

As a free-standing architectural structure, the Hindu temple can be recognized by several characteristic elements all related to its primary function as an enclosure for a deity or deities. The heart of the temple is the sanctuary where the image or symbol of the deity is located. This inner sanctum is known as the *garbhagriha* (womb chamber). Temples are often raised on high bases or plinths and are topped with towers, known in the north as *shikharas* and in the south as *vimanas*. The rock-cut "Shore Temple" at Mamallapuram (or Mahabalipuram), from ca. 700 CE, shows these forms (see Figure 12.6). Two major shrines are topped by impressive pyramidal towers with elaborate details, resembling a series of balconies and parapets. In general, Hindu temples in the south tend to show this pyramidal form of tower (see Figure 12.7), whereas northern-style temples show towers with more rounded profiles (see Figure 12.8).

The exterior sculptured decoration of Hindu temples tends to become even more complex through time. The narratives and symbols depicted in the sculptures are absolutely integral to the meaning of the architecture; they are placed in specific arrangements on the corners, buttresses, towers, and niches, and all relate to the purpose of the temple in serving as an appropriate residence or palace for the deity enshrined therein. "Axiality in relation to the sanctum and

Figure 12.5 Shiva with three aspects, stone sculpture, ca. 550 CE, Elephanta, India. Werner Forman / Art Resource, NY.

Figure 12.6 Shore Temple, ca. 700, Mamallapuram, India. Courtesy of Shutterstock.

Figure 12.7 Brihadeshvara Temple, early 11th century, Tanjavur, India. The Art Archive / Gianni Dagli Orti.

Figure 12.8 Brahmeswara Temple, mid 11th century, Bhubanesvar, India. Courtesy of Shutterstock.

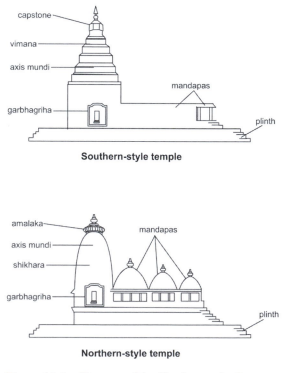

Figure 12.9 Diagram of the Hindu temple. Courtesy of Ricochet Productions.

door, compass direction, sequential arrangement, circumabulatory order, hierarchy within the wall, and visual coherence are all at play on the . . . temple exterior."[28]

EXAMPLES

The Kandariya Mahadeva Temple, Khajuraho, ca. 1025–50

The Kandariya Mahadeva Temple is an excellent example of the elements most characteristic of Hindu temple architecture during the flourishing medieval period (see Figure 12.10). Constructed under the patronage of the Chandella dynasty, the Kandariya is only one of many temples at the sacred site of Khajuraho. It is estimated that originally about 85 temples were located at the site; about 25 temples still exist there today in some form. These range in date from the 9th through the 12th century and are dedicated to a variety of Hindu deities. The Kandariya temple is dedicated to Shiva. The term Kandariya means "of the cave," and Mahadeva means "the Great God" (that is, Shiva).

The temple is raised on a high base or platform and is entered via a steep staircase on the front. The visitor then passes through a series of several small connected chambers (halls, or *mandapas*) before reaching the heart of the

Figure 12.10 Kandariya Mahadeva Temple, ca. 1025–1050, Khajuraho, India. Borromeo / Art Resource, NY.

temple: the *garbhagriha* (womb chamber) designed to enshrine the image of the deity. A narrow passageway with projecting porches and an open-air zone allows visitors to circumambulate the inner sanctum, which is signaled on the exterior also by the very tall tower (or *shikhara*). This shows the slightly rounded form typical of northern-style temple towers, and it is capped with an *amalaka* or ring-like form.

Altogether, this temple has a highly complex profile. In addition to the main tower, the *mandapas* (halls) are topped with roofs in semi-rounded, stepped, pyramidal form of progressively greater height that lead up to the main tower, which is itself surrounded by a cascade of connected smaller towers and spires. The tower symbolizes the center of the universe (the *axis mundi*) rising upwards with the divine energy radiating from the deity deep within the structure. Additional lines of divine energy are signaled by sculptures on the exterior walls and corners. The sculpture and architecture work together to create a structure that not only serves as a symbol of the divine but also offers a vehicle for seeing and experiencing the divine.

The elaborate exterior sculptures on the Kandariya temple cover virtually every surface. There are horizontal friezes with narrative reliefs and niches filled with images of deities. There are guardian figures (*karnas*), attendant figures (notably celestial females known as *apsaras*), mythical beasts (*vyalas*), and amorous couples (*maithunas*) in an enormous variety of poses. The temple as a whole represents the "universe in microcosm,"[29] and the images serve as "visual 'theologies' . . . and visual scriptures."[30] The densely packed sculptures covering the temple surface "need to be looked at from the perspective of architectural logic rather than as individual units,"[31] all working together to create a grand, cosmic display of divine energy. On the Kandariya temple, "curving lines and sinuous solids [are] paramount and the whole temple [pulsates] to a stupendous linear crescendo."[32] Although but one example among thousands, the Kandariya Mahadeva at Khajuraho is an especially famous and well-studied example of a grand and complex Hindu temple.

Images of Hindu Deities

These bronze sculptures (see Figure 12.11 and Plate 23), both from southern India, represent two of the most important and widely venerated Hindu gods: Vishnu and Shiva. Although many centuries separate these examples in terms of their dates, they both typify many shared and traditional characteristics of Hindu religious images.

These types of sculptures were created for important ritual purposes. Housed in temples, they would have played particularly important roles during festivals and processions. Sculptures of this type are known as *utsava murtis* (the bodies of the gods); they served as mobile and secondary images of the deities otherwise enshrined in non-moveable images or symbols in the inner sanctum of the temple. These processional images "are awakened during the festival time to provide the gods with the mobile bodies they need to move out into the daily world."[33] "During the rest of the year, when they are not in use, these bronze sculptures are stored away from the center of the temple, although in some temples they are enshrined within the sanctum."[34]

Although both examples illustrated are iconic images, depicting the deities in fundamentally human form, they also show symbols, gestures, and actions that present specific aspects of the divine forces. The forms that these images take assist viewers in grasping the nature of the essentially limitless and formless divine. "The things of the world we can see well enough all about us, but for the Indian religious artist the task of image-making was giving shape to those things we cannot readily see."[35]

Vishnu (the Preserver) is "consistently seen as the preserver of harmony and the maintainer of order and tradition."[36] As such, he plays a critical role as a member of the triad of major male Hindu gods, between Brahma (the Creator) and Shiva (the Destroyer).

Figure 12.11 Vishnu, bronze sculpture, 17th century, southern India. The Art Archive / Musée Guimet Paris / Gianni Dagli Orti.

Vishnu's role is to maintain and sustain the universe. Perhaps ultimately derived from the ancient Vedic sun god, Varuna (the keeper of cosmic order), the name Vishnu comes from the Sanskrit term meaning "to work." "He is indeed regarded as the all-doing presence"[37] and embodies goodness, mercy, and sustenance.

This 17th-century example shows many characteristics of his traditional iconography. He is depicted as a tall, stately figure with his feet planted firmly on the ground (base); he is wearing a high crown (or *kiritamukuta*—the highest crown), a richly decorated belt or hip-band (*katibandha*), a symbolic sacrificial cord, and elaborate jewelry (necklaces, earrings, armlets) symbolic of his power, prestige, and importance. In this typically four-armed form he holds two of his chief attributes: the conch shell (the sound of which wards off demons and the spiral form of which represents constantly expanding infinity) and the solar disk or wheel (the symbol of infinity—life and death). His remaining two hands show symbolic gestures (or *mudras*) of blessing, protection, reassurance, and mercy. His four arms and hands may also be seen as symbolic of the stages of human life and his control over all spatial directions. "The interpretation of Vishnu's attributes cannot be precise. Understanding has to be associated with vision or enlightenment, which comes as much from unconscious perception as from a conscious reading of symbols."[38]

In addition to this form, Vishnu is also widely depicted in other ways, specifically in his 10 chief avatars, or manifestations on earth. According to tradition, Vishnu has come to earth at various moments of political and spiritual need, to protect and guide humans. Several of his avatars were animal forms (fish, turtle, boar, half-man/half-lion); in other forms he appeared as a powerful dwarf, as Rama with an axe, as the King Rama (the hero of the epic *Ramayana*), as Balarama (the brother of Krishna), as Krishna (the most popular and widely venerated of all his avatars), and as the Buddha. The tenth and final avatar of Vishnu is yet to come. Known as Kalki, this figure will signal the end of the world, or the conclusion of the present time cycle.

The god Shiva (the Destroyer) also has a highly complex and multifaceted iconography bespeaking his various aspects. "Like a complex personality [he] has multiple forms and a paradoxical character. He is a deity who often inhabits the extremes of human behavior."[39] Shiva represents creation as well as destruction; he symbolizes the forces of regeneration as well as removal; he has an ascetic as well as a highly sexual nature. Frequently worshiped in the aniconic and phallic *linga* form, in iconic guise Shiva may appear as an ascetic, as a teacher, as a fierce and wild demonic type, and most popularly, as *Nataraja*, the Lord of the Dance, as shown in the 11th to 12th century bronze sculpture illustrated in Plate 23.

Shiva Nataraja dances in a ring of flames, symbolizing the fiery forces of destruction and transformation. He stands atop and crushes a demonic dwarf named Apasmara, who represents ignorance and forgetfulness. Shiva's long, matted hair streams out energetically on both sides of his head. Caught within the strands of his hair is a small figure of the goddess Ganga, the personification of the sacred river Ganges, whose descent from heaven Shiva assisted. His four arms represent his power over the four directions. His *mudras* include gestures of protection (raised hand) and salvation (downward pointing hand).

> Nataraja, the lord of dancers, dancing, shows his fivefold activity, the expression of his divine totality. His dancing limbs convey by their movements and symbols the fivefold action of creation, maintenance, dissolution, veiling-unveiling, and liberation. Nataraya dances the cosmos into existence, upholds its existence, and dances it out of existence. . . . The raised leg of the dancer shows the liberating freedom of his dance, the drum raised by the right hand sounds the note of creation, the flame in the left hand flickers in the change brought about by destruction. . . . The movement of the dancer . . . self-enclosed in balanced gyration, is encircled by flames.[40]

The image of the dancing Shiva Nataraja is one of the most popular representations of this deity, and great numbers of bronzes of this type, with minor variations, survive. In the 1988 court case in London mentioned earlier, it was a Shiva Nataraya bronze sculpture that was at the heart of the dispute. Indeed, "most of the large bronze images of Hindu deities displayed in museum collections were originally *utsava murtis*"[41] (processional images) that have lost their power and sacredness as a result of damage, theft, deterioration, or mistreatment.

Krishna and Radha, Miniature Painting, ca. 1760

Krishna is one of the most popular Hindu deities. An avatar of Vishnu, his deeds and adventures are frequently illustrated in art (see Plate 24). These scenes derive from literary sources, such as the *Mahabharata* (including the *Bhagavad Gita*—primarily a conversation between Krishna and the warrior Arjuna) and many other *puranas* or tales concerning this widely venerated deity.

Among the many episodes in Krishna's biography, one that is most celebrated involves his early relationship with his beloved Radha and her companions among the *gopis* (cowgirls or milkmaids). The romantic exploits of Krishna and the *gopis* were especially popular in later Indian miniature painting, such as seen in this example from the middle of the 18th century. Small paintings such as these were created in great numbers, especially at the various royal courts (both Muslim and Hindu) between the 16th and 19th centuries. Created with gouache (vegetable and mineral colors mixed with gum arabic) on specially prepared paper, these miniature paintings were designed to be kept in albums (either bound or loose) for the enjoyment of the courtly patrons. "They were made above all to delight the eye by their rich color harmonies and fluent clarity of line . . . to impart mainly auspicious or pleasurable sentiments, whether of royal grandeur, devotional wonder, or a refined eroticism."[42]

There are a number of distinctive styles of Indian miniature painting associated with various regions, time periods, and patronage. This particular example was produced at the Rajput court in Kishengarh, Rajasthan, during the time of the refined and accomplished ruler and art patron Savant Singh (1699–1764; reigned 1748–57). The delicate and detailed rendering of the figures, drapery, and landscape reflect the elegance and sophistication of the courtly context. They mirror the type of clothing and jewelry favored at the court, as well as the garden settings. In this illustration, Krishna, typically blue-skinned (his name means "dark blue or black"), is in a dancing pose and is being offered a betel leaf by the elegantly dressed Radha. To either side of these famous lovers are groups of Radha's companions, the *gopis*, who are also elegantly dressed and bearing various gifts, jewelry, flowers, vases, and fans made of peacock feathers. According to some of the tales, the *gopis* left their husbands and children in order to follow Krishna, who multiplied himself so as to achieve a personal relationship with each one of them. This symbolizes the intense connection between devotees and deities, especially reflective of *bhakti* (devotional) practices. "Krishna and Radha in the grove are models, as divine lovers, of human love but especially of the soul's devotion to God."[43]

NOTES

1. Julius Lipner, *Hindus: Their Religious Beliefs and Practices* (London: Routledge, 1994), 6.

2. Richard H. Davis, "A Brief History of Religions in India," in *Religions of Asia in Practice: An Anthology,* ed. Donald Lopez (Princeton, NJ: Princeton University Press, 2002), 5.

3. Davis, 37.

4. Davis, 46–47.

5. Lipner, 6.

6. Lipner, 12–13.

7. Pratapaditya Pal, *Art of the Himalayas: Treasures from Nepal and Tibet* (New York: Hudson Hills Press, 1991), 15.

8. Vasudha Narayanan, "Hinduism," in *The Illustrated Guide to World Religions*, ed. Michael Coogan (New York: Oxford University Press, 2003), 134.

9. Diana Eck, *Darsan: Seeing the Divine in India* (New York: Columbia University Press, 1998), 24.

10. Paul Courtright, *Ganesa: Lord of Obstacles, Lord of Beginnings* (New York: Oxford University Press, 1985).

11. Pika Ghosh, Edward Dimock, Lee Horne, and Michael Meister, *Cooking for the Gods: The Art of Home Ritual in Bengal* (Newark, NJ: The Newark Museum, 1995).

12. Richard Davis, "The Origin of Linga Worship," in *Religions of Asia in Practice: An Anthology*, ed. Donald Lopez (Princeton, NJ: Princeton University Press, 2002), 150–61.

13. Joseph Dye, *Ways to Shiva: Life and Ritual in Hindu India* (Philadelphia: Philadelphia Museum of Art, 1980), 73.

14. Paul Courtright, "On This Holy Day in My Humble Way: Aspects of Puja," in *Gods of Flesh/Gods of Stone: The Embodiment of Divinity in India*, ed. Joanne Waghorne and Norman Cutler (New York: Columbia University Press, 1996), 33.

15. Simon Coleman and John Elsner, *Pilgrimage: Past and Present in the World Religions* (Cambridge, MA: Harvard University Press. 1995), 136–65; and Surinder Mohan Bhardwaj, *Hindu Places of Pilgrimage in India: A Study in Cultural Geography* (Berkeley: University of California Press, 1973).

16. Eck, *Darsan*, 65.

17. Diana Eck, *Banaras: City of Light* (Princeton, NJ: Princeton University Press, 1982), 3.

18. Partha Mitter, *Much Maligned Monsters: A History of European Reactions to Indian Art* (Chicago: University of Chicago Press, 1992); and Robert Inden, "Orientalist Constructions of India," *Modern Asian Studies* 20, no. 3 (1986): 401–46.

19. Mitter, xiv.

20. Vishakha Desai, "Beyond the Temple Walls: The Scholarly Fate of North Indian Sculpture, AD 700–1200," in *Gods, Guardians, and Lovers: Temple Sculptures from North India A.D. 700–1200*, ed. Vishakha Desai and Darielle Mason (New York: Asia Society Galleries, 1993), 19–31.

21. Eck, *Darsan*, 1.

22. Alistair Shearer, *Forms of the Formless: The Hindu Vision* (London: Thames and Hudson, 1993), 15.

23. Eck, *Darsan*, 3.

24. Stephen Huyler, *Meeting God: Elements of Hindu Devotion* (New Haven, CT: Yale University Press, 1999), 36.

25. Richard Davis, *Lives of Indian Images* (Princeton, NJ: Princeton University Press, 1997), 33.

26. Richard Davis, "Loss and Recovery of Ritual Self among Hindu Images," *Journal of Ritual Studies* 6, no. 1 (1992), 44; and Richard Davis, *Lives of Indian Images* (Princeton, NJ: Princeton University Press, 1997), 248–52.

27. Michael Meister, "De- and Re-Constructing the Indian Temple," *Art Journal* 49, no. 4 (1990): 395–400.

28. Darielle Mason, "A Sense of Time and Place: Style and Architectural Disposition of Images on the North Indian Temple," in *Gods, Guardians, and Lovers: Temple Sculptures from North India A.D. 700–1200*, ed. Vishakha Desai and Darielle Mason (New York: Asia Society Galleries, 1993), 135.

29. Eck, *Darsan*, 59.

30. Eck, *Darsan*, 41.

31. Desai, "Beyond the Temple Walls," 25.

32. Mason, "A Sense of Time and Place," 217.

33. Joanne Waghorne, "Dressing the Body of God: South Indian Bronze Sculpture in Its Temple Setting," *Asian Art* 5, no. 3 (1992): 17.

34. Huyler, 166.

35. Eck, *Darsan*, 39.

36. Heather Elgood, *Hinduism and the Religious Arts* (London: Cassell, 1999), 55.

37. Elgood, 55–56.

38. Elgood, 64.

39. Elgood, 45.

40. Stella Kramrisch, *The Presence of Siva* (Princeton, NJ: Princeton University Press, 1981), 440.

41. Huyler, 169.

42. Andrew Topsfield, *An Introduction to Indian Court Painting* (Owings Mills, MD: Stemmer House, 1984), 5.

43. Albert Moore, *Iconography of Religions: An Introduction* (Philadelphia: Fortress Press, 1977), 114.

BIBLIOGRAPHY AND FURTHER READING

Alles, Gregory. "Surface, Space, and Intention: The Parthenon and the Kandariya Mahadeva." *History of Religions* 28, no. 1 (1988): 1–36.

Bhardwaj, Surinder Mohan. *Hindu Places of Pilgrimage in India: A Study in Cultural Geography*. Berkeley: University of California Press, 1973.

Coleman, Simon, and John Elsner. *Pilgrimage: Past and Present in the World Religions*. Cambridge, MA: Harvard University Press, 1995.

Coogan, Michael, ed. *The Illustrated Guide to World Religions*. New York: Oxford University Press, 2003.

Courtright, Paul. *Ganesa: Lord of Obstacles, Lord of Beginnings*. New York: Oxford University Press, 1985.

Courtright, Paul. "On This Holy Day in My Humble Way: Aspects of Puja." In *Gods of Flesh/Gods of Stone: The Embodiment of Divinity in India*, ed. Joanne Waghorne and Norman Cutler, 33–50. New York: Columbia University Press, 1996.

Dallapiccola, Anna. *Dictionary of Hindu Lore and Legend*. New York: Thames and Hudson, 2002.

Dallapiccola, Anna. *Hindu Visions of the Sacred*. London: British Museum, 2004.

Davis, Richard. "A Brief History of Religions in India." In *Religions of Asia in Practice: An Anthology*, ed. Donald Lopez, 3–50. Princeton, NJ: Princeton University Press, 2002.

Davis, Richard. *Lives of Indian Images*. Princeton, NJ: Princeton University Press, 1997.

Davis, Richard. "Loss and Recovery of Ritual Self among Hindu Images." *Journal of Ritual Studies* 6, no. 1 (1992): 43–61.

Davis, Richard. *Ritual in an Oscillating Universe: Worshiping Siva in Medieval India.* Princeton, NJ: Princeton University Press, 1991.

Desai, Devangana. *Erotic Sculpture of India, A Socio-Cultural Study.* New Delhi: Tata McGraw-Hill, 1975.

Desai, Vishakha, and Darielle Mason, eds. *Gods, Guardians, and Lovers: Temple Sculptures from North India A.D. 700–1200.* New York: Asia Society Galleries, 1993.

Dye, Joseph. *Ways to Shiva: Life and Ritual in Hindu India.* Philadelphia: Philadelphia Museum of Art, 1980.

Eck, Diana. *Banaras: City of Light.* Princeton, NJ: Princeton University Press, 1992.

Eck, Diana. *Darsan: Seeing the Divine in India.* New York: Columbia University Press, 1998.

Elgood, Heather. *Hinduism and the Religious Arts.* London: Cassell, 1999.

Ghosh, Pika, Edward Dimock, Lee Horne, and Michael Meister. *Cooking for the Gods: The Art of Home Ritual in Bengal.* Newark, NJ: The Newark Museum, 1995.

Goswamy, B.N. *Essence of Indian Art.* San Francisco: The Asian Art Museum of San Francisco, 1986.

Gray, Basil, ed. *The Arts of India.* Oxford: Phaidon, 1981.

Huyler, Stephen. *Meeting God: Elements of Hindu Devotion.* New Haven, CT: Yale University Press, 1999.

Huyler, Stephen. "Respecting Material Spirit." *Asian Art* 5, no. 3 (1992): 2–7.

Inden, Robert. "Orientalist Constructions of India." *Modern Asian Studies* 20, no. 3 (1986): 401–46.

Jansen, Eva Rudy. *The Book of Hindu Imagery: Gods, Manifestations and Their Meaning.* Diever, Holland: Binkey Kok, 1993.

Klostermaier, Klaus. *Hinduism: A Short History.* Oxford: Oneworld, 2000.

Kramrisch, Stella, ed. *Discourses on Shiva.* Philadelphia: University of Pennsylvania Press, 1984.

Kramrisch, Stella. *Painted Delight: Indian Paintings from Philadelphia Collections.* Philadelphia: Philadelphia Museum of Art, 1986.

Kramrisch, Stella. *The Presence of Siva.* Princeton, NJ: Princeton University Press, 1981.

Lipner, Julius. *Hindus: Their Religious Beliefs and Practices.* London: Routledge, 1994.

Lopez, Donald. *Religions of Asia in Practice: An Anthology.* Princeton, NJ: Princeton University Press, 2002.

McGee, Mary. "Hinduism." In *Eastern Wisdom: An Illustrated Guide to the Religions and Philosophies of the East,* ed. C. Scott Littleton, 14–53. New York: Henry Holt, 1996.

Meister, Michael. "De- and Re-Constructing the Indian Temple." *Art Journal* 49, no. 4 (1990): 395–400.

Michell, George. *Hindu Art and Architecture.* London: Thames and Hudson, 2000.

Michell, George. *The Hindu Temple: An Introduction to Its Meaning and Forms.* Chicago: University of Chicago Press, 1988.

Mitter, Partha. *Much Maligned Monsters: A History of European Reactions to Indian Art.* Chicago: University of Chicago Press, 1992.

Mookerjee, Ajit. *Ritual Art of India*. London: Thames and Hudson, 1985.

Moore, Albert. *Iconography of Religions: An Introduction*. Philadelphia: Fortress Press, 1977.

Narayanan, Vasudha. "Hinduism." In *The Illustrated Guide to World Religions*, ed. Michael Coogan, 124–61. New York: Oxford University Press, 2003.

Pal, Pratapaditya. *Art of the Himalayas: Treasures from Nepal and Tibet*. New York: Hudson Hills Press, 1991.

Pinney, Christopher. *Photos of the Gods: The Printed Image and Political Struggle in India*. New York: Oxford University Press, 2004.

Sharma, Arvind. *Classical Hindu Thought: An Introduction*. New York: Oxford University Press, 2000.

Shearer, Alistair. *Forms of the Formless: The Hindu Vision*. London: Thames and Hudson, 1993.

Stutley, Margaret. *The Illustrated Dictionary of Hindi Iconography*. London: Routledge and Kegan Paul, 1985.

Tadgell, Christopher. *The History of Architecture in India*. London: Phaidon, 1990.

Topsfield, Andrew. *An Introduction to Indian Court Painting*. Owings Mills, MD: Stemmer House, 1984.

Waghorne, Joanne. "Dressing the Body of God: South Indian Bronze Sculpture in Its Temple Setting." *Asian Art* 5, no. 3 (1992): 8–33.

Waghorne, Joanne, and Norman Cutler, eds. *Gods of Flesh/Gods of Stone: The Embodiment of Divinity in India*. New York: Columbia University Press, 1996.

−13−

Buddhism

ORIGINS AND DEVELOPMENT

Buddhism, one of the world's major religions today, has a lengthy history and exists in many different variations. The origins of Buddhism can be attributed to a historical figure, Siddhartha Gautama, who was born in what is now southern Nepal ca. 566 BCE and who, after a long life of teaching and travels, died at age 80 in 486 BCE.[1] The details of his life have long formed the subject matter for many Buddhist tales and elaborations, notably the *jataka* or "birth" narratives, frequently featured in art, which tell of the Buddha's previous lives before his incarnation as Siddhartha Gautama. He was a royal prince of the Shakya family, who were Indian rulers over a territory at the base of the Himalayan foothills spanning part of present-day northern India and Nepal. He is thus sometimes also known as Shakyamuni—the Sage of the Shakya clan.

The fundamental narrative of his life might be summarized as a journey from worldly wealth to spiritual richness. Traditions recount that, as a young man, Siddhartha enjoyed a very privileged and opulent lifestyle. He was deliberately sheltered from the world outside the royal household by his father, who wished to protect him and prepare him for life as a royal leader. Siddhartha followed these familial expectations; he married a beautiful wife who bore him a son. But he became increasingly curious about the world outside the palace, and in his late twenties (shortly after the birth of his son), he took a series of trips to the local village and there encountered a number of sights that influenced him profoundly. For the first time in his previously sheltered existence, Siddhartha witnessed aspects of human suffering in the form of disease, old age, and death. He also encountered a wandering ascetic (a Hindu *sadhu* or holy man) and was inspired by this example to renounce his previously opulent lifestyle and search for answers about the meaning and purpose of human life and suffering.

Ultimately, and after many subsequent years of extreme self-denial, discipline, travels, and encounters with others who offered him various forms of guidance and inspiration, Siddhartha sat down to make a final effort in his quest by meditating beneath a tree (later known as the Bodhi Tree, or Tree of Awakening) at Bodh Gaya in northern India. After prolonged meditation, he received profound insights about the nature of human life and existence, and he became the Buddha—a Sanskrit term that means the "Awakened One."

It is very important to realize that the cultural and religious milieu in India that ultimately gave birth to Buddhism represents a period of time when aspects of Hinduism were continuing to develop as well. Hinduism had long been dominated by the Brahmin priestly class and focused especially on rituals performed by these priests. But Buddha's lifetime, the sixth century BCE, was a period "of great intellectual speculation, when many religious leaders questioned and even rejected the authoritarian structures of traditional Indian religion."[2] Both Buddhism and Jainism (also founded in India in the sixth century BCE by Mahavira the Jina—or "Victorious One") represented significant critical challenges to traditional Hinduism while retaining and reinterpreting many of the concepts and vocabulary of Hindu beliefs.

After Buddha's enlightenment at Bodh Gaya, he ultimately determined to share the fruits of his awakening to the "truth" or "law" of human existence (the *dharma*) with others. He first offered his teachings to a small group of his previous companions of ascetics who gathered at a deer park in Sarnath. These followers became the first members of the Buddhist community (the *sangha*), which expanded greatly through the next several decades of the Buddha's travels and teaching in northern India.

After the Buddha's peaceful death, his teachings continued to be orally disseminated as well as interpreted by a growing number of schools and increasingly settled monastic communities. However, doctrinal controversies arose about the specifics and nature of his teachings and about the nature of the Buddha himself. Traditions tell of several early Buddhist meetings or councils that were held to resolve these differences in interpretation; nevertheless, regional sects and schools continued to develop as Buddhism spread widely through India and beyond. Within these early centuries, 18 different schools of Buddhism eventually emerged, including the Theravadan ("Wisdom of the Elders") branch that today continues to be followed in southeast Asia and Sri Lanka. A critical stage in the historical development of Buddhism took place around the first century CE with the reform movement known as Mahayana (or "Great Vehicle"). The term "Great Vehicle" contrasts Mahayana Buddhism with the several Hinayana ("Lesser Vehicle") schools. Theravada and Mahayana are considered to be the two major branches of Buddhism, although many widely different variations of Mahayana Buddhism, in particular, also developed in subsequent centuries.

Both Theravada and Mahayana schools trace their history back to the teachings of the Buddha himself, although it should be noted that no Buddhist texts were written down, in any language, during the lifetime of the Buddha or even shortly thereafter. The Buddha's teachings were memorized and transmitted orally and translated into a variety of languages and dialects through many centuries before the earliest scriptures were committed to writing. This took place in the first century BCE and first century CE in the Theravadan context of Sri Lanka. This vast body of writings is known as the Pali Canon, after the ancient language (Pali) in which it is written. It is divided into three major sections (or "baskets") of teachings concerning monastic life, discourses of the Buddha, and commentary. The Pali Canon (also known as the *Tripitaka*—or Three Baskets) is the oldest and most conservative collection of Buddhist scriptures.

With the development of Mahayana Buddhism in the first and second centuries CE, many additional texts (*sutras*) were created that also traced their origins to the foundational teachings of the Buddha—teachings that had been hidden but later mystically revealed to enlightened beings, or *bodhisattvas*. Major authors such as Nagarjuna (ca. 150–250 CE) were instrumental in promoting the authority of these later texts, which were seen as adding to, if not fulfilling and superseding, the previous teachings, which were regarded as foundational, but preparatory. "The enormous range and variety of Buddhist scripture has led to many controversies about scriptural authority and interpretation,"[3] as different schools understand a variety of texts to be authoritative. Nevertheless, these all indicate ways of understanding the Buddha's message and represent the flourishing growth, spread, and remarkable ability of Buddhism to adapt to different cultures and settings.

The Mahayana branch of Buddhism is, in itself, extremely diverse and represents a wide range of practices. Buddhism spread to China in the first and second centuries CE and thence to Korea in the fourth century and to Japan in the sixth century. Two waves of Buddhism entered Tibet in the 7th and in the 10th centuries. All of these different styles or branches of Buddhism were also transformed by the already-existing and continuously developing religious systems in these world regions. In China, Buddhism encountered, influenced, and was transformed by preexistent Chinese popular religious traditions, plus Taoism and Confucianism. In Japan, Buddhism merged, to a large extent, with Japanese Shinto practices and resulted in a uniquely Japanese Shinto-Buddhist synthesis. In Tibet, Buddhist practices developed differently as well, assimilating some of the indigenous traditions of Bon shamanistic practices and influencing the continued development of the Bon religion itself.[4] New branches of Buddhism continued to develop in India and in Asia through the medieval period and were transmitted across cultures.

Among the most influential of these later Mahayana developments are Pure Land, Zen, and Tantric Buddhism. The former two are associated particularly with China and Japan, respectively, and the latter primarily with Tibet. The specifics of these (also multivaried) systems are especially well demonstrated in the diversity of texts and art works that enliven and characterize these movements.

Although Buddhism began in India, and during several periods of history was supported and encouraged by major political leaders (notably the early Emperor Asoka in the third century BCE and the Pala dynasty in southern India in the 8th through 12th centuries CE), by the 13th century Buddhism had significantly declined in India. Several cultural and political factors were doubtless influential in this process of decline, such as the growth and popularity of devotional and revival movements within Hinduism, the reabsorption of many Buddhist concepts and deities into the ever-expanding Hindu pantheon, and the Islamic invasions of India that began in the 12th century. Buddhist monasteries were attacked and looted in the Islamic conquests, and by the 13th century, Buddhism was virtually extinct in its Indian birthplace. Islam and Hinduism are today the dominant religions in India, and Buddhism is widely practiced in world regions outside the Indian subcontinent.

PRINCIPAL BELIEFS AND KEY PRACTICES

The lengthy history of Buddhism—combined with the complexities of its historical development and transformations in different world regions—may, at first, seem to make a discussion of principal beliefs and key practices a very daunting task. Although Buddhism has taken on many diverse guises, there are certainly some core concepts that all facets of Buddhism share. The historical Buddha (in whatever ways he is variously perceived, honored, or worshiped by various Buddhist sects) is understood to have been a person of remarkable abilities who transmitted highly important knowledge about the ultimate meaning of life.

These teachings can be, and often are, summarized as the Four Noble Truths and the Eightfold Path. In the Buddha's personal encounters with and sorrowful concern for human suffering on earth, his enlightenment resulted not only in awareness of human suffering but also in ways in which to alleviate this suffering. This wisdom is contained in the Four Noble Truths.

The first noble truth is the truth of suffering. The Buddha saw and understood that human life will inevitably involve some degree of hardship and suffering (*duhkha*)—whether emotional or physical. His own experience with life, and his witnessing of disease, old age, and death, led him to the painful realization that human life, although often pleasant and happy, is also filled with challenges, difficulties, and disappointments. The second noble truth that he conveyed to his followers regards the origins and causes of suffering. Sufferings and difficulties in life are caused by qualities often seen as simply characteristic of human nature, such as desire, greed, selfishness, ignorance, and attachment to and grasping for material goods, status, power, and relationships. This is all reflective of human misperceptions of the inherent nature of reality. Humans delude themselves by their ego-based thinking in which they set themselves—as individual beings—apart from the dynamic unity of the universe, which they mistakenly feel they can control and manipulate to some extent by their own positions, actions, and achievements. According to the third noble truth, suffering can be avoided if one frees oneself from inappropriate cravings and attachments that reflect an ego-driven perception of the self. Avoiding attachment can be achieved, according to the fourth noble truth, by following the Eightfold Path of right understanding, right purpose, right speech, right conduct, right livelihood, right effort, right alertness, and right concentration.[5]

The Four Noble Truths and the Eightfold Path represent the core of Buddhist teaching, regardless of sectarian divisions. In his lengthy career as a teacher, the Buddha offered many additional insights about the nature of reality and the universe. He established and provided guidance for numerous monastic communities of both men and women, and he promoted a balanced, disciplined, and measured lifestyle to achieve liberation from suffering. This state of liberation is known as *nirvana*. Indeed, many Buddhist concepts (such as *nirvana*) derive from and significantly reinterpret Hindu beliefs in reincarnation (*samsara*), actions and their consequences (*karma*), and liberation (*moksha*) from *samsara*, to achieve a cessation of all ego-based cravings and attachments.

As Buddhism continued to develop in the centuries following the Buddha's death, differing interpretations arose about these teachings and how to follow the ideals in actual practice. Especially after the advent of Mahayana Buddhism in the first and second centuries CE, many new teachers—through the subsequent centuries to the present day—have promoted and emphasized different manners in which to achieve true awareness of the Four Noble Truths and how to correctly enact the guidance offered by the Eightfold Path. The great diversity of schools and branches of Buddhism is actually rather akin to the situation of Protestant Christianity, where vast numbers of adherents consider themselves to be Christians first and foremost, while also maintaining firm allegiances to specific denominations that are themselves characterized by significantly different interpretations of the core Christian teachings and that enact their beliefs through vastly different liturgical practices.

For example, Theravadan Buddhists (often considered to be the most strictly conservative of Buddhist sects) believe that the historical Buddha (Siddhartha Gautama) was the final incarnation of an enlightened being, who appeared on earth, lived, and died and transmitted great wisdom. Mahayana Buddhists, in contrast, regard the historical Buddha as only one manifestation among many related exemplars or incarnations of enlightenment. *Arhats* (saints, ascetics, or worthy ones) feature prominently in Theravada Buddhism because of their achievement of great spiritual discipline, awareness, and ability to provide inspiring examples to others. In Mahayana Buddhism, focus is directed instead on the many manifestations of the Buddha and on the numerous *bodhisattvas* (*buddhas*-to-be) who compassionately postpone their own achievement of *nirvana* to assist other beings in their own process to achieve this liberation. The celestial *bodhisattvas*

> can intervene miraculously in the world, and can even create heavenly realms where people may be reborn into bliss for reasons that depend as much on the compassion of the *bodhisattvas* as on the merit of the individual worshipper. At the end of their careers as *bodhisattvas* they become "celestial *buddhas*" and attain even more remarkable powers.[6]

Among the most important of these *bodhisattvas* are Avalokiteshvara (who embodies the compassion of the Buddha and is worshiped in Japan and China as the female deity Kannon or Guan Yin), Maitreya (the future-age Buddha), Manjushri (the *bodhisattva* of wisdom), and Kshitigarbha (who consoles and protects.)

Among the most revered of celestial *buddhas* is Amitabha (the *buddha* of Infinite Light), who is believed to have established a Pure Land paradise in the western heavens where his faithful followers will be reborn. Pure Land Buddhism is one of the most influential branches of later Mahayanist developments; it has roots in India but was developed especially in China from the fifth century CE and also became enormously popular in Japan during the 12th century and later. Pure Land Buddhism is often seen as a more accessible and popular form for both lay and monastic practitioners. Adherents to this form of Buddhism rely extensively on chanting and repeated invocations of the name of Amitabha Buddha. Pure Land Buddhists believe that prayers faithfully directed to Amitabha will be accepted compassionately by the deity, who is often visualized and depicted as residing in a magnificent universe.

Meditation practices are especially emphasized in the Ch'an (Chinese) and Zen (Japanese) branches of Buddhism. According to traditions, Ch'an practices were brought to China from India in the late fifth century CE by the legendary figure known as Bodhidharma (whose name means "Enlightened Tradition"). Ch'an Buddhism was later conveyed to Korea and Japan. There are numerous branches (for example, Soto and Rinzai) of this style of Buddhism, many of which rely extensively on practices of rigorous disciplined and formal sitting meditation (*zazen*) to still the mind and allow insights and enlightenment to arise directly. Order and simplicity designed to provide quiet harmony and minimal distractions are especially characteristic of Zen aesthetics, well demonstrated, for example, in the style of "dry gardening" seen at the Ryoan-ji Temple in Kyoto, Japan (see Figure 13.1).

Colorful imagery and complex iconography are, in contrast, especially characteristic of Tantric (or Vajrayana, Thunderbolt or Diamond Vehicle) Buddhism, which emphasizes elaborate ritual practices and visually aided meditation on esoteric symbols and diagrams designed to assist adherents in attaining immediate experiences and stages of awakening and enlightenment. Tantric practices have roots in ancient India also and were especially developed later in Tibet

Plate 17 Synagogue at Dura Europos, interior, mid-third century CE. Replica, Tel Aviv, Israel: Museum of the Diaspora. Erich Lessing / Art Resource, NY.

Plate 18 The "Golden Haggadah," ca. 1320, Northern Spain. London: British Library Ms Add 27210, ff. 4v-5. Erich Lessing / Art Resource, NY.

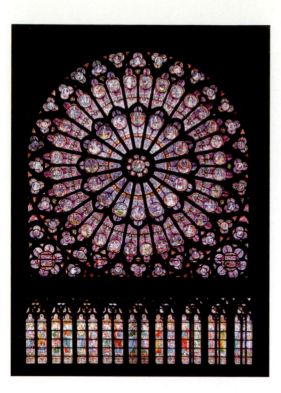

Plate 19   Notre Dame Cathedral in Paris, France, north transept rose window, 13th century. Courtesy of Shutterstock.

Plate 20   Matthias Grunewald, *The Isenheim Altarpiece*, crucifixion panel, ca. 1510–15. Colmar: Musée d'Unterlinden. Scala / Art Resource, NY.

Plate 21 The Dome of the Rock, Jerusalem, Israel, begun 691, interior. Erich Lessing / Art Resource, NY.

Plate 22 The Ascent of Muhammad, manuscript illustration attributed to Sultan-Muhammad in a *Khamsa* of Nizami, 1539–43, Tabriz. London: British Library Ms Or 2265, f. 195. Art Resource, NY.

Plate 23 Shiva Nataraja, bronze sculpture, 11th to 12th century, southern India. The Art Archive / Musée Guimet Paris / Gianni Dagli Orti.

Plate 24 Krishna and Radha, miniature painting, mid-18th century, Kishengarh, Rajasthan, India. Victoria & Albert Museum, IS 40-1980, London / Art Resource, NY.

Plate 25 Avalokiteshvara, wood, 11th to 12th century, China. London: British Museum. Erich Lessing / Art Resource, NY.

Plate 26 Satchakravarti Samvara Mandala, thangka, 15th century, Tibet. The Philadelphia Museum of Art / Art Resource, NY.

Plate 27 *Divine Immortals of the Five Paths and Transcendents Who Have Obtained the Tao,* 1454, hanging scroll. Paris: Musée Guimet. Réunion des Musées Nationaux / Art Resource, NY.

Plate 28 Jade plaque of a Taoist Paradise, 17th century. Bath, England: Museum of East Asian Art. HIP / Art Resource, NY.

Plate 29 The Hall of Supreme Harmony, the Imperial City, Beijing, China, early 15th century. Vanni / Art Resource, NY.

Plate 30 Zhu Bang, Officials in front of the Forbidden City, ca. 1500, Ming Dynasty, silk painting. The Art Archive / British Museum, London.

Plate 31 Utagawa Kunisada (1785–1864), *Amaterasu, Shinto Goddess of the Sun*, woodblock print, ca. 1860. Victoria & Albert Museum, London / Art Resource, NY.

Plate 32 Kasuga Shrine *mandara*, ca. 1300, Kamakura period, hanging scroll. The Art Archive / Sylvan Barnet and William Burto Collection.

and Nepal as well as in Japan—as Shingon Buddhism. Vajrayana Buddhists also have their own sets of sacred scriptures and have developed into several distinct schools.

Buddhism spread very widely and was avidly transmitted by missionary activity in Asian regions outside of India during the many centuries following the lifetime of the Buddha. It should certainly be noted that Buddhism today has also developed a significant body of adherents in the West—in Europe and America.[7] Buddhist practices, of diverse types, have been transmitted to and transformed via their adoption by, and adaptation to, a great many cultures. The many forms of Buddhism, nevertheless, all represent approaches to the principal teachings of the Buddha about the possibility of achieving enlightenment via ethical behavior and via the development of wise attitudes reflective of an awareness of the realities of human life in the cosmos.

Figure 13.1 Ryoan-ji Temple, garden, late 15th century, Kyoto, Japan. Courtesy of Shutterstock.

TRADITIONAL ART AND ARCHITECTURAL FORMS

Buddhist art and architecture is as multivariant as the many different world venues into which the religion has spread. From the birthplace of Buddhism in India, the religion spread rapidly to many other Asian regions, adapting to and adopting local building and iconographic traditions and, in turn, adding to the development of indigenous styles of art and architecture. "One of the keys to the success of the religion was the ability of Buddhism to adapt to and evolve within different cultures and their existing beliefs. . . . Buddhist art serves to remind, to support and to reinforce the eternal truths of the religion, and its development and style remain integral to the history of the religion, the two not being easily separated."[8]

It is possible to approach the study of Buddhist art and architecture through a variety of lenses. A traditional chronological survey focusing on the development of specific styles in architecture, sculpture, and painting reveals a consistently evolving diversity as the religion spread from India through Asia and beyond. Similarly, studies that focus on the development of specifically Buddhist symbols and narrative imagery will reveal a diversity not only in the use of aniconic symbols but also in the ways of representing the Buddha himself.

Some symbols, forms, materials, and styles of art are particularly characteristic of specific world regions and different branches of Buddhism. These art forms and styles reflect different doctrinal emphases and differing liturgical practices. For example, Theravadan Buddhist art generally tends to focus attention on the life and deeds of the historical Buddha (and the *jataka* narratives—stories of his previous lives), whereas Mahayana Buddhist art developed an expansive visual vocabulary of celestial Buddhas, *bodhisattvas*, and realms of heavenly paradises.[9] The arts associated with the Vajrayana schools are especially rich in complex symbols and images reflective of the esoteric Tantric teachings and use of art in ritual practices. "Thus, the Buddhist religion, despite having a founder who had. . . . preached a doctrine against material possessions, acquired the world's richest and most varied system of visual support."[10]

Although, as wisely stated, "to many students of Buddhism and its arts, the task of deciphering Buddhist iconography and symbolism can seem as challenging as the search for enlightenment itself,"[11] there is nevertheless some degree of consistency in this diversity. Sacred sites of Buddhist pilgrimage in India were identified soon after the Buddha's death, and tradition recounts that the Buddha himself gave directions about the dispersal of his bodily relics during his final sermon to his disciples before his death (or final transcendence, *parinirvana*). He directed his followers to place his cremated remains into funeral mounds (or *stupas*), which would serve as memorials of his life and teaching and provide focal sites for meditation and pilgrimage. Although no visible evidence remains of these purportedly eight original Buddhist memorials (presently existing structures on the sites all date to later centuries), it is extremely significant to note that the concepts of marking sacred sites with physical structures, and the activity of making pilgrimages to visit these sites, have played a critical role in Buddhist practices through the centuries. "For the Buddha, pilgrimage was a spiritual practice capable of easing the heart, bringing happiness and taking the practitioner to a heaven-realm. Relics and pilgrimage monuments, such as *stupas*, were important as the material focus of such spiritual activity."[12]

In certain senses, it could be said that all Buddhist art has similar commemorative and symbolic purposes. Stupas mark and create sacred sites; they serve as symbols of the Buddha and his teachings, and the entire cosmos is also symbolized in a stupa. Symbols have always played a critical role in Buddhist art, and it appears that for the first several centuries after the Buddha's lifetime, symbols were primarily used to refer to the Buddha and his teachings and to represent the objects venerated at the sacred sites of Buddhist pilgrimage.

> This was not due to an explicit prohibition of images during these centuries. . . .
> It is due to the nature of early Buddhism and its Indian background. The Buddha
> was essentially a reforming sage who taught truths about existence. . . . Like a
> prophet, he was embodied in his message and to "see" his word was to see him.[13]

Among the earliest and still most widespread and prevalent symbols in Buddhism are wheels, lions, lotus flowers, trees, and footprints (see Figures 13.2

and 13.3). The lion was a traditional Indian symbol of royalty and power and thus referred to the noble lineage of the Buddha as well as the immense power of his teachings (*dharma*). The *dharma* (law) itself is most often symbolized by a wheel—indicating that the teaching "is in constant motion and provides a path toward spiritual enlightenment and eventual release."[14] The Wheel of the Law may have differing numbers of spokes depending on the context and other symbolism intended; for example, an eight-spoked wheel references the Eightfold Path.

Trees in Buddhist art refer to various events in the life of the Buddha, primarily his attainment of enlightenment

Figure 13.2 Lion capital, Asoka pillar at Sarnath, India, 273–32 BCE. The Art Archive.

under the *bodhi* tree at Bodh Gaya. The lotus flower is also an extremely important Buddhist symbol of spiritual purity and enlightenment, for "just as the lotus flower rises up from the depths of muddy ponds and lakes to blossom immaculately above the water's surface, the human heart or mind can develop the virtues of the Buddha and transcend desires and attachments."[15]

Reminders of the path to enlightenment, for those who aspire to follow in the footsteps of the Buddha, are frequently found in the form of carved stone footprints of the Buddha. Legends tell that the Buddha, shortly before his death, left his footprints impressed into stone as a deliberate memorial of his life and teachings. Like stupas, footprints of the Buddha are ubiquitous visual symbols found wherever Buddhism itself has traveled. The footprints, of course, also serve as reminders of the physical journeys of the Buddha during his decades of teaching and traveling in northern India.

Representations of the Buddha in human form do not appear to have developed until about the first century BCE. Much discussion has been devoted to the questions of "when, where, and why" the first images of the physical Buddha were created.[16] The explanations are doubtless multifaceted. The rich iconography associated with Hinduism in India and the related *bhakti* or devotional practices involving veneration of images, the influence from figural styles associated with Greco-Roman art in the Gandhara region of northern India,[17] the

Figure 13.3 Footprints of the Buddha, limestone panel from the Great Stupa at Amaravati, India, first century BCE. London: British Museum. Erich Lessing / Art Resource, NY.

spread of Buddhism generally with larger and more settled monastic communities plus its growing widespread appeal to the laity, and perhaps most significantly, the development of Mahayana Buddhist schools are all factors that have been cited as contributory in the further elaboration of figural and narrative Buddhist art.[18]

The veneration and worship of the Buddha as a sacred being, characteristic of the popular piety associated with the Mahayana schools, may be the most significant factor in the growth and proliferation of Buddha images, as well as the expanding Buddhist pantheon in general. In painting and sculpture, the image of the Buddha rapidly takes on specific standard forms and develops an iconographic vocabulary of attributes and hand gestures (*mudras*) that symbolize particular qualities of the Buddha or that refer to events in his life. The *mudras* ultimately derive from Hindu traditions but were adapted to suit Buddhist needs. They include gestures indicating teaching, protection, and reassurance, as well as the distinctive "turning the wheel of the law," or *Dharmachakra-mudra*, and the *Bhumisparsha-mudra*, or "touching the earth," a gesture that Buddha performed at the moment of his enlightenment.

Paintings and sculptures of the Buddha have been abundantly produced through the centuries. Although these images may be primarily understood as reminders and symbols of the Buddha and his teachings, images also often serve as objects of devotion in and of themselves.[19] This is akin to some Hindu practices involving anointing, bathing, and offering food and gifts to statues of deities housed in shrines and temples.[20]

The practice, characteristic of early Buddhism, of enclosing a stupa in a worship or assembly (*chaitya*) hall in a monastery eventually burgeoned into the creation of very elaborate temples filled with numerous Buddha images. The forms and styles of Buddhist temple architecture (both associated with monastic complexes or independent of monasteries) reflect the regional building practices of the Asian regions to which the religion spread (see Figures 13.4 and 13.5). In Japan and China, traditional wooden construction techniques are used, and large Buddhist monastery complexes often have many different structures, assembly halls, pagodas (derived from the *stupa* form plus regional styles of secular gate and watch towers as well as religious ritual towers), dwell-

Figure 13.4 Todaiji Temple, Hall of the Great Buddha; founded 743, rebuilt in the 18th century, Nara, Japan. Courtesy of Shutterstock.

ing quarters for monks, facilities for visitors, and so on. The layout and enclosures of these complexes often mirror imperial or palace styles as well, with, for example, large halls filled with Buddha images in a form resembling the style of imperial audience halls.

EXAMPLES

Two Great Stupas: The Great Stupa at Sanchi, India, Third to First Centuries BCE and Borobudur, Java, ca. 800 CE

The site of Sanchi, in central India, provides some of the earliest and most important evidence of the development and forms of early Buddhist art (see Figure 13.6). The site is traditionally associated with the Mauryan Emperor Asoka (c. 279–32 BCE), who is of extreme significance in Buddhist history for his conversion to and support of Buddhism. Asoka, after his highly successful military campaigns (which preceded his conversion to Buddhism and adoption of

Figure 13.5 Auspicious Light Pagoda, 3rd century, rebuilt 12th century, Suzhou, China. Vanni / Art Resource, NY.

Figure 13.6   Great Stupa at Sanchi, India, third to first century BCE. Scala / Art Resource, NY.

nonviolent policies), came to rule over a large territory in central and southern India. His political and cultural influence extended widely. Not only did Asoka support Buddhism as the official state religion, but he also actively promoted Buddhist missionary work. Tradition tells that his own son and daughter were among the Buddhist missionaries sent to Sri Lanka.

Asoka is also credited with having been an art patron of overwhelming magnitude. Legends tell that he directed the creation of over 84,000 Buddhist memorials throughout his kingdom. Admittedly, this number is improbable—and only a few examples from his period survive to the present day, including the Great Stupa at Sanchi. *Stupa* is a Sanskrit term for mound or artificial mountain. The form can partially be traced to the practice of erecting funerary memorials over the grave sites of important rulers and Hindu holy men. Of course, the architectural marking of the burial sites of significant figures has a long history in the religious and political practices of many world regions, and marking important sites with physical memorials is a cross-cultural phenomenon. The stupa is, however, one of the most distinctive and common forms of Buddhist architecture and is the foundation for many later Buddhist architectural forms, such as pagodas (characteristic of Buddhist architecture in China and Japan) and the distinctive Tibetan *chorten* form, plus variations in Thailand, Indonesia, and elsewhere.[21]

It is somewhat problematic to describe a stupa as a form of architecture, however, because stupas (of whatever size) are not buildings into which people can enter. In contrast, stupas are fully solid structures, generally formed of mounded rubble covered with stones, brick, or plaster, and their function is to mark sacred places, serve as relic-containing memorials of holy figures, and symbolize religious concepts. The Great Stupa at Sanchi is a large, excellent exemplar of the form. It is close to 120 feet in diameter and 54 feet tall. One walks around (circumambulates) the exterior of the stupa on a specified (clockwise) devotional path, but one does not enter into any architecturally enclosed or roofed interior space. Access to the sacred precincts of a stupa is often signaled by gates (*torana*) set in a surrounding fence-enclosure. After visitors pass through the gates and enter the precincts, they make their way around the *stupa* on a ground-level path or slightly elevated platform. Stupas are generally topped with distinctive elements—a cubical form (*harmika*) and a shaft (*yasti*) that supports one or more umbrella-like disks (*chatra*). These are placed at the apex of the *stupa* and symbolize the axis of the world or cosmic world mountain (Mount Meru), which is at the center of the universe.[22] The relics are placed deep inside the stupa in line with the *yasti*.

The sculptured gates that give access to the Great Stupa at Sanchi are also remarkable survivals from the early eras of Buddhism in India. The 35-foot-tall gates were set at the four cardinal points, symbolizing the cosmos, and are enriched with narrative and symbolic sculptures that demonstrate the development of Buddhist imagery as well as the adaptation of traditional Hindu forms. The creation and sculptural elaboration of these gates is traced to the post-Asokan era, in the first century BCE, giving evidence of the continued importance of this site.

A number of other stupas were also erected at Sanchi, several of which survive today in somewhat fragmentary condition. The site appears to have functioned as a very significant center of Buddhist pilgrimage and monastic retreat under the initial patronage of the Emperor Asoka. Later additions and re-buildings on the site appear to have taken place up until the 11th and 12th centuries CE, after which the site was abandoned during the decline of Buddhism in India and its spread to other Asian regions.

The continued importance of the stupa form in Buddhism and its later development and elaboration are extremely well demonstrated by the great monument of Borobudur on the island of Java, Indonesia[23] (see Figures 13.7 and 13.8). This impressive monument was constructed in the early ninth century and is still today considered to be the largest Buddhist structure in the world. Created under the direction of the Shailendra rulers, this unique and well-studied monument is unlike any other in size and complexity of symbolism. It serves not only as a memorial to the Shailendra rulers and their devotion to Buddhism but also as a visual representation of core Buddhist teachings.

The floor plan of Borobudur shows its complex mandala-like layout. The square structure is placed on top of a low hill and rises upward in a shape resembling

Figure 13.7 Borobudur, Java, ca. 800 CE. Courtesy of Shutterstock.

Figure 13.8 Borobudur, Java ca. 800 CE, floorplan. Courtesy of
Ricochet Productions.

a stepped pyramid. There are nine levels that the visitor ascends via staircases and walled galleries. The top three levels are circular, and the apex of the monument is topped with a large stupa. Borobudur is, itself, a *stupa,* but it contains a number of smaller *stupas* (72 on the three upper levels) filled with seated Buddha sculptures. Altogether there are over 500 free-standing Buddha figures plus several miles of elaborate relief carving on the base and middle terraces.

Borobudur dramatically symbolizes the Buddhist path from ignorance and attachment to enlightenment and release via the physical ascent of pilgrims to the apex of the monument and via the subjects found in the carvings on the different levels. The base represents the sphere of earthly desire, with relief carvings of various human actions and their causes and consequences. The middle four levels (where the majority of relief carvings are found) depict scenes from the life of the Buddha and other stories of spiritual quests. These levels represent the sphere of forms. The three upper levels symbolize the world of formlessness—the highest sphere. Thus, in journeying to and ascending Borobudur, "the visitor is transported by powerful, mystical forces that combine to make this enormous creation a remarkable evocation of earthly and divine worlds."[24]

Three Buddhas and Two Bodhisattvas

Three different free-standing sculptures of the Buddha from different world regions demonstrate some consistencies as well as divergences in form, style, and symbolism. Both the Great Bronze Buddha, from the middle of the 13th century, originally created for an important temple near Kamakura in Japan, and the much smaller bronze Buddha from 13th-century Thailand show specific types of seated Buddhas in meditation poses. The hand gestures (*mudras*) of the two seated Buddhas, as well as the sixth- or seventh-century Chinese standing Vairochana Buddha, represent standardized and oft-repeated forms.

The Japanese example shows Buddha in the *dhyana-mudra* pose, seated in intense meditation with closed eyes (see Figure 13.9). His large hands rest on his legs, palms upward with thumbs touching. This gesture refers to Buddha's long period of meditation preceding his enlightenment, and it is one of the most frequent forms of images of the Buddha. The pose was used for representations of the historical Buddha as well as the many important celestial Buddhas of the Mahayana schools, such as, as in this case, Amida (or Amitabha) Buddha (the Buddha of Infinite Light, especially venerated in the Pure Land traditions). This colossal, hollow bronze sculpture is close to 40 feet tall.

Although similar in basic format, the 13th-century seated Buddha from Thailand exhibits the *bhumisparsha* (touching the earth) *mudra,* indicating the moment of Buddha's enlightenment when "he called the earth to witness his good achievement"[25] (see Figure 13.10). Although still wrapped in stoic meditation, this Buddha reaches one hand downward to touch the earth with his fingertips. The slimmer and elongated body proportions of this Buddha are

Figure 13.9   Seated Amida Buddha, bronze, ca. 1252, Kotukuin, Kamakura, Japan. Werner Forman / Art Resource, NY.

Figure 13.10   Seated Buddha, bronze, 13th century, Thailand. Paris: Musée Guimet. Réunion des Musées Nationaux / Art Resource, NY.

typical of the images produced in Thailand during the period of the Sukhothai kingdom. The flame-like protuberance on the top of Buddha's head is also characteristic of this style. The protuberance (*ushnisha*) is a distinctive aspect of Buddha images generally, probably derived from the Indian royal hairstyle of topknot and/or turban. Other distinctive physical marks of the Buddha include a small dot or whorl of hair in the middle of his forehead (the *urna*, which symbolizes great wisdom) and his elongated earlobes. These represent another mark of nobility, resultant from the wearing of heavy jewelry (which of course the Buddha had discarded), and serve as a reminder that we also must leave behind attachment to worldly riches in order to attain enlightenment.

These features can also be seen in the sixth- or seventh-century Chinese bronze example of a standing Buddha (see Figure 13.11). A variety of types and poses were developed for standing Buddha figures also. This example shows Vairochana, the cosmic Buddha or Illuminator. He is shown with one palm raised and the other hand reaching towards the viewer, demonstrating the *vitarka-mudra* of teaching, welcome, and reassurance.

A range of forms and styles is also well demonstrated in depictions of the numerous *bodhisattvas*. Among the most popular and widely worshiped, in various guises, throughout the Buddhist world is Avalokiteshvara (the Protector of the World, Bodhisattva of Compassion). This figure can appear in dozens of different forms, of which the two illustrated here represent only two major types. This deity has an especially interesting history and evolution.[26] Venerated as a male deity in Indian Buddhism,

> Avalokiteshvara became associated with a female bodhisattva called Tara, who embodied the feminine side of his compassion. In China, where Avalokiteshvara is worshiped under the name Guanyin, the bodhisattva's male and female identities became compounded and Guanyin came to be worshiped mainly in female form. Tibetans feel a special kinship for Avalokiteshvara. . . . They claim that he has taken a vow to protect the nation of Tibet and is manifested in the person of every Dalai Lama.[27]

Figure 13.11 Standing Buddha Vairochana, bronze, 581–618 CE, China. The Art Archive / Musée Guimet Paris / Gianni Dagli Orti.

The beautifully painted 11th- to 12th-century wooden example from China shows the goddess in elaborate and elegantly flowing robes, seated casually with one knee drawn up and arm resting lightly atop the knee (see Plate 25). This pose is often called "royal ease," and—versus more formal and sometimes frightening depictions of deities—it conveys balance, relaxation, calmness, warmth, and welcome to all who call upon her merciful nature.[28]

A much more startling depiction of this deity is the 17th-century Tibetan example illustrated in Figure 13.12. The figure is seated in a lotus pose of meditation, with two hands placed together across the chest in the *anjali mudra* of prayer. Numerous additional arms radiate out from the figure, and the multiple hands demonstrate a variety of other *mudras* or hold various ritual objects. This symbolizes the *bodhisattva* with 1,000 arms (other examples will show 11 heads, 6 arms, and so on), indicating the deity's limitless powers and endless different ways to assist and lead all to enlightenment. The exquisitely detailed and precious nature of this gem-encrusted bronze statuette is typical of the arts associated with the esoteric Vajrayana schools of Tibetan Buddhism.

Figure 13.12 Avalokiteshvara, bronze and semi-precious stones, 17th century. Tibet: Werner Forman / Art Resources, NY.

A Tibetan Mandala, 15th Century

"No subject in Tibetan art has drawn more attention than the mandala. These works have an appeal beyond their original liturgical role; to psychologists they are universal images that reflect fundamental human instincts, while, for many, they attract through their blend of order and harmony and their multiple levels of mystery."[29] For many centuries, the arts of Tibet were relatively inaccessible to and unstudied by Western scholars. But especially following the Chinese takeover of Tibet in the mid-20th century and the resultant diaspora of Tibetans and their art objects, a vast amount of Tibetan art materials have been collected, studied, and displayed in the West.[30] Many studies—both popular and scholarly—have been devoted to all aspects of Tibetan art, with mandalas being among the most prominent sources of fascination and wide-ranging interpretation (see Plate 26).

Mandalas are not unique to Tibet or to Buddhism; they are used in Hindu and Jain religious practices and have been widely produced in India and throughout Asia generally.[31] Many would argue that the symmetrical diagram format of the mandala has an archetypal kinship with many other cross-cultural forms, such as labyrinths and the rose windows of medieval European cathedrals. The term mandala is said to derive from Sanskrit words meaning a "sacred center," "container," "essence," and something "set apart."[32] Mandalas, thus, are sacred diagrams that represent the cosmos, universe, paradises, and abodes of deities. They exist in both two- and three-dimensional forms and are used by practitioners as aids in visualizing and in communicating with deities who are able to assist with the search for enlightenment.

Typically, mandalas are highly complex symmetrical diagrams with circles, squares, and other geometric forms filled with images of deities and esoteric symbols. The 17th-century Tibetan example illustrated shows a mandala painted in watercolor on cloth, mounted on a cloth background. This hanging scroll (or *thangka*) format is very typical of portable mandalas, which could be displayed and used as aids in meditation and visualization practices.[33]

This particular example shows the "palace architecture" format, a style of mandala that became especially popular in Tibet in the 12th and 13th centuries and that grew in complexity of style through the 14th and 15th centuries, when this example was created. This work was produced in a monastery of the Sakya order, one of the major orders of Tibetan Buddhism.[34] The Sakya order was especially active in the production of sacred art and in maintaining and classifying the formats and styles of mandalas. The "palace architecture" type is meant to be understood and experienced as the two-dimensional floor plan for a multifaceted, three-dimensional structure. Set within the inner circle and visually entered through elaborate gateways at the four cardinal points, the square palace itself, in this case, contains six smaller palaces or mansions that are inhabited by deities. These deities are identified as six *chakravartins* (world rulers or kings) accompanied by female consorts in "father-mother" or *yab-yum* pose. This particular iconography of deities in sexual union, so frequent in Tibetan art, is "not meant to be regarded sensually. Rather, they are symbolic of the union of wisdom (female) and compassion (male), the two qualities necessary to achieve enlightenment."[35]

The gates and corners of the large palace are guarded by eight fearsome female deities, and these and other deities are repeated again in rows on the top and bottom of the mandala. Twenty additional deities are found in circles in the corners of the composition, plus various symbols and ritual objects. Elaborately detailed foliage scrolls in traditional and symbolic color schemes are repeated throughout the background, the palace, and the mansions. The specific proportions and layouts for mandalas adhere to standard conventions and maintain these fixed traditions due to their spiritual potency.

Each figure in a mandala has several purposes, functioning as a specific deity, as a manifestation of the central deity's power, as a focus of visualization and meditation, and as a signpost for a spiritual process. Each plays many roles during rites and visualizations which presumes a constant dialogue between the deity at the heart of the mandala (and in its various components) and the practitioner who moves, at least metaphorically, from outside the mandala to its core. On this journey he encounters the various forces radiating from the inside out, identifies with the central deity, apprehends all manifestations as parts of a single whole, and moves closer to the goal of perfect understanding or enlightenment.[36]

NOTES

1. Some branches of Buddhism accept slightly different birth and death dates for the Buddha; for example, in southeast Asian traditions, his dates may be charted as 623–543 BCE.

2. Vasudha Narayanan, "Hinduism," in *Eastern Religions: Origins, Beliefs, Practices, Holy Texts, Sacred Places*, ed. Michael Coogan (New York: Oxford University Press, 2005), 18.

3. Malcolm Eckel, "Buddhism," in *The Illustrated Guide to World Religions*, ed. Michael Coogan (New York: Oxford University Press, 1998), 181.

4. For information on the Bon religion, see Christoph Baumer, *Tibet's Ancient Religion: Bon* (Trumbull, CT: Weatherhill, 2002); and Per Kvaerne, *The Bon Religion of Tibet: The Iconography of a Living Tradition* (Boston: Shambhala, 1995).

5. Needless to say, the Buddha, in his practical fashion, also specified the details of these four truths and eight goals much more fully, and masses of later commentary have been devoted to analysis and understanding of these. A very useful summary may be found in Huston Smith and Philip Novak, *Buddhism: A Concise Introduction* (San Francisco: Harper San Francisco, 2003), 31–49.

6. Eckel, 176.

7. Smith and Novak, 123–83.

8. Robert Fisher, *Buddhist Art and Architecture* (London: Thames and Hudson, 1993), 8.

9. Joji Okazaki, *Pure Land Buddhist Painting* (Tokyo: Kodansha International, 1977).

10. Fischer, 10.

11. Meher McArthur, *Reading Buddhist Art: An Illustrated Guide to Buddhist Signs and Symbols* (London: Thames and Hudson, 2002), 8.

12. Simon Coleman and John Elsner, *Pilgrimage: Past and Present in the World Religions* (Cambridge, MA: Harvard University Press, 1995), 172.

13. Albert Moore, *Iconography of Religions: An Introduction* (Philadelphia: Fortress Press, 1977), 142.

14. McArthur, 123.

15. McArthur, 125.

16. Susan Huntington, "Early Buddhist Art and the Theory of Aniconism," *Art Journal* 49, no. 4 (1990), 401–8.

17. The complex discussion surrounding the influence of Western figural styles on Buddhist art and the interpretations of these decades-long and still ongoing scholarly debates are well covered by Stanley Abe, "Inside the Wonder House: Buddhist Art and the West," in *Curators of the Buddha: The Study of Buddhism under Colonialism*, ed. Donald Lopez (Chicago: University of Chicago Press, 1995), 63–106.

18. For early narrative art, see Patricia Karetzky, *The Life of the Buddha: Ancient Scriptural and Pictorial Traditions* (Lanham, MD: University Press of America, 1992).

19. Donald Swearer, *Becoming the Buddha: The Ritual Image Consecration in Thailand* (Princeton, NJ: Princeton University Press, 2004).

20. Donald Lopez, ed., *Buddhism in Practice* (Princeton, NJ: Princeton University Press, 1995).

21. Anna Dallapiccola, ed., *The Stupa: Its Religious, Historical, and Architectural Significance* (Wiesbaden: Franz Steiner, 1980).

22. I. W. Mabbett, "The Symbolism of Mount Meru," *History of Religions* 23, no. 1 (1983): 64–83.

23. Luis Gomez, *Barabudur: History and Significance of a Buddhist Monument* (Berkeley: Regents of the University of California, 1981).

24. Fisher, 197.

25. Moore, 151.

26. The bibliography on Kuan Yin is extensive. See John Blofeld, *Bodhisattva of Compassion: The Mystical Tradition of Kuan Yin* (Boulder, CO: Shambhala, 1978); and Chün-fang Yü, *Kuan-yin: The Chinese Transformation of Avalokitesvara* (New York: Columbia University Press, 2001).

27. Eckel, 176.

28. A very poignant, personal description of a contemporary woman's first encounter with a very similar statue of Kwan Yin can be found in Sandy Boucher, *Discovering Kwan Yin, Buddhist Goddess of Compassion* (Boston: Beacon Press, 1999), 2–3.

29. Fisher, 82.

30. Donald Lopez, *Prisoners of Shangri-La: Tibetan Buddhism and the West* (Chicago: University of Chicago Press, 1998).

31. Okazaki, 37–64.

32. Fisher, 82; McArthur, 73; and Denise Leidy and Robert Thurman, *Mandala: The Architecture of Enlightenment* (New York and Boston: Asia Society Galleries, Tibet House, and Shambhala, 1997), 9.

33. A helpful and readable description of these meditation and visualization practices can be found in John Blofeld, *The Tantric Mysticism of Tibet: A Practical Guide* (New York: Causeway Books, 1974). For more information on the materials and techniques of *thangka* painting, see David and Janice Jackson, *Tibetan Thangka Painting: Methods and Materials* (Ithaca, NY: Snow Lion, 1988).

34. The major orders of Tibetan Buddhism are the Nyingma (founded in the 8th century); Kardam, Sakya, and Kagyu (all founded in the 11th century); and Gelug (founded in the 14th century).

35. Barbara Lipton and Nima Ragnubs, *Treasures of Tibetan Art: Collections of the Jacques Marchais Museum of Tibetan Art* (New York: Oxford University Press, 1996), 32.

36. Leidy and Thurman, 4.

BIBLIOGRAPHY AND FURTHER READING

Abe, Stanley. "Inside the Wonder House: Buddhist Art and the West." In *Curators of the Buddha: The Study of Buddhism under Colonialism*, ed. Donald Lopez, 63–106. Chicago: University of Chicago Press, 1995.

Baumer, Christoph. *Tibet's Ancient Religion: Bon.* Trumbull, CT: Weatherhill, 2002.

Blofeld, John. *Bodhisattva of Compassion: The Mystical Tradition of Kuan Yin.* Boulder, CO: Shambhala, 1978.

Blofeld, John. *The Tantric Mysticism of Tibet: A Practical Guide*. New York: Causeway Books, 1974.

Boucher, Sandy. *Discovering Kwan Yin: Buddhist Goddess of Compassion*. Boston: Beacon Press, 1999.

Brauen, Martin. *The Mandala: Sacred Circle in Tibetan Buddhism*. Boston: Shambhala, 1997.

Buddhist Temples. http://www.buddhist-temples.com/.

Colman, Simon, and John Elsner. *Pilgrimage: Past and Present in the World Religions*. Cambridge, MA: Harvard University Press, 1995.

Coogan, Michael. *The Illustrated Guide to the World Religions*. New York: Oxford University Press, 1998.

Dallapiccola, Anna, ed. *The Stupa: Its Religious, Historical, and Architectural Significance*. Wiesbaden: Franz Steiner, 1980.

Davidson, J. Le Roy. *The Lotus Sutra in Chinese Art: A Study of Buddhist Art to the Year 1000 AD*. New Haven, CT: Yale University Press, 1969.

Eckel, Malcolm. "Buddhism." In *The Illustrated Guide to the World Religions*, ed. Michael Coogan, 162–97. New York: Oxford University Press, 1998.

Fisher, Robert. *Buddhist Art and Architecture*. London: Thames and Hudson, 1993.

Gomez, Luis. *Baradudur: History and Significance of a Buddhist Monument*. Berkeley: Regents of the University of California, 1981.

Huntington, Susan. "Early Buddhist Art and the Theory of Aniconism." *Art Journal* 49, no. 4 (1980): 401–8.

Jackson, David. *A History of Tibetan Painting: The Great Tibetan Painters and Their Traditions*. Vienna: Verlag der Österreichischen Akademie der Wissenshaften, 1996.

Jackson, David, and Janice Jackson. *Tibetan Thangka Painting: Methods and Materials*. Ithaca, NY: Snow Lion, 1988.

Karetzky, Patricia. *The Life of the Buddha: Ancient Scriptural and Pictorial Traditions*. Lanham, MD: University Press of America, 1992.

Klimburg-Salter, Deborah. *The Silk Route and the Diamond Path: Esoteric Buddhist Art on the Trans-Himalayan Trade Routes*. Los Angeles: University of California Art Council, 1982.

Kvaerne, Per. *The Bon Religion of Tibet: The Iconography of a Living Tradition*. Boston: Shambhala, 1995.

Lancaster, Lewis. "An Early Mahayana Sermon about the Body of the Buddha and the Making of Images." *Artibus Asiae* 36, no. 4 (1974): 287–91.

Leidy, Denise Patry, and Robert Thurman. *Mandala: The Architecture of Enlightenment*. New York and Boston: Asia Society Galleries, Tibet House, and Shambhala, 1997.

Ling, Haicheng. *Buddhism in China*. Beijing: China Intercontinental Press, 2004.

Lipton, Barbara, and Nima Ragnubs. *Treasures of Tibetan Art: Collections of the Jacques Marchais Museum of Tibetan Art*. New York: Oxford University Press, 1996.

Lopez, Donald. *Buddhism in Practice*. Princeton, NJ: Princeton University Press, 1995.

Lopez, Donald, ed. *Curators of the Buddha: The Study of Buddhism under Colonialism*. Chicago: University of Chicago Press, 1995.

Lopez, Donald. *Prisoners of Shangri-La: Tibetan Buddhism and the West*. Chicago: University of Chicago Press, 1998.

Lopez, Donald. *Religions of Asia in Practice: An Anthology*. Princeton, NJ: Princeton University Press, 2002.

Mabbett, I. W. "The Symbolism of Mount Meru." *History of Religions* 23, no. 1 (1983): 64–83.

McArthur, Meher. *Reading Buddhist Art: An Illustrated Guide to Buddhist Signs and Symbols*. London: Thames and Hudson, 2002.

Moore, Albert. *Iconography of Religions: An Introduction*. Philadelphia: Fortress Press, 1977.

Okazaki, Joji. *Pure Land Buddhist Painting*. Tokyo: Kodansha International, 1977.

Ooka, Minoru. *Temples of Nara and Their Art*. New York: John Weatherhill, 1973.

Paine, Robert Treat, and Alexander Soper. *The Art and Architecture of Japan*. New Haven, CT: Yale University Press, 1981.

Pal, Pratapaditya. *Art of the Himalayas: Treasures from Nepal and Tibet*. New York: Hudson Hills, 1991.

Pal, Pratapaditya. *Himalayas: An Aesthetic Adventure*. Chicago: The Art Institute of Chicago, 2003.

Rhie, Marilyn, and Robert Thurman. *Wisdom and Compassion: The Sacred Art of Tibet*. New York: Harry N. Abrams, 1991.

Smith, Huston, and Philip Novak. *Buddhism: A Concise Introduction*. San Francisco: Harper San Francisco, 2003.

Swearer, Donald. *Becoming the Buddha: The Ritual Image Consecration in Thailand*. Princeton, NJ: Princeton University Press, 2004.

Walpola, Sri Rahula. *What the Buddha Taught*. London: Gordon Fraser, 1959; reprinted 1982.

Wassman, Bill. *Buddhist Stupas in Asia: The Shape of Perfection*. Melbourne: Lonely Planet, 2001.

Yü, Chün-fang. *Kuan-Yin: The Chinese Transformation of Avalokitesvara*. New York: Columbia University Press, 2001.

Zwalf, Wladimir. *Buddhism: Art and Faith*. London: British Museum, 1985.

−14−

Taoism

ORIGINS AND DEVELOPMENT

Taoism (or Daoism) is a complex and multifaceted philosophical and religious system with origins in ancient China. It has a very lengthy history, has developed numerous aspects and different branches, and is still practiced in various forms today. The ultimate origins of Taoism are shrouded in mystery and mythology. Some traditions credit the legendary or semi-historical Yellow Emperor of ancient China (Huangdi or Huang Ti, ca. 2000 BCE) with establishing many aspects of civilization, culture, and religious practices that ultimately formed the foundations for later developments in Chinese religious history, including Taoism. Many of the beliefs and practices associated with Taoism thus significantly predate the teachings and writings attributed to the scholar Lao Tzu (or Lao Zi), who is said to have lived in the sixth to fifth century BCE. His name means "old teacher," "old master," or "wise old man." Some consider him to have been an actual historical person, an older contemporary of Confucius (ca. 551–479 BCE), whereas others believe he is simply a legendary (or semi-legendary) figure. Lao Tzu is often considered to be the founder of Taoism, although it might be much more accurate to describe him as the most well-known name in a long line of ancient philosophers whose teachings provide the basis for Taoism (see Figure 14.1).

According to traditions, late in his life Lao Tzu became disenchanted with the social and political situation in which he worked in China as a minor government official and decided to leave the country and travel to central Asia, in order to devote his remaining years to quiet meditation and study. On his way

Figure 14.1 Chinese scroll painting, 17th century, Lao Tzu and his servant. Paris: Bibliothèque National. Snark / Art Resource, NY.

out of the country, he was stopped by a border guard or customs official, Yin Hsi, who recognized his wisdom and who asked him to write down his ideas and teachings. Lao Tzu did so, purportedly in a matter of just a few days, and this text is known as the *Tao Te Ching* (*Daode jing*—often translated as *The Way and Its Power*). This work is considered to be the first and still preeminent Taoist text. Although Lao Tzu is traditionally credited with the authorship of this work, it is much more likely that the *Tao Te Ching* was actually composed and edited over time by several different contributors, reaching its final form in the fourth to second centuries BCE (see Figure 14.2).

The *Tao Te Ching* is a relatively short but very dense and comprehensive treatise on the position of humans in the universe, the nature of reality, the ultimate meaning of human life, and the proper actions and attitudes required to achieve and maintain harmony in life, in society, and in the natural world. It has been described as a book that "can be read in half an hour or a lifetime."[1] It is a highly poetic and metaphorical work consisting of a series of often terse statements concerning the Tao—the indescribable guiding principle of the universe—and the fundamental importance of seeking and maintaining harmony with the Tao. The text advises simplicity in life and recommends the

Figure 14.2 Scribes copying the *Tao Te Ching* and presenting it to the Emperor. Paris: Bibliothèque National. Erich Lessing / Art Resource, NY.

avoidance of contentious and ambitious striving and useless activity of any sort that goes against nature, the Tao. Power and virtue (*Te*) will, instead, be achieved via *wu wei* (which can be translated as "non-action" or "unmotivated action"). The *Tao Te Ching* is a much-studied work, still highly popular (and popularized) today, and can be seen as a combination of social and political philosophy, ethical guidance, poetic mysticism, and religious teaching.

Other important Taoist texts, such as the fourth- to third-century *Book of Zhang Zi* (composed by disciples of Zhang Zi, who lived ca. 369–286 BCE) and the much later *Book of Lie Zi* (ca. 300 CE) continue and expand the fundamental themes of the *Tao Te Ching* while adding more popular tales and anecdotes. This also reflects the gradual development of Taoism as a religious system (with specific sets of beliefs and practices, a pantheon of deities, a priesthood, temples and monasteries, and related art) that took place in China largely during the second and third centuries CE, especially after the fall of the Han dynasty in 220 CE. Previous to this, Confucianism had become the official state religion, and Taoism was considered to be a complementary and largely philosophical movement. Many scholars thus separate "philosophical Taoism" from "religious Taoism," although in practice the distinction is far from clear cut. "Much ink has been spilled on this matter, but usually, it must be admitted, by people who have not studied the texts of 'religious Taoism.'"[2]

The founder of religious Taoism is traditionally said to have been the scholar and healer Zhang Daoling, who, in the middle of the second century (142 CE), had a vision of "the personified god of the Tao, Taishang laojun, the Highest Venerable Lord. This deity is the Tao, but also a mythological development of the ancient philosopher Laozi."[3] This mystical and deified Lao Tzu communicated directly with him in a series of revelations. Zhang Daoling is credited with founding the Taoist sect known as the Way of the Celestial (or Heavenly) Masters (or Orthodox Unity), which remained a major branch of Taoism for many centuries and is still active today.[4] Other Taoist sects soon developed, such as the school of Highest Clarity (Shangqing), which was founded in the late fourth century,[5] and the school of Numinous Treasure (Lingbao.)[6]

The introduction of Buddhism from India to China in the second century CE also had an enormous impact on the development of religious Taoism and Taoist art. Taoism was seen as a native or indigenous tradition, although Taoists adopted and modified several aspects of Buddhism to suit their own needs and enhance their own followings. It is at this point also that many popular legends arose about the life of Lao Tzu, for example, that he was able to prolong his life greatly through spiritual and meditation practices, that he had met Confucius (who was very impressed with the "truth" of his teachings), and that after his departure from China, he spread the word of the Tao widely (including converting the Buddha to Taoism, or himself becoming the Buddha.)[7]

Religious Taoism ultimately grew into several different schools, branches, or sects, some of which placed special emphasis on religious ritual, practices of meditation, and other physical and sexual exercises to promote harmony with the Tao and to achieve longevity. External practices (involving the occult, magic, divination, and alchemy) also characterize religious Taoism and have played a very significant role in the development of Chinese medicine and martial arts. Many of these Taoist practices were taken over from other much earlier Chinese traditions, especially those of the second- and first-century BCE "magico-technicians (fangshi),"[8] who were adept at the arts of healing, divination, and various mystical, magical, and alchemical endeavors.[9]

As religious Taoism developed, so did the pantheon of deities. Lao Tzu was elevated to the status of a god by the second century, and eventually, "the deified Laozi was identified with the Tao itself and credited with the creation of the universe."[10] Lao Tzu (as the Lord Lao) had appeared in a vision to Zhang Daoling, as mentioned previously, and the earliest record of Lao Tzu being formally worshiped as a divinity occurred in 165 or 166 CE when Emperor Huan "decided to perform . . . a sacrifice to Laozi and the Buddha, in a ceremony accompanied by the sacral music belonging to the semi-annual sacrifice to Heaven."[11] The deified Lao Tzu was joined quickly by many other deities, some of whom derived from much earlier native or folk traditions. The deities in this expanding pantheon were associated with specific geographical locales, natural phenomena, animals, stars and planets, various activities, and occupations. A number of historical (or semi-historical or completely legendary) humans of special wisdom and holiness were also considered to have become immortal deities. Stories about the Taoist immortals are especially filled with brilliant and fantastic details about their abilities and magical powers.[12] "The Taoist pantheon is vast and has grown constantly over the centuries, with each school, each revelation, adding its own gods to the older ones, who have usually been retained rather than replaced."[13]

Religious Taoism continued to expand and was very popular in China through most of the medieval period. It was generally supported, with some periods of exception, by the imperial dynasties of the Tang (618–907), Song (960–1279), and Yuan (1276–1386) eras. The Tang emperors, because of their sharing of Lao Tzu's surname (Li), claimed to be his direct descendants and thus further legitimized their position as godly rulers. They founded and supported temples and monasteries and made the *Tao Te Ching* required reading for government employees. Confucianism was always a strong rival for imperial support, however, and in spite of mutual interchanges, Confucianism was often more in favor with the government. Additionally, Taoist–Buddhist relations have varied through the centuries from mutually supportive to downright hostile at times.

Of course, all religions in China suffered during the mid-20th-century rise of Communism, and during the Cultural Revolution, Taoism in particular was especially targeted, for its "superstitious" practices. Today, various forms of Taoism are practiced in China alongside various closely related "Chinese Community Traditions." Taoism remains highly popular in Taiwan and has developed European and American followers and variations as well.

PRINCIPAL BELIEFS AND KEY PRACTICES

As mentioned earlier, many scholars distinguish "philosophical Taoism" from "religious Taoism." This distinction has much to do with how the original teachings and primary texts associated with Lao Tzu and his initial followers and commentators are regarded, as well as what regard is given to the later Taoist writings. The fundamental Taoist text, the *Tao Te Ching* is a highly complex, challenging, and extremely intriguing set of thought-provoking sayings about the nature of reality and human life. The *Tao Te Ching* recommends and demonstrates the wisdom and benefits to be gained from living in harmony with the Tao; it emphasizes certain modes of human attitude and behavior as being most beneficial to achieving the ideal state of being in harmony with the universe; it speaks about the values of non-contentious and non-gainfully-motivated action (*wu-wei*), and it offers readers, who may wisely choose to be open to the teachings, a set of ideas to consider carefully. It does not contain specific directions about worship practices or identify particular deities to be revered; it does not contain any specific commandments, rules, or set of strictly specified virtues that adherents are required to follow; instead, it makes a series of wise (and sometimes contradictory) assertions about the nature of life and the universe.

Thus, at the risk of oversimplifying, it could be said that Taoism evolved from a set of complex philosophical teachings into a religious system—which adherents were motivated to expand and codify by their need to have more specific information and directions about whom and what to venerate and how exactly to enact their beliefs by specific actions and practices. Hence, the "wise old sage" (Lao Tzu) ultimately became regarded as a deity, and in competition, assimilation, and coordination with Buddhist beliefs and practices, as well as Confucianism, Taoism developed into a religious system with a vast canon of holy scriptures and specific (but extremely diverse) religious rituals and practices. The *Tao Te Ching*, in religious Taoism, is thus regarded as a "revealed" text that offers religious teachings and revelations directly from the Tao—or God, the Lord Lao—in the form of the deified Lao Tzu.

> One of the most complicated aspects of Taoism is its transformation from a philosophy to a religion. The West is just beginning to become aware of the long history of religious Taoism. Even scholars who are familiar with Laozi and the *Daode jing* are generally unaware of the later history of religious Taoism . . . or of the role of this religion in Chinese political history.[14]

In the centuries after Lao Tzu and the composition of the *Tao Te Ching*, literally hundreds of independent Taoist texts were produced. By the mid-15th century, when the present Taoist canon (*Daozang*) was collected, it included well over one thousand volumes.[15] Many of these Taoist writings were also seen as divinely inspired: "the manifestation of the Tao on earth."[16] Founders of various Taoist sects were inspired by visions and revelations received from various deities and spirits in the ever-growing pantheon, and the texts they composed are esteemed and regarded as divine revelations. Other Taoist writings include biographies and hagiographies of worthy people and holy figures. Many texts recount tales of the Immortals—humans who, by various deeds and practices, achieved immortality and who perpetually reside in various heavenly realms. Some Taoist texts describe sacred places, holy mountains, important temples, monasteries and shrines, sites of physical pilgrimage, while other Taoist texts include information (often couched in arcane terms) on ritual, exorcism, healing, alchemy, divination, medicine, and meditation practices. This truly vast and complex variety of writings and practices may explain why the religious aspects of Taoism are often misunderstood and seen as "nothing more than superstition and folk religion."[17]

> Despite its influence on Chinese civilization, Taoism has been notoriously difficult to define—this is largely attributable to the many different and distinctive forms the tradition has adopted through its history. . . . The schools of Taoism have never been united under a central authority, and the development of systematic teachings has not been an overriding concern.[18]

Nevertheless, in spite of the complexity and diversity of Taoist teachings and the many different schools and practices, the belief that human life can be enhanced and prolonged by living in harmony with the Tao is one of the fundamental principles of Taoism in general. This can be achieved in a variety of ways—via adopting a wise attitude toward life that involves awareness of the Tao and the principles of the complementary forces of *yin* and *yang*, via seeing the importance of maintaining harmony and balance in one's actions, and via demonstrating by action (and non-action) the Taoist goal of *wu-wei*. Such harmonious living, letting nature take its course, will result in contentment and enjoyment of life, rather than useless striving, contentious behavior, discontent, and unhappiness. The many benefits to be gleaned from such a desirable and enhanced life experience are obvious—achieving harmony with the nature of reality (the Tao) will necessarily result in a prolonged and happy life. So harmony with the Tao should be cultivated and maintained.

"To be alive is good; to be more alive is better; to be always alive is best."[19] This quest for longevity and immortality has been understood differently by various schools of Taoism through the centuries. The life-prolonging and life-enhancing techniques developed by many Taoist practitioners can be understood as having symbolic as well as literal goals. Taoist practitioners of various forms of internal and external alchemy may approach the quest for immortality in a mystical or physical or psychological sense, or with a combination of various understandings. Immortality can be understood as being free from earthly life and worldly limits; it can involve maintaining a sense of stability by going along with changes.[20]

> More than just a pattern of belief or a doctrine, Taoism is a way of life. . . . it has always remained the province of initiates who are the respectful possessors of revealed texts not divulged to the masses. Preaching plays no part in it, but replies are given to questions. . . . Taoism has evolved in a world apart, like those constructs in its meditations and ritual, a world always somehow marginal to society, within but testifying to another world beyond.[21]

TRADITIONAL ART AND ARCHITECTURAL FORMS

Taoist forms of art and architecture evolved as Taoism itself evolved in China over the course of many centuries. It is a matter of some scholarly discussion when the first specifically Taoist art appeared out of previous and parallel artistic traditions or whether or not the search to identify the first Taoist art is a useful scholarly endeavor.

> It is critical to remember that the meaning and content of Taoism have undergone many changes over the course of its long history. . . . any definition of Taoist art must be a historical and dynamic one, taking into account the continuity of this art as well as its specific manifestations in different places and times.[22]

Based on surviving evidence, art works that can be seen or clearly identified as specifically Taoist date only from the fourth or fifth centuries CE, when Taoism had developed into a formal religious system rather than a purely philosophical movement. As a formal religion (albeit with different branches or schools) Taoism required architecture (temples and monasteries) and all manner of visual arts (painting, sculpture, calligraphy) in order not only to house monastic communities and provide worship spaces, but also to teach and offer insight and understanding into the often arcane and increasingly complex development of Taoist schools of thought and practices.

The visual arts have always played an extremely important role in religious Taoism, and Taoist teachings have had a great deal of influence on the development of Chinese art. The Taoist respect for nature and harmonious natural surroundings, for example, has had a great impact on the history of Chinese landscape painting and garden design, and Taoist temples and monasteries are often located in extremely beautiful surroundings on or near sacred mountains (see Figure 14.3). Taoist art, however, is closely related to Buddhist and Confucian art in China, and the forms and styles of the arts produced for all three of these continually intersecting traditions are often indistinguishable—and logically so, given that firm distinctions between these systems were most often not formally maintained. It is wise to remember that "Chinese religion is an amalgam of the 'Three Teachings' (Confucianism, Taoism, Buddhism) and the folk tradition. . . . In the modern era, just as in the past, rather than professing a single doctrinal affiliation most Chinese people draw simultaneously from elements of all the teachings."[23]

Figure 14.3 Chuan Long Tiong (Yellow Dragon Cave), Hang-zhou, Chekiang, China. Werner Forman / Art Resource, NY.

The sharing of art styles and forms across traditions is well seen, for example, in Taoist architecture, which uses the same wooden-frame construction techniques typical of Chinese architecture through the ages. "If it is sometimes difficult to determine whether a particular work of art is Taoist, it is a far greater challenge to identify a Taoist building. . . . Taoist architecture, first and foremost, is part of the mainstream of the Chinese building tradition."[24] The basic principles of Chinese architectural construction, for both secular and religious buildings, involve the placement of spatial modules around courtyards and in axial layout. Post-and-beam construction is used, and tiled roof structures with overhanging eaves are often supported by a series of intricate wooden brackets. This type of wooden construction has remained consistent through centuries of Chinese architectural history. Certain periods, of course, are characterized by specific styles of bracketing, roof profiles, sculptural elaboration, and painted decoration; and the importance or status of buildings and their patrons is evident by size, extensiveness, and degree of elaboration. Nevertheless, the style of grouping series of smaller structures into neat clusters arranged axially (north–south) and around courtyards does reflect Confucian concerns with demonstrating hierarchical patterns as well as Taoist concerns with harmonious living in nature. The careful placement and orientation of buildings and the arrangement of interior spaces reflect the practices of *feng shui*—the art of locating, orienting, and ordering space in such as way as to maximize positive energies (*ch'i*). *Feng shui* is not exclusively Taoist or demonstrated only in Taoist structures; it pervades Chinese architectural planning regardless of secular or religious context.

A variety of terms can apply to Taoist religious structures. The word *guan* often denotes a monastic temple complex; *gong* (palace) is the term often used for larger Taoist complexes; and smaller temples may be called *dao yuan* (Taoist courtyards). The larger temple complexes often contain scores of structures, including many individual halls and worship and offering areas devoted to the vast panoply of Taoist deities.

Some of the most impressive Taoist temple complexes are located on sacred mountains or near rivers and caves. These sites of natural beauty are believed to be especially powerful places where *ch'i* (energy) is focused. A number of mountains in China are generally considered sacred by the several related Chinese religions, whereas some mountains are especially associated with specific Taoist schools or branches. Many of these sites are major centers of pilgrimage—notably Mount T'ai, which has hundreds of shrines and temples, and the Abbey of the Holy Ancestor, founded on the site where Lao Tzu is said to have composed the *Tao Te Ching*.

In the same way that Taoist architecture follows the mainstream styles and materials of Chinese architecture generally, Taoist art also uses the same forms and styles of Buddhist, Confucian, and popular religious art in China. Through the centuries, much intermingling and sharing of symbolism and iconography took place. Some of the very earliest Taoist images per se date to the fifth century and depict the deified Lao Tzu accompanied by heavenly worthies (*tianzun*) in a manner that draws from earlier traditional Chinese depictions of deities and that also resembles Buddhist imagery.[25] Although literary evidence indicates that Lao Tzu had been worshiped as a deity as early as the second century CE, it seems that his visual presentation as a god was avoided at first.[26] The development of Taoist iconography was certainly influenced by previous religious imagery in China and, in turn, was influential on, as well as influenced by, Buddhist imagery.[27] Often Buddhist and Taoist images and themes are found together. The developing Taoist and Buddhist pantheons shared a number of gods and goddesses, although certain symbols and deities are more fundamentally Taoist in nature.

These include figures such as Yu Huangdi (or Yu-huang), the Jade Emperor, who derived from Chinese folk religion to become an extremely important

Figure 14.4 Boxwood pendant, China, 18th century. Werner Forman / Art Resource, NY.

figure in religious Taoism, overseeing a vast heavenly administration. His cult became especially popular in the 11th century, and he is frequently depicted in art wearing imperial ceremonial robes and headdress. The Mother Empress of the West (Xiwangmu or Hsi-wang-mu) is the highest female deity in the Taoist pantheon and is most often shown in splendid imperial attire as well. Many Taoist deities are depicted wearing Chinese official or imperial costume, and men are frequently shown with beards. In contrast, Buddhist figures are more likely to be depicted in robes or monastic attire, and men are rarely bearded in Buddhist art.

The Eight Immortals, the Spirits of the Five Holy Mountains, city gods, local deities, warrior and guardian figures, and a great number of female deities make up the complex Taoist pantheon. The Eight Immortals have specific attributes by which they can be recognized. Other symbols traditionally associated with Taoism include the *yin-yang* and the Eight Trigrams (see Figure 14.4). The *yin-yang* symbolizes the universe with the two basic energies of *yin* (feminine, passive, receptive; associated with the moon, water, and clouds) and *yang* (masculine, active, creative; associated with the sun, fire, and dragons) in harmony and partaking of each other. The concept of *yin* and *yang* appears in the *I Ching* (or *Yi Jing;* the Book of Changes), an ancient Chinese manual on philosophy and divination. The complex process of divination described in the *I Ching* involves casting sticks, on which patterns of broken (*yin*) or unbroken (*yang*) lines are inscribed, into patterns. The Eight Trigrams represent the total possible combinations of groups of triads, which in turn are further combined in pairs (hexagrams—total of 64). The Eight Trigrams of the *I Ching* and the *yin-yang symbol*, although not exclusively Taoist, feature frequently in Taoist art.

EXAMPLES

The White Cloud Monastery, Beijing, 14th–15th Century

The White Cloud Monastery (or *Baiyun Guan*) is an extremely important Taoist complex in Beijing (see Figures 14.5, 14.6 and 14.7). It is the headquarters for the Quanzhen (or Ch'an-chen tao) school of Taoism (the Perfect Realization, or Complete Truth, or Way of the Realization of Truth), one of the two major Taoist sects surviving today.[28] This monastic branch of Taoism is said to have been founded in the middle of the 12th century (ca. 1167–68) by Wang Ch-un-yang (ca. 1112/23–70 CE), who was the recipient of secret teach-

Figure 14.5 The White Cloud Monastery, Beijing, China, 15th century, Sanqing and Siyu Halls. Vanni / Art Resource, NY.

ings received from two notable immortals. This school of Taoism combines and synthesizes elements from Taoism, Confucianism, and Zen Buddhism with an emphasis on meditation and study in quiet and enclosed settings removed from the distractions of the external world.

The monastery is again today a functioning Taoist center.[29] Although it was established on the site earlier, most of the structures date to the 14th and 15th centuries when the complex was rebuilt under Ming imperial patronage. The buildings show the typical Chinese wood construction techniques, with overhanging eaves supported by elaborate brackets. It is an extensive complex of about 15 acres and is laid out on a narrow and rectangular north–south axis, again typical of Chinese architectural planning and siting. There are over 50 different halls of diverse sizes dedicated to various deities, ranged around seven major courtyards, plus living, study, and meditation areas for the monks and spaces for visitors. There are four main halls, among which is the hall dedicated to the Sanqing (or: San-ch'ing, the Three Pure Ones), who are major Taoist deities believed to inhabit different heavenly realms. The Heaven of Jade Purity is inhabited by the Lord of the Heavenly Jewel (or the Venerable Celestial One of the Original Beginning); the Heaven of Great Purity is inhabited by the Lord of the Tao; and the Heaven of Highest Purity is inhabited by the Supreme Master Lao (the deified Lao Tzu). The Three Pure Ones are venerated with offerings and incense; it is believed that incense smoke carries prayers directly to the deities.[30]

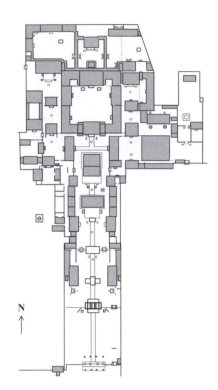

Figure 14.6 The White Cloud Monastery incense burner, Beijing, China, 15th century. Vanni / Art Resource, NY.

Figure 14.7 The White Cloud Monastery, Beijing, China, floorplan. Courtesy of Ricochet Productions.

Divine Immortals of the Five Paths and Transcendents Who Have Obtained the Tao, 1454

This hanging scroll, created of ink, colors, and gold on silk, is typical of the development of later Taoist imagery (see Plate 27). It dates from the mid-15th-century Ming period, and the extremely fine details and crisp, clear painting style are characteristic of imperial art production of the time. The scroll is part of a series of paintings that were designed for use by the imperial court in the Forbidden City in Beijing, specifically for a Buddhist-based ceremony known as the Water and Land Ritual (*Shuilu zhai*). This important religious rite was periodically held "for the universal salvation of all sentient beings . . . [and] . . . was intended to establish merit (*gong*) for both the living and the souls of the dead."[31]

Taoist deities and notables play prominent roles in this set of scrolls, evidencing the Taoist–Buddhist synthesis embraced by this era. This particular example features a group of Divine Immortals and Transcendents, human beings who, through careful study and practice of the Tao, became spiritually and physically transformed; "they achieved realization (*zhen*) and a state of being beyond *yin* and *yang*."[32]

There is a vast body of literature on the Taoist immortals, and many lively tales describe their lives on earth and their different paths toward achievement of enlightenment. Many biographies (or hagiographies) of specific immortals exist, although the immortals are also understood to represent generic types, such as shown in this scroll. Several of the figures are wearing the distinctive headgear of Taoist priests; one of the figures is dressed in a garment of leaves (indicating that he is a hermit saint); others hold books and scrolls (indicating that they are scholars); and others hold plants and mushrooms (indicating their adeptness at the medicinal arts). One of the figures is accompanied by a three-legged toad, which clearly identifies him as Liu Haichan, a famous practitioner of inner alchemy who lived during the early 10th century and who is also associated with the Quanzhen—or Perfect Realization school of Taoism.

These immortals and transcendent beings are, befittingly, depicted as if they are floating above the world in a heavenly cloud-filled realm. At the same time, the variety of body types and facial details and the different costumes they wear emphasize a sense of their original earthly individuality as well.

Vase with the Eight Taoist Immortals, 14th Century

The Taoist immortals provide subject matter for art in a wide variety of media. This porcelain vase (Figure 14.8), produced in the 14th century, is an excellent example of the continued popularity of these figures. Although there are many Taoist tales of people who achieved immortality, a group of Eight Immortals was especially recognized by the 12th and 13th centuries, under the influence of the Quanzhen (Perfect Realization) school of Taoism. By the 15th century, whole temples were often dedicated to the Eight Immortals, the majority of whom were believed to have lived on earth during the 7th through 10th centuries.

Each one of the Eight Immortals is generally represented with specific iconography symbolic of their life on earth or other aspects of their biography and attainment of immortality. Han Xiang may be depicted with flowers or a flute; Lu Dongbin often holds a sword; Lan Caije may be shown with a basket of fruit; Zhang Guolao is often depicted with a bag

Figure 14.8 Vase with the Eight Taoist Immortals, 14th century. London: The Trustees of The British Museum / Art Resource, NY.

containing his magical mule, which could be folded up; and He Xian-gu (the only female immortal among the eight) is often shown with a basket of medicinal mushrooms or a lotus flower. They frequently appear as a group and were very popular during the Yuan dynasty when this porcelain vase was produced.

The creation of fine ceramics has a very lengthy history in China. This particular vase is an example of Longquan ware, which was highly valued in China and frequently exported as well. Longquan refers to the town in southeastern China where a number of workshops were highly active especially from the 10th through 17th centuries, creating the characteristic cool green, celadon-glazed pieces of great elegance and refinement. In this case, the eight reddish brown relief plaques circling the center of the octagonal vase were left unglazed and covered with wax and grease when the vase was fired. The reddish brown plaques set off the relief molded figures of the Eight Immortals from the cool, jade green celadon glaze. Other examples of this style indicate that the relief plaques might have once been gilded, but this appears not to have been the case with this example.

Figure 14.9 *The Lady of the Highest Primordial and the Empress of the Earth,* hanging scroll, ca. 1600. Paris: Musée Guimet. Réunion des Musées Nationaux / Art Resource, NY.

The Lady of the Highest Primordial and the Empress of the Earth, ca. 1600

Female deities, immortals, healers, and practitioners have always played prominent roles in religious Taoism.[33] The Taoist pantheon includes a number of high-ranking female deities, notably the Mother Empress (or Queen Mother) of the West, the Lady of the Highest Primordial, and the Empress of the Earth. The latter two are shown in this Ming dynasty hanging scroll (see Figure 14.9). Like the example discussed previously (*Divine Immortals of the Five Paths*), this painting on silk was created for use in an important Buddhist ritual that included recognition of these important Taoist deities.

The Lady of the Highest Primordial appears at the top of the scroll. She represents the heavens and is accompanied by three female attendants holding various symbolic items. They are all elegantly dressed in colorful and flowing courtly style robes and have elaborate hairstyles and headdresses. According to legends, this female deity appeared in a vision (along with the Queen Mother of the West—the highest female deity in the Taoist pantheon) to an early Han dynasty emperor. She was later believed to have served as the teacher for several early legendary Taoist scholars. She is also known as the Realized Mother of the Three Heavens and, as such, "serves as a divine matriarchal figure."[34] The fact that she is accompanied by three attendants may reflect the fact that *yang* (active, heavenly) energy is associated with odd numbers in ancient Chinese systems of divination.

Yin (passive, earthly) energy is associated with even numbers, and the Empress of the Earth, depicted on the lower section of the scroll, is accompanied by four female attendants. The Empress of the Earth is a figure from ancient and pre-Taoist Chinese religion who was adopted into the Taoist pantheon. She often appears with the Queen Mother of the West or, as here, with the Lady of the Divine Primordial. The Empress of the Earth is "a divine manifestation of the earth . . . [and] has secondary connotations as a protector spirit of graves and the deceased."[35]

These personifications of heavenly and earthly realms, the pairing of *yin* and *yang,* and the sense of elegant balance and coordination seen here are exemplary of not only fundamental Taoist concepts but also the later growth and development of courtly styles associated with Taoism in late imperial China.

Jade Plaque of a Taoist Paradise, 17th Century

Carved objects of jade, for various uses, have been produced in China since the Neolithic period (ca. 6500 BCE). "Jade" is actually a generic term for several different types of stones (nephrite, jadeite, and other composite minerals). Jade appears in a variety of colors, especially various shades of green. This 17th-century example from the late Ming or early Qing era attests to the continued popularity of jade objects throughout the history of Chinese art (see Plate 28). Jade carvings such as this example were avidly collected and admired by imperial patrons, scholars, and connoisseurs. These prized objects, often exquisitely carved and highly polished, frequently served devotional or ritual purposes or functioned as decorative objects for adorning scholars' desks or collectors' cabinets.

This particular 17th-century example is replete with Taoist iconography and symbolism. The representation of landscape scenes, sacred mountains and caves, and paradisiacal locales are especially common in Taoist art. The creation of miniature mountains in jade was especially popular from the 12th century onward.[36] Often these micro-scenes include exquisite details of humans, animals, trees, caves, and architectural elements. The viewer who contemplates one of these miniature sculptural landscapes takes an extensive visual journey through the scene in the same fashion as viewers of much larger-scale painted landscapes.

Frequently, these miniature jade landscapes are inhabited by various deities, as is the case here. This plaque represents Xi Wangmu (or Hsi Wang Mu), the Queen Mother of the West. She is depicted wearing an elaborate crown and flowing robes and is seated in a landscape of trees and rocks. Perhaps this setting is meant to represent her abode in the sacred K'un-lun mountain ranges of western China. Wild and remote mountains figure prominently in Taoist art and literature, as realms of the gods and immortals.

The Queen Mother of the West, the most important Taoist goddess, has a long history in Chinese popular religion and appears to derive from pre-Taoist goddess worship.[37] Early descriptions characterize her as a rather wild figure with magical powers over the natural world. She features in a number of early Taoist texts and has continued to play a major role in religious Taoism through the centuries. Her image gradually transformed to take on courtly, imperial connotations and iconography.[38]

> She not only resides in the splendid palaces of Mount Kunlun, but is the ruler of immortals, the controller of fate, the giver of good fortune, and the bestower of celestial blessings. She manages the holy scriptures of the religion, assuring their exactness and providing suitable transmission to earth; she creates protective talismans; she gives instructions on internal cultivation; and to the very fortunate she appears in person and bestows upon them the peaches of immortality which will grant a better and faster access to the divine realms.[39]

In the example illustrated, the Queen Mother of the West is accompanied by a number of symbols that emphasize her power and importance. The pine tree under which she sits is a symbol of strength and immortality, as are the crane and tortoise, all traditional symbols of longevity. The tortoise (lower right) is emitting clouds of smoke from his mouth, and a small pagoda appears to float in these clouds. On the upper left side, a figure appears floating in a bank of clouds. Stories of the miraculous powers of the immortals, including their abilities to fly and bi-locate, abound in Taoist literature and frequently feature in art as well.

The material from which this piece is carved—jade—is also a traditional symbol of strength, perseverance, and longevity. Hence, the material used to create this piece combined with the symbols and images depicted render this an excellent example of important Taoist themes and concepts.

NOTES

1. Huston Smith, *The Illustrated World's Religions* (San Francisco: Harper San Francisco, 1994), 124.

2. Isabelle Robinet, *Taoism: Growth of a Religion* (Stanford, CA: Stanford University Press, 1997), 3.

3. Livia Kohn, ed., *The Taoist Experience: An Anthology* (Albany: State University of New York Press, 1993), 3.

4. "Still continuing the tradition, the sixty-fourth Celestial Master resides today in Taiwan. The school is a form of communal religion, with a heavy emphasis on morality, ritual, purifications, and exorcism." Kohn, 4. See also Robinet, 53–77.

5. "Shangqing practice was highly individual and aimed at transferring the practitioner into the realms of the immortals, first by visualizations, then by ecstatic journeys, and finally through the ingestion of a highly poisonous alchemical elixer." Kohn, 5. See also Robinet, 114–48.

6. "Much simpler than the practice of Highest Clarity, Numinous Treasure required merely the recitation of its scriptures and participation in its rites to guarantee a place among the perfected." Kohn, 5. See also Robinet, 149–83.

7. The story of Lao Tzu's visit to the "barbarian lands" (*Laozi huahu*) was especially popular during the later Han era (c. 300 CE). "In attempting to account for the many similarities between the doctrines of Buddhism and Taoism . . . the belief was conceived of that Laozi had traveled to India and had become Buddha and/or converted its inhabitants (barbarians) to his doctrines. Thus Buddhism was nothing but the doctrine preached by Laozi after his departure to points west." Arthur Pontynen, "The Deification of Laozi in Chinese History and Art," *Oriental Art* 26, no. 2 (1980): 193.

8. Kohn, 4.

9. Rolf A. Stein, "Religious Taoism and Popular Religion from the Second to Seventh Centuries," in *Facets of Taoism,* ed. Holmes Welch and Anna Seidel (New Haven, CT: Yale University Press, 1979), 53–81.

10. Stephen Little, *Taoism and the Arts of China* (Chicago: The Art Institute of Chicago, 2000), 19.

11. Pontynen, 193.

12. Isabelle Robinet, "The Taoist Immortal: Jesters of Light and Shadow, Heaven and Earth," *Journal of Chinese Religions* 13/14, no. 1 (1985–86): 87–105.

13. Robinet, *Taoism: Growth of a Religion*, 18.

14. Little, 16.

15. Ninji Ofuchi, "The Formation of the Taoist Canon," in *Facets of Taoism*, ed. Holmes Welch and Anna Seidel (New Haven, CT: Yale University Press, 1979), 253–67.

16. Jennifer Oldstone-Moore, *Taoism: Origins, Beliefs, Practices, Holy Texts, Sacred Places* (New York: Oxford University Press, 2003), 38.

17. Little, 13.

18. Oldstone-Moore, 7.

19. Smith, 130.

20. Livia Kohn, "Transcending Personality: From Ordinary to Immortal Life, *Taoist Resources* 2, no. 2 (1990): 1–20; and Livia Kohn, "Eternal Life in Taoist Mysticism," *Journal of the American Oriental Society* 110, no. 4 (1990): 622–40.

21. Robinet, *Taoism, Growth of a Religion, 20.*

22. Wu Hung, "Mapping Early Taoist Art: The Visual Culture of Wudoumi Dao," in *Taoism and the Arts of China*, ed. Stephen Little, 77.

23. Oldstone-Moore, 8–9.

24. Nancy Steinhardt, "Taoist Architecture," in *Taoism and the Arts of China*, ed. Stephen Little, 57.

25. Arthur Pontynen, "The Dual Nature of Laozi in Chinese History and Art," *Oriental Art* 26, no. 3 (1980): 308–13.

26. "The reason is simple: as the personification of the Dao, Laozi was considered to have neither matter nor form; he could therefore only be symbolized. . . . not represented by a figurative likeness. This early Taoist convention persisted until at least the fifth century." Hung, 87.

27. Yang Liu, "Origins of Daoist Iconography," *Ars Orientalis* 31 (2001): 31–64.

28. The other major Taoist sect surviving today is the earliest one to have been founded: the school of the Celestial Masters. See Kohn, *Taoist Experience,* 7.

29. Yoshitoyo Yoshioka, "Taoist Monastic Life," in *Facets of Taoism*, ed. Holmes Welch and Anna Seidel (New Haven, CT: Yale University Press, 1979), 229–52.

30. On the symbolism of incense burning generally, see Stephan Feuchtwang, *Popular Religion in China: The Imperial Metaphor* (Richmond, Surrey: Curzon, 2001), especially chapter 5: "The Incense-Burner: Communication and Deference," 135–60.

31. Little, 227.

32. Little, 251.

33. See Catherine Despeux and Livia Kohn, *Women in Daoism* (Cambridge, MA: Three Pines Press, 2003); and Eva Wong, "Taoism," in *Her Voice, Her Faith: Women Speak on World Religions*, ed. Arvind Sharma (Boulder, CO: Westview Press, 2002), 119–43.

34. Shawn Eichman, catalogue entry number 97 in *Taoism and the Arts of China*, ed. Stephen Little, 281.

35. Eichman, 281.

36. Rolf Stein, *The World in Miniature: Container Gardens and Dwellings in Far Eastern Religious Thought* (Stanford, CA: Stanford University Press, 1990).

37. See Despeux and Kohn, 25–47.

38. Suzanne Cahill, *Transcendence and Divine Passion: The Queen Mother of the West in Medieval China* (Stanford, CA: Stanford University Press, 1993).

39. Despeux and Kohn, 29.

BIBLIOGRAPHY AND FURTHER READING

Cahill, Suzanne. *Transcendence and Divine Passion: The Queen Mother of the West in Medieval China*. Stanford, CA: Stanford University Press, 1993.

Despeux, Catherine, and Livia Kohn. *Women in Daoism*. Cambridge, MA: Three Pines Press, 2003.

Feuchtwang, Stephan. *Popular Religion in China: The Imperial Metaphor*. Richmond, Surrey: Curzon, 2001.

Fischer-Schreiber, Ingrid. *The Shambhala Dictionary of Taoism*. Trans. Werner Wünsche. Boston: Shambhala, 1996.

Hung, Wu. "Mapping Early Taoist Art: The Visual Culture of Wudoumi Dao." In *Taoism and the Arts of China*, ed. Stephen Little, 76–93. Chicago: The Art Institute of Chicago, 2000.

Ji, Sang. *Religions and Religious Life in China*. Beijing: China Intercontinental Press, 2004.

Kohn, Livia. "Eternal Life in Taoist Mysticism." *Journal of the American Oriental Society* 110, no. 4 (1990): 622–40.

Kohn, Livia. *God of the Dao: Lord Lao in History and Myth*. Ann Arbor: University of Michigan, Center for Chinese Studies, 1998.

Kohn, Livia. "The Looks of Laozi." *Asian Folklore Studies* 55, no. 2 (1996): 193–236.

Kohn, Livia. *The Taoist Experience: An Anthology*. Albany: State University of New York Press, 1993.

Kohn, Livia. "Transcending Personality: From Ordinary to Immortal Life." *Taoist Resources* 2, no. 2 (1990): 1–20.

Little, Stephen. *Realm of the Immortals: Daoism in the Arts of China*. Cleveland, OH: Cleveland Museum of Art, 1988.

Little, Stephen, ed. *Taoism and the Arts of China*. Chicago: The Art Institute of Chicago, 2000.

Liu, Yang. "Origins of Daoist Iconography." *Ars Orientalis* 31 (2001): 31–64.

Ofuchi, Ninji. "The Formation of the Taoist Canon." In *Facets of Taoism: Essays in Chinese Religion*, ed. Holmes Welch and Anna Seidel, 253–67. New Haven, CT: Yale University Press, 1979.

Oldstone-Moore, Jennifer. *Taoism: Origins, Beliefs, Practices, Holy Texts, Sacred Places*. New York: Oxford University Press, 2003.

Pontynen, Arthur. "The Deification of Laozi in Chinese Art and History." *Oriental Art* 26, no. 2 (1980): 192–200.

Pontynen, Arthur. "The Dual Nature of Laozi in Chinese History and Art." *Oriental Art* 26, no. 3 (1980): 308–13.

Qingxi, Lou. *The Architectural Art of Ancient China*. Trans. Li Zhurun. Beijing: China Intercontinental Press, 2002.

Robinet, Isabelle. *Taoism: Growth of a Religion*. Stanford, CA: Stanford University Press, 1997.

Robinet, Isabelle. "The Taoist Immortal: Jesters of Light and Shadow." *Journal of Chinese Religions* 13/14, no. 1 (1985–86): 87–105.

Schipper, Kristofer. "The Taoist Body." *History of Religions* 17, no. 3/4 (1978): 355–86.

Seidel, Anna. "The Image of the Perfect Ruler in Early Taoist Messianism." *History of Religions* 9, no. 2/3 (1969–70): 216–47.

Sharma, Arvind, and Katherine Young, eds. *Her Voice, Her Faith: Women Speak on World Religions*. Boulder, CO: Westview Press, 2003.

Smith, Huston. *The Illustrated World's Religions*. San Francisco: Harper San Francisco, 1994.

Stein, Rolf A. "Religious Taoism and Popular Religion from the Second to the Seventh Centuries." In *Facets of Taoism: Essays in Chinese Religion*, ed. Holmes Welch and Anna Seidel, 53–81. New Haven, CT: Yale University Press, 1979.

Stein, Rolf A. *The World in Miniature: Container Gardens and Dwellings in Far Eastern Religious Thought*. Stanford, CA: Stanford University Press, 1990.

Steinhardt, Nancy. "Taoist Architecture." In *Taoism and the Arts of China*, ed. Stephen Little, 57–75. Chicago: The Art Institute of Chicago, 2000.

Taoism and the Arts of China. http://www.artic.edu/taoism/.

Welch, Holmes, and Anna Seidel, eds. *Facets of Taoism: Essays in Chinese Religion*. New Haven, CT: Yale University Press, 1979.

Wong, Eva. "Taoism." In *Her Voice, Her Faith: Women Speak on World Religions*, ed. Arvind Sharma and Katherine Young, 119–43. Boulder, CO: Westview Press, 2002.

Yoshioka, Yoshitoyo. "Taoist Monastic Life." In *Facets of Taoism: Essays in Chinese Religion*, ed. Holmes Welch and Anna Seidel, 229–52. New Haven, CT: Yale University Press, 1979.

−15−

Confucianism

ORIGINS AND DEVELOPMENT

Confucianism is traditionally included in studies of the world's religions as a philosophy/belief system developed by the ancient Chinese scholar Confucius (Kongzi or Kong Fu Zi, the Venerable Master Kong, 551–479 BCE). His teachings primarily represent suggestions on ethical codes of conduct that he developed and advanced during the course of his career as a government official, political reformer, sage, and itinerant scholar. Confucianism has often been described as an ethics-based philosophy and a way of life, rather than a strict set of religious beliefs.[1] However, although Confucianism is largely philosophical in content, it cannot be fully understood without recognition of its religious context, dimensions, and function.

> Those interpretations that have sought to define Confucianism as a form of humanism devoid of religious character have failed to realize the central feature that persists throughout the tradition. . . . Confucianism is an ethical system and humanistic teaching. It is also, however, a tradition that bears a deep and profound sense of the religious, and any interpretation that ignores this quality has missed its quintessential feature.[2]

Confucianism has been of supreme influence and importance in shaping centuries of history and cultural traditions in China and numerous other Asian regions including Japan, Korea, and Vietnam.

It is often pointed out that the origins of Confucianism can be traced far back into ancient Chinese history, many centuries before the life and teaching of

Confucius himself. Confucius regarded himself less as an innovator and more as a transmitter and correct interpreter of ancient, inherited traditions and beliefs about society, government, politics, and the roles of rulers and individuals in maintaining earthly and cosmic order through proper adherence to their social responsibilities.

He was born in eastern China, in the city of Qufu in the state of Lu, during a highly troubled and turbulent period in Chinese history. This was during the last centuries of the Zhou Dynasty (ca. 1050–256 BCE), which preceded and overlapped with the Warring States Period (475–221 BCE), during which the Zhou rulers ultimately lost their power and territorial control. By this time, "real power resided with the aristocratic rulers of various principalities, who constantly sought to strengthen their positions and enlarge their domains at the expense of their neighbors."[3] Confucius attributed this social and political deterioration to a loss of ancient values and traditions, "the behavioral norms, rituals, and etiquette laid down by the founders of the Zhou Dynasty to bring about civility, order, peace, and harmony in the community from the top of society on down."[4] A restoration of harmonious social order and effective government, according to Confucius, could be achieved by reforms of conduct based on ethical principles: "honor, respect, love, and service." He believed that "attention to rank, obligations, and ritual duties will lead ultimately to the perfection of oneself and the transformation of society."[5]

The ultimate foundations for many of Confucius's ideas are thus derived from his study of ancient Chinese texts, associated primarily with the early Zhou Dynasty. Now known as the Five Classics, these include the *Yi Jing* (*I Ching*, or *Book of Changes*), *Shi Jing* (*Book of Odes*), *Li Ji* (*Book of Rites*), *Shu Jing* (*Book of Documents*), and *Chun Qiu* (*Springs and Autumns*). These texts range from manuals of divination to accounts of historical events, to records of traditional poetry and rituals. They overall contain much information and guidance on ancient customs, morality, protocol, and propriety. These classic works represent the basis for Confucian thought and for its later developments.

Although some traditions credit Confucius with editing or even authoring sections of these classics, the teachings of Confucius are primarily found in the work known as *Lunyu* or *The Analects of Confucius*, which was compiled in several stages during the fourth century BCE, decades after his death. This work has been called the "most influential book ever written in East Asia,"[6] which has "probably exercised a greater influence on the history and culture of the Chinese people than any other work in the Chinese language."[7] The word *Lunyu* means "conversations," and the book largely takes the form of dialogue between Confucius (the Master teacher) and his students.

The reader of the Analects should be prepared to encounter not a formal treatise but conversations that seek to illuminate or grapple with important concepts, sometimes in clear and succinct form, at other times in more oblique fashion, colored by the sort of surprise, misunderstanding, pleased reaction, displeased reaction, humor, or sarcasm that characterize conversations in real life.[8]

Although during his life, Confucius did not succeed in his efforts to convince contemporary political leaders of the importance of his advice, he gleaned a wide following of students and disciples who continued to promulgate his ideas after his death. Known as the *Ru* or *Rujia* school (scholars or moralists), later important figures include Mencius (or Mengzi, ca. 372–289 BCE) and Xun Zi (ca. 370–286 BCE), both of whom also strove for political reform based on Confucian ethical principles, but who also developed their own divergent ideas about human nature and social roles.

During the period of the Qin Dynasty (221–207 BCE), Confucian teachings were suppressed. However, in the Han Dynasty (206 BCE–220 CE), Confucianism reemerged to become the official state doctrine under the emperor Wu Di (reigned 140–87 BCE). A Confucian academy was established in 124 BCE in the Han capital of Chang-an. All aspiring government employees and officials were required to study the Classics and Confucianism and to pass a rigorous examination on this material. It was during this period, as well, that temples dedicated to Confucius began to be constructed, and ritual commemorations were held to honor his spirit.

During the Tang Dynasty (618–907 CE) Confucian temples were extended by imperial decree to all major cities throughout the land. Local governors had to go and pay their respects to the Master at the temple before taking up their appointments. Ceremonies were conducted there annually, and the temples became especially connected with education and the examination system.[9]

At the same time, Buddhism (see chapter 13), which had reached China in the first century CE, and Taoism (see chapter 14), which had developed much earlier in China, became increasingly influential, although Confucianism continued to be the political philosophy of the imperial court and government. The Neo-Confucian revival of the Song Dynasty (960–1279) ushered in another significant era characterized by important degrees of dialogue between the three systems of Confucianism, Buddhism, and Taoism. Important Neo-Confucian thinkers include Zhu Xi (1130–1200), whose reinterpretations and augmentations of Confucian teachings dominated educational and government practices in China through the early 20th century. Later Ming Dynasty syncretic thinkers such as Lin Chao-en (or Lin Zhaoen, 1517–98) sought to unify the three traditions of Confucianism, Buddhism, and Taoism.[10] Indeed, the relationships between Confucianism, Buddhism, and Taoism in Chinese culture and history are often so intertwined that it can be difficult to clearly separate their unique characteristics from the shared elements. In practice, elements of all three may be combined. Chinese community traditions, Chinese imperial traditions, and elements of Confucianism, Buddhism, and Taoism often blend together. Even so, it is possible to identify several distinctive beliefs and practices associated with Confucianism.

PRINCIPAL BELIEFS AND KEY PRACTICES

Religion and politics have been very closely entwined in China since very ancient times. The belief that earthly rulers are divinely mandated to carry out the will of heaven can be traced far back into Chinese history and mythology. The effective functioning of earthly society depends on the ruler's awareness of and adherence to heaven's will. In the ancient Shang Dynasty (ca. 1766–1050 BCE), a remote supreme being, *Shang Di* ("the Lord on High"), was worshiped. The practice of ancestral veneration is also attested at this early date. The spirits of royal ancestors were believed to be able to communicate their continued guidance to earthly rulers and were often consulted by the Shang aristocracy via divination practices. Many examples of ancient "oracle bones" give evidence of the divination practice known as pyroscapulimancy[11] (see Figure 15.1). Questions posed were answered via the diviner's interpretation of cracks and patterns created when heated rods were placed on the bones (especially shoulder blades) taken from sacrificial oxen or sheep. The bottom shells of turtles were also used; this practice is known as plastromancy. The answers recorded on these bones and shells are also evidence of the early development of Chinese ideographic writing.

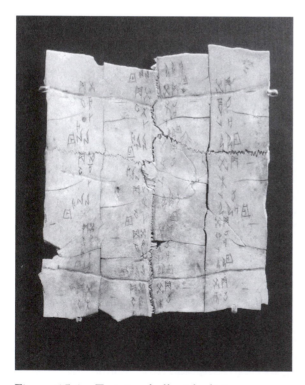

Figure 15.1 Tortoise shell with divinatory text, Shang Dynasty, 14th to 13th century BCE. The Art Archive / Musée Guimet Paris / Gianni Dagli Orti.

When the Shang Dynasty was overthrown by the Zhou Dynasty in the middle of the 11th century BCE, "the Zhou proclaimed that they had received the 'Mandate of Heaven,' the divinely sanctioned right to rule, because of their virtue in contrast to the depravity of the last Shang rulers. The idea that virtue and beneficent rule are the basis of the state was firmly established by this date."[12] The belief that *Tian* (or "Heaven") was the source of cosmic and earthly order replaced the worship of Shang Di. Tian was seen as "a nonanthropomorphic force that was able to control and influence events."[13]

A sense of connectedness between earthly and heavenly realms, the supreme significance of virtuous behavior, and a belief in the importance of venerating ancestors, all provide the background for the teachings of Confucius and for the later development of Confucianism. Confucian thought is fundamentally based on the premise of an orderly universe guided by moral principles. Heavenly and earthly order is not characterized by capricious, whimsical, or self-serving behavior, but rather by a virtuous adherence to ethical principles. Foremost among these is the quality of *ren* (goodness, benevolence, human-heartedness), which requires that all people be treated with respect. "*Ren* has been described as the sum total of virtues, because Confucius once said that endurance, fortitude, simplicity and reticence are all close to the meaning of *ren*. When one of his disciples asked him how to practice *ren*, he replied, 'Love people.'"[14] The virtue of *ren* is directly manifested in righteous behavior (*yi*), the ability to make morally correct and proper decisions in one's actions and relationships with others, especially with "regard to the Five Relationships upon which society was believed to be based: those between sovereign and subject, father and son, husband and wife, elder and younger brother, and friend and friend."[15] *Xiao* (filial piety) is thus an essential virtue for Confucianism. The respect and honor that dutiful children demonstrate to their parents is ideally mirrored in all social relationships within the Confucian hierarchy. "An ordered, harmonious society depends on each person playing his or her part appropriately and with good intent."[16]

Confucian ethics are thus fundamentally focused on the concerns of humans in society rather than in supernatural or other-worldly realms. The pursuit of *ren* via study, contemplation, and moral cultivation is the ultimate goal. The achievement of *ren* in society and human relationships will reflect the orderliness of the cosmic will (*li*). *Li* "was held to be immanent in all phenomena, including human relationships, and it was held to be manifested in the laws of the empire."[17] Confucius and his later followers emphasized the qualities of superior moral behavior demonstrated by "gentlemanly" modes of self-cultivation, including "intensive scholarship, a reverent attitude and disciplined mind, and 'quiet sitting'—meditation for purifying and focusing the mind which can produce a profoundly transformative experience."[18] The ideal Confucian gentleman-scholar was most often a member of the *literati* class of elite, well-educated government officials and administrators who oversaw imperial functions and the rituals performed under imperial directives.

The maintenance of ancient rituals was of critical importance for Confucius and his followers, who visualized the earthly imperial bureaucracy as a reflection of the heavenly realm. On earth, the emperor resided at the apex of the social hierarchy, just as heaven was visualized as the dwelling place of the gods, presided over by the heavenly counterpart of the emperor on earth. This celestial realm also included numerous deities and ancestral spirits who served to guide and influence earthly matters.

The imperial pantheon was a meticulously regulated hierarchical nexus of cults that extended from the temples and altars in the capital to the county level though the empire. Imperial cults were bureaucratically distinct from those of

Buddhism, Daoism, and popular religion in that they were served by officers of the court and bureaucracy and sanctioned by the Confucian canon.[19]

Ancestral veneration is long attested in China, "but as a matter for the court, not for the general public. Confucius popularized the practice, teaching that it could strengthen family ties and play an important role in ensuring the continuity of the family."[20] The veneration of ancestors, the performance of imperial rituals (including animal sacrifice), the belief in a celestial pantheon of deities, and the veneration of local tutelary gods all have roots in ancient Chinese traditions and were embraced and promulgated by Confucius and his followers. Although it certainly can be said that Confucianism devotes greatest attention to understanding and cultivating human behavior on earth, the development of the veneration of Confucius and the centrality of this cult in Chinese imperial and ritual traditions cannot be underestimated.[21]

TRADITIONAL ART AND ARCHITECTURAL FORMS

Confucianism has had such a profound influence on Asian culture and art that it is extremely challenging to attempt to define or separate "Confucian art" from the larger historical and stylistic contexts. Narrowly defined, Confucian art would include examples of statuary depicting Confucius and later Confucian scholars, paintings and illustrations of events in the life of Confucius and his followers, illustrations of Confucian teachings, and the many examples of Confucian temples found throughout Asia. At the same time, however, Confucian themes and values are also demonstrated in art and architectural forms not specifically or necessarily designed for strictly Confucian purposes. The Confucian values of order, harmonious relationships, and scholarly contemplation can be sensed in architectural planning of both public and private spaces, in the venerable traditions of Chinese landscape painting, and in the contemplative appreciation of nature as also demonstrated in garden design.

Temples

The first temple to Confucius was dedicated soon after his death (see Figure 15.2). Located in Confucius's birthplace, Qufu (Shangdong province), it originally consisted simply of the three-room house where Confucius had lived. In 478 BCE, the ruler of Lu declared this structure to be a sacred site dedicated to the memory of Confucius. In subsequent years, many scholars settled in the town, and many visitors came to pay their respects to Confucius at the temple and his nearby grave site. Over the centuries, the Confucius Temple at Qufu expanded greatly to cover an area of close to 25 acres, with multiple buildings arranged in axial fashion around a series of nine courtyards. Numerous renovations, repairs, and expansions transformed the site into an

Figure 15.2 Temple of Confucius, Qufu, China. Werner Forman / Art Resource, NY.

impressive and richly decorated architectural complex dating primarily to the 17th- and 18th-century Qing Dynasty period.[22]

The enlargement of the architectural complex reflects the growth and expansion of Confucianism under imperial patronage as well as the worship and veneration of Confucius himself. Emperor Gao (reigned 206–195 BCE), founder of the Han Dynasty, established the custom of offering sacrifices at the temple in 195 BCE, a practice that continued through subsequent centuries.[23] The close association of Confucianism and imperial rituals and traditions is also reflected by the layout of the temple complex that, in its axial balance, symmetry, and scale, mirrors the design of the Imperial Palace complex in Beijing.

> Confucian temple architecture echoes the architecture of the emperor's palace—notably the north–south axis on which the important halls are located. The temples are built on a square base, and internally they are symmetrical, with each hall a mirror-image of the one opposite, conveying the order associated with Confucian thought. Temples were public spaces—results of civil service examinations were posted in them and they were also used for training in music and ritual.[24]

In 630 CE, during the Tang Dynasty, an imperial decree was issued requiring that Confucian temples be constructed in all schools across the empire. This, too, reflected the increasing importance of Confucianism as an integral aspect of government administration and educational programs. During the Tang and Song dynasties, the state sacrifices and rituals associated with the veneration of Confucius and his followers became increasingly complicated and officially regulated, a process that continued through the Ming and Qing periods. The growth of the cult of Confucius can also be traced via the many prestigious titles he was granted, such as Great Completer, Ultimate Sage, Exalted First Teacher, and the Sage of Culture.[25]

> As the domain of the cosmos over which Confucius presided, culture (*wen*) encompassed the imperium and its orderly operations based on the teachings of the ancient sage-kings as recorded in the Confucian canon. This culture was also embodied in the Confucian literati devoted to the primacy of ritual and music, which gave perfect expression to human sentiments and generated the orderly principles (*wen*) that governed the human world.[26]

Confucian temples, regardless of date, reflect the traditional and often conservative styles of Chinese architecture based on interlocking modules of wooden construction.[27] Often elevated on low platforms, temples show the basic post-and-lintel forms typical of Chinese architecture, often with elaborate bracketing systems and impressive roof lines. The upward sloping eaves of the much-restored Confucius Temple in Taipei, Taiwan, are characteristic of southern Chinese forms of the Qing Dynasty (see Figure 15.3). Tile roofs of imperial yellow, carved columns decorated with traditional Chinese symbols such as protective dragons, and painted and carved friezes of similar motifs abound.

Figure 15.3   Temple of Confucius, Taipei, Taiwan. SEF / Art Resource, NY.

The interiors of Confucian temples are often richly decorated as well, though often in a slightly less flamboyant style than Taoist or Buddhist temples (see Figure 15.4). Altars to Confucius and major Confucian thinkers were commonly enriched with sculptures of these figures until the early

Figure 15.4   Temple of Confucius, Jiading, China. Vanni / Art Resource, NY.

16th century, when, by imperial decree, many of these carved likenesses were replaced by memorial "spirit tablets" simply bearing their names. Statues of Confucius are still found in many temples, however. Because Confucian temples were often associated with schools or academies, the names of those successful in passing the rigorous exams required for entry into government service were frequently displayed on stone tablets within the temple/academy precinct, such as the stone steles found in the garden of the Temple of Confucius in Beijing (see Figure 15.5).

Images of Confucius and Confucian Themes in Art

Records indicate that commemorative portraits of Confucius and his disciples (either in painting or in sculpture) were produced at an early date and certainly during the Han Dynasty, when Confucianism became the state cult, and the practice of imperial offerings to his spirit became established. Although no early examples exist, engraved stone steles of the Tang Dynasty (seventh century CE) probably suggest the appearance of earlier examples (see Figure 15.6). Confucius is often depicted in a dignified frontal pose, with his hands clasped in front of him. He is represented as a scholar-official with appropriate regalia and demeanor. "The formality of the pose, the generic physical appearance, and the absence of specific context or activity invest [these images] with the timeless quality of an icon."[28] The conventions of commemorative portraiture

Figure 15.5 Temple of Confucius, Beijing, China; scholar's tablets. Erich Lessing / Art Resource, NY.

Figure 15.6 Portrait of Confucius, carved stone stele, Tang Dynasty (618–906 CE). Werner Forman / Art Resource.

were established in the Han Dynasty. In addition to being made for use in funerary rites and memorial ceremonies, commemorative portraits also served didactic functions by perpetuating role models in visible (albeit idealized) form. Model figures were portrayed not with idiosyncratic physical features, but with the characteristics appropriate to their categorical "type," as expressed through posture, bodily proportions, clothing, and objects held. The background is typically blank, rather than delineating a particular setting.[29]

Images of Confucius and his disciples were widely produced in the subsequent centuries and featured (in both painted and sculptural form) in the numerous temples and academies established throughout the empire.[30] Within temples, these images provided a focus for commemorative ceremonies and rituals; "however, the proliferation of temples containing iconic images of Confucius and his numerous disciples, and the religious character of the sacrifices themselves, also prompted his cult to develop certain characteristics of devotional religion, like Buddhism and Daoism."[31] This became a matter of concern especially during the Ming period (1368–1644), when, in spite of some opposition, iconic images were removed from Confucian temples and replaced with inscribed tablets bearing only the names of important figures.

Concomitantly, during the Ming period, illustrated narratives of the life of Confucius began to appear in increasing numbers in various media including woodblock prints, paintings on silk, and incised stone tablets.[32] Some scholars believe that this upsurge in Confucian pictorial narrative imagery in the Ming period reflects the removal of images from the Confucian temples. The illustrated narratives addressed "an enduring desire for representational embodiment"[33] on the part of scholars as well as members of the literate public. Many woodblock printed pictorial biographies of Confucius were produced by an increasing number of commercial publishers in the Ming period. These editions were more accessible to a less-than-exclusive or elite audience. The ultimate sources for many of these narrative illustrations have been traced to previous traditions of Buddhist illustrated biography, and "in a sense, the pictures of Confucius' life offered a means for his cult to continue to compete with Buddhism and various deity cults."[34] The production of illustrated scenes from the lives of Confucius and his disciples continued well into the Qing Dynasty (1644–1912) (see Figure 15.7).

Illustrations of Confucian texts and Confucian themes also appear widely in Asian art of various dates and media, including illustrated scrolls, woodcuts, silk paintings, and painted screens. The utmost Confucian virtue of *xiao* (filial piety) was expounded by many writers and was often shown in sequential narrative illustrations focusing on the proper and decorous behavior of dutiful

Figure 15.7   Scenes from the Life of Confucius, Qing Dynasty, early 19th century. Bridgeman-Giraudon / Art Resource, NY.

persons. Scenes include children paying respect to their parents, subjects paying homage to rulers, and so on.

The influence of Confucian teachings outside China is well attested also by the revived popularity of Confucian themes in 16th- and 17th-century Japan. Members of Japan's ruling elite class (the Tokugawa shoguns), eager to increase their political influence and legitimacy, paid homage to Confucian virtues and commissioned works of art illustrating themes such as filial piety. *The Twenty-Four Paragons of Filial Piety*, depicted in two large six-panel folding screens attributed to the circle of Kano Mitsunobu (1565–1608), is an excellent example of the themes of self-sacrifice and humility (as well as the rewards for this behavior) in a series of both celestial and earthly exemplars (see Figure 15.8).

In addition to portraits of Confucius and his followers, narrative scenes from their lives, and illustrations of Confucian teachings, Confucianism has also had a profound influence on the arts of poetry, calligraphy, landscape painting, and garden design. This pervasive influence can be widely noted, perhaps most especially in the refined works associated with the *literati*, particularly those of the Ming Dynasty "Southern" and "Wu" Schools. The Confucian virtues of scholarship, self-cultivation, contemplation, and the development of skills with artistic pursuits were avidly demonstrated by gentleman-scholars, especially retired members of the government, who settled in the region of the city of Suzhou during the Ming period. The achievement of skill with the refined arts of calligraphy, poetry, music, and painting—long considered hallmarks of the cultivated gentlemanly character—flourished among many groups of scholar-amateurs centered in the Suzhou region during the 15th through 17th centuries. During this period especially, the venerable materials used for both calligraphy and painting (ink, inkstone, brush, and paper) were termed "the four treasures of the scholar's studio" (*wen fang si bao*).[35]

Figure 15.8 Circle of Kano Mitsunobu (1565–1608), *The Twenty-Four Paragons of Filial Piety*, painted screen, early 17th century. New Haven, CT: Yale University Art Gallery / Art Resource, NY.

Landscape painting has an extremely lengthy history in China. Evocative scenes of the beauty and power of nature have long been produced by Chinese artists. Indeed, landscape painting has been called "one of the greatest achievements of Chinese culture."[36] Many of the foundations for Chinese landscape painting traditions were established in the 10th century by several artists who specialized in creating expansive views (in either horizontal or vertical scroll format) of mountains, streams, trees, rocks, clouds, fog, and winding pathways. These often include architectural elements and small figures of people journeying through or admiring the extensive landscape. It might be said that, from its origins, Chinese landscape painting demonstrates far less interest in topographic or documentary recording of scenes and landscape elements, but is far more concerned with evoking moods and essences rather than simply outward appearances. In this sense, Chinese landscape painting generally has a highly spiritual/mystical dimension, which undercurrent permeates the various traditions and stylistic developments. "What was sought after was the essence of a scene and the metaphors it might offer for life, rather than a superficial attractive resemblance."[37] Purely realistic representations, it was felt, do not really reflect the depth and complexity of actual human experiences, perceptions, and understanding.

> At moments of extraordinary clarity, when the mind is receptive but at rest, uncluttered by distracting considerations . . . one's perceptions become a part of one's self, in an undifferentiated "passage of felt life." The cumulative absorption and ordering of such perceptions is the "self-cultivation" of the Confucian system, this in turn is the proper stuff of art.[38]

Artists of the Wu School (not a formal institution but rather a group related by shared interests) sought especially to create works of landscape painting that evoked poetic and personal concepts, finding "comfort and reassurance in the belief that they were the elite, upholding the Confucian virtues."[39] The scholar-painter Wen Zhengming (Wen Cheng-ming, 1470–1559) exemplifies this trend. He excelled in the arts of calligraphy, poetry, and painting, and many of his works, such as *The Hour That Mist Descends into the Shadows* (Figure 15.9), represent far more than simply literal rendering of landscape scenes. This vertical scroll painting done in ink on silk focuses attention on two tall and ancient pine trees surrounded by rocks and mountains with a small bridge visible in the distance. This scene shows the end of day, the descent of mist into the twilight, and thus poetically evokes themes of the passage of time, mortality, loss, and old age as well as the fleeting and enduring beauties of nature.

Figure 15.9 Wen Zhengming (1470–1559), *The Hour That Mist Descends into the Shadows*, scroll painting. Paris: Musée Guimet. Réunion des Musées Nationaux / Art Resource, NY.

Paintings of old trees, especially the pine and cypress, are conspicuous among Wen Cheng-ming's late works. Like waterfalls and rocks, they belonged to an austere, uncompromising environment, free of blandishments; that was the way Wen sometimes chose to see his world, as one in which survival required tireless effort, and in which life made a place for itself through steadfastness and integrity. . . . for Wen Cheng-ming, commitment to the austere was a matter of moral principle, not of physical circumstance.[40]

Wen Zhengming also served as a consultant in the design of one of the most renowned Ming Dynasty "Scholar's Gardens": the Garden of the Humble Administrator (or *Zhuozheng Yuan*), located in Suzhou (see Figure 15.10). The property was purchased in the early 16th century by a retired government administrator, Wang Xianchen, who created a large villa with extensive gardens to serve as an idyllic retreat for himself, family members, and honored guests. Although the gardens and buildings have been much altered, modified, and renovated since their original creation, the design retains much of the essence and purpose of its original conception as an enclosed private retreat for a scholarly gentleman trained in Confucian virtues, well educated in the classics, and with a refined aesthetic sensibility befitting his station. Numerous pavilions, towers, halls, bridges, covered walkways, and paths take the visitor through a series of precisely planned viewing experiences in the extensive landscape. Rocks, trees, and water are the typical buildings blocks of classical Chinese garden design, here brilliantly exploited to greatest potential in providing a sense of calm, repose, reflection, and inspiration for artistic pursuits.

Figure 15.10 The Garden of the Humble Administrator, Suzhou, China. Vanni / Art Resource, NY.

In early spring, plum flowers at the Fragrant Snow and Clouds Pavilion blossom against the cold, and crabapple flowers at the Spring Crabapple Flower Dock weave a brocade of colors; in summer time at Jiashi Pavilion the loquat trees are laden with golden fruit; in autumn the fragrance of the rice flowers wafts to inside the Fragrant Sorghum Wind House; and in winter time pines and bamboos at the Pine Wind and Water Pavilion keep their green in the cold. The Tower of Viewing feasts the eye, the Distant Fragrance Hall invigorates one's sense of smell, and the Rain Listening Hall pleases the ears with the sound of raindrops falling on banana leaves.[41]

EXAMPLES

The Imperial City and Temple of Heaven, Beijing

Confucian teachings emphasize adherence to traditions, the maintenance of hierarchical relations, and respect for authority. The achievement of earthly harmony in the social and political realms serves as a reflection of cosmic ordering principles.

> Confucius firmly believed that harmony within the court would result in a prosperous and powerful reign. Harmony within the family and with nature would bring good fortune and health to the household. Inner harmony and moderation of one's self could bring a well-balanced character, and it is the aim of self-cultivation. Attuning to Heaven came from harmony with nature, obedience to elders brought harmony to the family, therefore, it could be said that the most important of Confucius's teachings, which also influenced architecture, was harmony.[42]

The creation of "imposing buildings expressing a dignity inherent in the concept of the state,"[43] or what could be described as "the architecture of hierarchy,"[44] is, without doubt, no better demonstrated than in the extensive and resplendent Imperial City of Beijing with its numerous axially arranged structures and deeply symbolic program. It is impossible to overstate the vast scale of this architectural complex, "the largest and best-preserved palace complex in the world."[45] Created on the site of earlier Yuan Dynasty (1279–1368) structures, the Imperial City was largely created in the Ming period (1368–1644) and enlarged in the Qing (1644–1911) periods. It served as the center of Chinese government administration and as imperial residence for close to five centuries.

From very ancient times, Chinese emperors were believed to derive their power and authority through heavenly mandate. The emperors, as the Sons of Heaven, were required to offer sacrifices and prayers to heaven and earth to ensure the continued prosperity of the empire. "A principal duty of the Chinese court was to provide ritual feasts for the gods and spirits at imperial altars and temples. From ancient times to the early twentieth century, the emperor regularly offered a ritual feast or sacrifice (*ji*) to Heaven and Earth, the royal ancestors, the gods of grains and soils, sun and moon, stars, and other gods and spirits that reigned over different realms of the cosmos."[46]

Figure 15.11 The Temple of Heaven: Hall of Prayers for a Good Harvest, Beijing, China, early 15th century. Vanni / Art Resource, NY.

The Temple of Heaven complex, located in the outer city area of Beijing, just to the south of the Imperial and Forbidden city enclosures, was constructed to serve these traditional purposes in the early 15th century (ca. 1406–21.) The *Qinian Dian* (or Hall of Prayer for Good Harvests) is one of three major structures in the complex (see Figure 15.11). It is an imposing circular wooden building elevated on a series of three concentric stone platforms that are numerically mirrored in the triple-gabled roof of blue tiles, symbolizing the heavens. Numeric and astronomical symbolism are apparent in the repetition of sets of 12 pillars (signifying the 12 months of the year and hours of the day) and the sets of four columns (representing the seasons of the year). The interior of the building is richly decorated with painted geometric designs, cloud patterns, and imperial dragon emblems. At the apex of the ceiling is a carved and gilded design of a dragon and a phoenix. "In ancient times, the tablets of deceased emperors were placed on a table under the coffered ceiling. Approaching from the long, raised terrace, one crossed the high threshold of the great hall, gradually approaching the centre under the elaborate 60-foot high ceiling. The designer of this temple may have intended the emperor to experience an integration between himself, the heaven above and his ancestors."[47]

The extensive complex of the Imperial City, the core of which contains the Forbidden City, is altogether an absolutely stunning expression of hierarchical authority.

> From the very beginning, it was designed to be a place of display and spectacle . . . . a terrestrial refraction of the realm of the celestial Jade Emperor, or Heavenly Ancestor, and his court which was said to rule over the universe. . . . It was conceived on such a monumental scale so as to awe not only the subjects of China, but also the tributary peoples who lived along the extensive borders of Ming territory. It was also the focal point of imperial rituals and festivals designed to ensure the harmony of heaven, earth, and man.[48]

It consists of a series of imposing gates giving access to a vast and axially laid out, walled, and moated complex of ceremonial and residential structures that progress from south to north along the central axis. The northern area (off limits to all but imperial family and household) contains the imperial residences, including a series of palaces with thousands of rooms placed around courtyards in laby-rinthine complexity. The southern gate (*Tian'anmen*—Gate of Heavenly Peace) gives access into a large courtyard, beyond which the *Tuan Men* gate (Gate of Uprightness) opens into another vast courtyard before the *Wu Men* (Meridian) gate—the entrance into the Forbidden City. The Meridian gate actually comprises five separate entrances or gates, each of which had specific uses.

> The central gateway was reserved for the emperor, although the empress was allowed to pass through it once on her wedding day, and the three top examination candidates passed through it after they had accepted honors in the palace. Royal princes, civil and military officials used the gates on the two sides, while the outer gateways were opened only on the days when the emperor held court. On those days, civil ministers would enter through the east gate and military officials came through the west gate. Candidates for the palace examination filed out according to their examination number: those with odd numbers by way of the gate on the left and those with even numbers through the right.[49]

Inside the Meridian gate, five bridges (with use restricted as just noted) cross over a curved stream (Golden River) to the elevated *T'ai-ho Men* (Gate of Supreme Harmony), beyond which is located the first and most impressive in a series of imposing halls: the *T'ai-ho Tien* (Hall of Supreme Harmony) (see Plate 29). This large and richly decorated rectangular wooden structure, elevated on three marble platforms, served as the imperial audience hall where the emperors held court. The distance from the outer city gate (*Yung Ting Men*)—near which the Temple of Heaven is located—to the imperial audience hall is approximately three miles.

> This whole axial approach was consciously designed to provide a suitably impressive setting for emperors who considered themselves the mightiest rulers on earth. At no point can one see the entire route or final destination. The axis unfolds instead as a staged series of spaces, progressing logically from one to the next, and it is the cumulative experience of the sequence that gives it measured dignity and power. It may also be interpreted as a supreme expression of Confucian teachings regarding hierarchy and deference to authority.[50]

Beyond the Hall of Supreme Harmony are the axially located Hall of Complete Harmony and Hall of Preserving Harmony (used for preparation and rehearsing of ceremonies). The Gate of Heavenly Purity leads to the inner court area of the imperial residences: the Palace of Heavenly Purity (occupied by the emperor), the Palace of Earthly Tranquility (occupied by the empress), and the Hall of Union. The Hall of Mental Cultivation, numerous other courtyards and structures to the east and west (occupied by the emperor's concubines and children), and the imperial gardens are also found within the northern area of this vast complex. The *Shen Wu* gate (Gate of Divine Might or Spiritual Prowess) marks the northern end of the Forbidden City.

Although the specific functions of the various structures within the complex varied slightly through the centuries, and shrines for Taoist as well as Buddhist worship are found within the complex as well, the overall ambiance of authoritative organization, strict attention to protocol, and hierarchical order can be well seen as reflections of Confucian values founded in ancient Chinese rituals and traditions (see Plate 30).

NOTES

1. "The absence of the word 'religion' in the Chinese language before the nineteenth century . . . should alert us to the complex ways that the activities Western scholars tend to group together under the rubric of religion are themselves distributed and dispersed throughout some societies in uneven and unpredictable ways. In the ancient Chinese typology of ritual, 'religion'—specifically the liturgical form of religious practice on the auspicious rites—was subsumed under a broader category of 'ritual.'" Thomas Wilson, "Sacrifice and the Imperial Cult of Confucius," *History of Religions* 41, no. 3 (2002), 254–55.

2. Rodney Taylor, *The Religious Dimensions of Confucianism* (Albany: State University of New York Press, 1990), 1–2.

3. John Chinnery, "Confucianism," in *Eastern Wisdom: An Illustrated Guide to the Religions and Philosophies of the East,* ed. C. Scott Littleton (New York: Henry Holt, 1996), 92.

4. Barry Steben, "Confucius," in *Holy People of the World: A Cross-Cultural Encyclopedia,* ed. Phyllis Jestice, vol. 1 (Santa Barbara, CA: ABC-CLIO, 2004), 200.

5. Jennifer Oldstone-Moore, "Confucianism," in *Eastern Religions: Hinduism, Buddhism, Taoism, Confucianism, Shinto,* ed. Michael Coogan (New York: Oxford University Press, 2005), 324–25.

6. Chinnery, 94.

7. Burton Watson, trans., *The Analects of Confucius* (New York: Columbia University Press, 2007), 1.

8. Watson, 7.

9. Chinnery, 111.

10. Judith Berling, *The Syncretic Religion of Lin Chao-en* (New York: Columbia University Press, 1980).

11. Léon Vandermeersh, "From Pyroscapulimancy to Writing," in *A History of Writing: From Hieroglyph to Multimedia,* ed. Anne-Marie Christin (Paris: Flammarion, 2002), 90–91.

12. Oldstone-Moore, "Confucianism," in *Eastern Religions,* ed. Coogan, 323.

13. Oldstone-Moore, "Confucianism," in *Eastern Religions,* ed. Coogan, 323.

14. Chinnery, 102.

15. Chinnery, 102–3.

16. Jennifer Oldstone-Moore, "Chinese Traditions," in *The Illustrated Guide to World Religions,* ed. Michael Coogan (Oxford: Oxford University Press, 2003), 217.

17. Romeyn Taylor, "Official Altars, Temples, and Shrines Mandated for All Counties in Ming and Qing," *T'oung Pao* 83, no. 1–3 (1997): 94.

18. Oldstone-Moore, "Confucianism," in *Eastern Religions,* ed. Coogan, 336–37.

19. Wilson, "Sacrifice and the Imperial Cult of Confucius," 253.

20. Chinnery, 107.

21. Thomas Wilson, ed., *On Sacred Grounds: Culture, Society, Politics, and the Formation of the Cult of Confucius* (Cambridge, MA: Harvard University Press, 2002).

22. Wang Liang, "The Confucius Temple Tragedy of the Cultural Revolution," in *On Sacred Grounds: Culture, Society, Politics, and the Formation of the Cult of Confucius*, ed. Thomas Wilson (Cambridge, MA: Harvard University Press, 2002), 376–98.

23. Official documents record that this was "a 'large beast' (*tailao*) sacrifice of an ox, goat, and pig . . . The earliest record of this sacrifice, written a century later, provides no other details of the ceremony, and it gives no indication that any ancient precedent for the rite was explicitly invoked by the emperor, or the court historian who recorded the event." Wilson, "Sacrifice and the Imperial Cult of Confucius," 259.

24. Oldstone-Moore, "Confucianism," in *Eastern Religions*, ed. Coogan, 374.

25. Thomas Wilson, "The Ritual Formation of Confucian Orthodoxy and the Descendants of the Sage," *The Journal of Asian Studies* 55, no. 3 (1996): 559–84.

26. Wilson, "Sacrifice and the Imperial Cult of Confucius," 252. See also Leon Stover, *Imperial China and the State Cult of Confucius* (Jefferson, NC: McFarland, 2005).

27. See the excellent discussion and helpful diagrams in Laurence Liu, *Chinese Architecture* (New York: Rizzoli, 1989), 27–33.

28. Julia Murray, "Illustrations of the Life of Confucius: Their Evolution, Functions, and Significance in Late Ming China," *Artibus Asiae* 57, no. 1–2 (1997): 75.

29. Murray, "Illustrations," 75.

30. Julia Murray, "The Hangzhou Portraits of Confucius and Seventy-Two Disciples (*Shengxian tu*): Art in the Service of Politics," *The Art Bulletin* 74, no. 1 (1992): 7–18.

31. Murray, "Illustrations," 74.

32. Julia Murray, "The Temple of Confucius and Pictorial Biographies of the Sage," *The Journal of Asian Studies* 55, no. 2 (1996): 269–300; and Julia Murray, "Varied Views of the Sage: Illustrated Narratives of the Life of Confucius," in *On Sacred Grounds: Culture, Society, Politics, and the Formation of the Cult of Confucius*, ed. Thomas Wilson (Cambridge, MA: Harvard University Press, 2002), 222–64.

33. Murray, "Illustrations," 80.

34. Murray, "Illustrations," 80.

35. See Anne Farrer, *"The Brush Dances and the Ink Sings": Chinese Paintings and Calligraphy from the British Museum* (London: Hayward Gallery, 1990); and Chu-Tsing Li and James Watt, *The Chinese Scholar's Studio, Artistic Life in the Late Ming Period* (New York: Thames and Hudson, 1987).

36. Lothar Ledderose, "The Earthly Paradise: Religious Elements in Chinese Landscape Art," in *Theories of the Arts in China*, ed. Susan Bush and Christian Murck (Princeton, NJ: Princeton University Press, 1983), 165.

37. Anne Farrer, "Calligraphy and Painting for Official Life," in *The British Museum Book of Chinese Art*, ed. Jessica Rawson (London: The British Museum Press, 1992), 115.

38. James Cahill, *Parting at the Shore: Chinese Painting of the Early and Middle Ming Dynasty, 1368–1580* (New York: Weatherhill, 1978), 91.

39. Michael Sullivan, *The Arts of China* (Berkeley: University of California Press, 1999), 229.

40. Cahill, 238–39.

41. Lou Qingxi, *Chinese Gardens* (Beijing: China Intercontinental Press, 2003), 38.

42. Liu, 19.

43. Liu, 20.

44. Geremie Barmé, *The Forbidden City* (Cambridge, MA: Harvard University Press, 2008), 25.

45. Lou Qingxi, *The Architectural Art of Ancient China* (Beijing: China Intercontinental Press, 2001), 21.

46. Wilson, "Sacrifice and the Imperial Cult of Confucius," 251.

47. Liu, 39.

48. Barmé, xi.

49. Yu Zhuoyun, *Palaces of the Forbidden City* (New York: Viking, 1984), 39.

50. Marian Moffett, Michael Fazio, and Lawrence Wodehouse, *A World History of Architecture* (Boston: McGraw Hill, 2004), 96.

BIBLIOGRAPHY AND FURTHER READING

Barmé, Geremie. *The Forbidden City.* Cambridge, MA: Harvard University Press, 2008.

Berling, Judith. *The Syncretic Religion of Lin Chao-en.* New York: Columbia University Press, 1980.

Bush, Susan, and Christian Murck, eds. *Theories of the Arts in China.* Princeton, NJ: Princeton University Press, 1983.

Cahill, James. *Parting at the Shore: Chinese Painting of the Early and Middle Ming Dynasty, 1368–1580.* New York: Weatherhill, 1978.

Chinnery, John. "Confucianism." In *Eastern Wisdom: An Illustrated Guide to the Religions and Philosophies of the East,* ed. C. Scott Littleton, 92–115. New York: Henry Holt, 1996.

Christin, Anne-Marie, ed. *A History of Writing: From Hieroglyph to Multimedia.* Paris: Flammarion, 2002.

Coogan, Michael, ed. *Eastern Religions: Hinduism, Buddhism, Taoism, Confucianism, Shinto.* New York: Oxford University Press, 2005.

Coogan, Michael, ed. *The Illustrated Guide to World Religions.* Oxford: Oxford University Press, 2003.

Farrer, Anne. *"The Brush Dances and the Ink Sings": Chinese Paintings and Calligraphy from the British Museum.* London: Hayward Gallery, 1990.

Farrer, Anne. "Calligraphy and Painting for Official Life." In *The British Museum Book of Chinese Art,* ed. Jessica Rawson, 84–133. London: The British Museum Press, 1992.

Jestice, Phyllis, ed. *Holy People of the World: A Cross-Cultural Encyclopedia,* 3 vols. Santa Barbara, CA: ABC-CLIO, 2004.

Jiajin, Zhu. *Treasures of the Forbidden City.* New York: Viking, 1986.

Johnson, David. "'Confucian' Elements in the Great Temple Festivals of Southeastern Shansi in Late Imperial Times." *T'oung Pao* 83, no. 1–3 (1997): 126–61.

Ledderose, Lothar. "The Earthly Paradise: Religious Elements in Chinese Landscape Art." In *Theories of the Arts in China,* ed. Susan Bush and Christian Murck, 165–83. Princeton, NJ: Princeton University Press, 1983.

Li, Chu-Tsing, and James Watt. *The Chinese Scholar's Studio, Artistic Life in the Late Ming Period.* New York: Thames and Hudson, 1987.

Liang, Wang. "The Confucius Temple Tragedy of the Cultural Revolution." In *On Sacred Grounds: Culture, Society, Politics, and the Formation of the Cult of Confucius,* ed. Thomas Wilson, 376–98. Cambridge, MA: Harvard University Press, 2002.

Littleton, C. Scott, ed. *Eastern Wisdom: An Illustrated Guide to the Religions and Philosophies of the East*. New York: Henry Holt, 1996.

Liu, Laurence. *Chinese Architecture*. New York: Rizzoli, 1989.

Mac Farquhar, Roderick. *The Forbidden City*. New York: Newsweek, 1981.

Moffett, Marian, Michael Fazio, and Lawrence Wodehouse. *A World History of Architecture*. Boston: McGraw Hill, 2004.

Murck, Alfreda, and Wen Fong, eds. *Words and Images: Chinese Poetry, Calligraphy, and Painting*. New York: Metropolitan Museum of Art, 1991.

Murray, Julia. "The Hangzhou Portraits of Confucius and Seventy-Two Disciples (*Shengxian tu*): Art in the Service of Politics." *The Art Bulletin* 74, no. 1 (1992): 7–18.

Murray, Julia. "Illustrations of the Life of Confucius: Their Evolution, Functions, and Significance in Late Ming China." *Artibus Asiae* 57, no. 1–2 (1997): 73–134.

Murray, Julia. "The Temple of Confucius and Pictorial Biographies of the Sage." *The Journal of Asian Studies* 55, no. 2 (1996): 269–300.

Murray, Julia. "Varied Views of the Sage: Illustrated Narratives of the Life of Confucius." In *On Sacred Grounds: Culture, Society, Politics, and the Formation of the Cult of Confucius*, ed. Thomas Wilson, 222–64. Cambridge, MA: Harvard University Press, 2002.

Oldstone-Moore, Jennifer. "Chinese Traditions." In *The Illustrated Guide to World Religions*, ed. Michael Coogan, 198–235. Oxford: Oxford University Press, 2003.

Oldstone-Moore, Jennifer. "Confucianism." In *Eastern Religions: Hinduism, Buddhism, Taoism, Confucianism, Shinto*, ed. Michael Coogan, 315–416. New York: Oxford University Press, 2005.

Qingxi, Lou. *The Architectural Art of Ancient China*. Beijing: China Intercontinental Press, 2001.

Qingxi, Lou. *Chinese Gardens*. Beijing: China Intercontinental Press, 2003.

Rawson, Jessica, ed. *The British Museum Book of Chinese Art*. London: The British Museum Press, 1992.

Seckel, Dietrich. "The Rise of Portraiture in Chinese Art." *Artibus Asiae* 53, no. 1–2 (1993): 7–26.

Sickman, Laurence, and Alexander Soper. *The Art and Architecture of China*. New Haven, CT: Yale University Press, 1992.

Steben, Barry. "Confucius." Vol. 1 of *Holy People of the World: A Cross-Cultural Encyclopedia*, ed. Phyllis Jestice, 199–201. Santa Barbara, CA: ABC-CLIO, 2004.

Steinhardt, Nancy, ed. *Chinese Architecture*. New Haven, CT: Yale University Press, 2002.

Stover, Leon. *Imperial China and the State Cult of Confucius*. Jefferson, NC: McFarland, 2005.

Sullivan, Michael. *The Arts of China*. Berkeley: University of California Press, 1999.

Taylor, Romeyn. "Official Altars, Temples, and Shrines Mandated for All Counties in Ming and Qing." *T'oung Pao* 83, no. 1–3 (1997): 93–125.

Taylor, Rodney. *The Religious Dimensions of Confucianism*. Albany: State University of New York Press, 1990.

Vandermeersh, Léon. "From Pyroscapulimancy to Writing." In *A History of Writing: From Hieroglyph to Multimedia*, ed. Anne-Marie Christin, 90–91. Paris: Flammarion, 2002.

Watson, Burton, trans. *The Analects of Confucius*. New York: Columbia University Press, 2007.

Watson, William. *The Arts of China 900–1620*. New Haven, CT: Yale University Press, 2000.

Wilson, Marc, and Kwan Wong. *Friends of Wen Cheng-Ming: A View from the Crawford Collection*. New York: China Institute in America, 1974.

Wilson, Thomas, ed. *On Sacred Grounds: Culture, Society, Politics, and the Formation of the Cult of Confucius*. Cambridge, MA: Harvard University Press, 2002.

Wilson, Thomas, ed. "The Ritual Formation of Confucian Orthodoxy and the Descendants of the Sage." *The Journal of Asian Studies* 55, no. 3 (1996): 559–84.

Wilson, Thomas, ed. "Sacrifice and the Imperial Cult of Confucius." *History of Religions* 41, no. 3 (2002): 251–87.

Zhuoyun, Yu. *Palaces of the Forbidden City*. New York: Viking, 1984.

–16–

Shinto

ORIGINS AND DEVELOPMENT

Shinto has often been described as one of the world's oldest religious systems that is still practiced today. On the other hand, Shinto has also been described as an invention of the modern period. Both descriptions of Shinto are true, to some extent. The term *Shinto* derives from the translation, into Japanese, of the Chinese words *shen* (spirit) and *dao* (way). Shinto thus means the "way of the spirits" (or gods, or *kami*). Shinto is the native religion of Japan and still today, to a large extent, influences significant aspects of Japanese culture.

The roots of Shinto can be traced to the prehistoric period in Japan. Although the belief systems and religious practices of the very ancient Jomon period (12,500–300 BCE) are far from clearly understood, many scholars believe that the origins of Shinto practices of ancestral and spirit veneration are evidenced in the Jomon period. Certainly, by the later prehistoric period and specifically in the Yayoi culture (ca. 300 BCE–300 CE), archaeological finds reveal artifacts that seem to clearly indicate the development of beliefs and practices characteristic of later Shintoism. These artifacts (ritual objects and grave goods) include miniature grain storehouses, vessels for food and offerings, curved jewels (*magatama*), sacred spears and swords (*katana*), and ceremonial mirrors (*kagami*). Many of these objects figure prominently in later Shinto art and are associated with specific values; honesty is symbolized by the mirror, compassion is symbolized by the jewels, and wisdom is associated with the sword (see Figures 16.1 and 16.2).

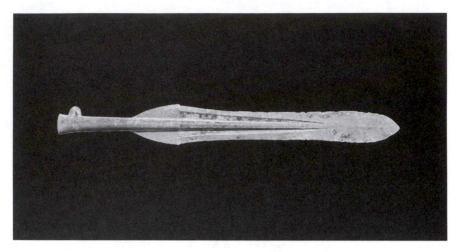

Figure 16.1 Ritual spear blade, Yayoi period, Japan, ca. 300 BCE to 300 CE. London: British Museum. Erich Lessing / Art Resource, NY.

Through subsequent eras of Japanese history, Shinto beliefs became increasingly more defined, especially with the introduction of Buddhism, Confucianism, and Taoism, belief systems that reached Japan (through China and Korea) in the middle of the sixth century CE. Previous to this, it is doubtful that the religion was understood as anything other than the ancient, local, traditional beliefs that varied somewhat from region to region. Patron deities and the venerable ancestors of individual clans were worshiped; there were no written texts that described specific tenets or practices. "The concept of Shinto itself, in many respects, came about as a result of the entry of Buddhism into Japan."[1]

Buddhism was declared the official religion of the Japanese imperial court between the late sixth and early seventh century, and Shinto continued to exist in harmony with Buddhism, often with no sense of great distinction between the two. "Buddhists did not attempt to undermine or supplant Shinto, but simply founded their temples next to Shinto shrines and proclaimed that there was no fundamental conflict between the two faiths."[2] Indeed, as both Buddhism and Shintoism continued to develop in Japan during the medieval period, mutual influences and modifications resulted in what is known as *Ryobu* or "Double Shinto"—a sharing of deities and practices understood to have similar or supporting roles and meanings. "*Ryobu* Shinto became a form . . . that could be performed . . . without much concern about whether the practice was 'Shinto' or 'Buddhist.'"[3] Under the influence of Buddhism, Shinto adopted many Buddhist deities; conversely, many Shinto deities were subsumed into Buddhism and significantly influenced the development of Buddhism in Japan. Shinto and Buddhist art and architectural forms also mutually influenced each other.

Although Buddhism was the dominant belief system in Japan under the Tokugawa shogunate (1603–1867), the renewed interest in ancient Japanese texts during the 18th century by a number of Japanese scholars ultimately contributed to the greater understanding of Shinto as the native or indigenous religion of Japan. The Native Studies or National Learning Movement was especially led by the scholar Motoori Norinaga (1730–1800) whose studies and interpretations of ancient historical and mythological texts were instrumental in defining Shinto as the true religion of Japan. His writings, as well as those by Hirata Atsutane (1776–1843), ultimately intermingled dramatically with politics in the later 19th century and the first half of the 20th century. "A nostalgic, romanticized view of the past developed around the idea that there was something especially special and distinctive about being Japanese—and this essence was intricately intertwined with Shinto."[4]

Figure 16.2 Bronze mirror, middle Kofun period, Japan, fourth century CE. The Art Archive / Musée Guimet Paris / Gianni Dagli Orti.

Thus, following the formal restoration of imperial power under Emperor Meiji in 1868, Shintoism, with its emphasis on the divine lineage of Japanese rulers, became seen as the official religion of Japan. State Shinto or Shrine Shinto, with definitively nationalistic and political connotations, existed in Japan up until the end of World War II. Buddhism and Shinto were formally separated during the Meiji period. "Shinto precincts within former Buddhist complexes had to be walled off into separate compounds containing no images or structures related to Buddhism; only Shinto priests could head a shrine; government support of Buddhist temples ended."[5] The policy of *shimbutsu bunri*—the dissociation of Shinto and Buddhist deities—had very dramatic consequences on the history of Japan and on the arts. Much Buddhist art in Japan was destroyed; monasteries and temples were closed down; statues, paintings, ritual implements, and documents were obliterated; and "the government pretended to return to the 'real' source of Japanese identity and religious consciousness."[6]

Although the Meiji Constitution of 1889 ostensibly granted religious freedom in Japan, practitioners of all faiths and sects needed to recognize Shrine Shinto. According to government directives, Shrine Shinto was not considered or construed to be a religion, but rather a civic responsibility, and hence could be supported, funded, and promulgated by the government.

> Nowhere else in modern history do we find so pronounced an example of state sponsorship of a religion—in some respects the state can be said to have created Shinto as its official "tradition," but in the process Shinto was irrevocably changed . . . [and] in the end, Shinto, as adopted by the modern Japanese state, was largely an invented tradition.[7]

In 1945, at the end of World War II, the Japanese emperor renounced his claims to divinity, and the 1947 Constitution of Japan prohibited the new Japanese government from being formally involved with religion. In modern-day Japan, however, Shinto "continues to thrive and to command the affection, if not absolute loyalty, of the majority of the Japanese people. Indeed, in a great many respects, to be Japanese is to be Shinto, no matter what other religions one espouses."[8]

Although the roots of Shintoism can be traced back to prehistoric times in Japan, it is important to note that Shinto claims no single founder, enlightened being, or prophet whose personal experiences with the divine inspired the belief system. Shinto is not understood to be a revealed religion in the same sense that, for example, Christianity, Buddhism, and Islam are seen by adherents to those faiths, which follow the words, teachings, and revelations of Jesus, Buddha, and Muhammad. In contrast, Shinto appears to confidently assert the fundamental correctness and inherent naturalness of the basic beliefs that are intimately connected with the experiences and history of the Japanese people.

Similarly, Shinto does not have scriptural texts—any body of writings that are seen as especially sacred or divinely inspired. Although extremely significant texts about Shinto (including descriptions of creation stories and the early history of Japan) were composed in the eighth century CE and later, these writings are generally not regarded with quite the same degree of reverence with which Christians, for example, regard the Bible, and with which Muslims regard the Qur'an. Shinto texts such as the *Kojiki* (Record of Ancient Matters, ca. 712—the oldest surviving text written in Japanese, authored by Ono Yasumaro),[9] the *Nihonshoki* (Chronicles of Japan, ca. 720),[10] the *Manyoshu* (Collection of 10,000 Leaves, ca. 760), and the *Engishiki* (a collection of laws, prayers, and directions for Shinto ritual, composed in the late 10th century) contain mixtures of legends, history, mythology, and poetry. Although these writings can be described as sacred texts for Shinto and are certainly regarded with great esteem, they are not generally seen as divinely inspired.

> Shinto . . . is amazingly slippery and various. It has no doctrine, no consensus of philosophy or theology. It does not have the formidable logical tradition of the Buddhist sects. In fact, it is nonintellectual. Shinto likes names and forms and dislikes description. It appears at times to be without content, while at other times it seems to have caught the purest essentials of religion.[11]

PRINCIPAL BELIEFS AND KEY PRACTICES

The most important and fundamental belief for Shinto involves the existence of *kami*. The word *kami* is often translated as deities, gods, spirits, "but in fact it designates an extremely wide range of spirit-beings together with a host of mysterious and supernatural forces and 'essences.'"[12] Kami reside in, and give energy to, both animate and inanimate objects throughout the universe. The number of kami is immeasurable. Kami are present in natural landscape features, such as trees, rocks, and waterfalls. The souls of deceased humans are believed to become kami after death, and there are particular kami that are especially significant. Chief among these is the sun goddess, Amaterasu (see Plate 31). Other especially important kami are Susanoo (the god of the sea and storms, the brother of Amaterasu), Tsukiyomi (the moon god), Inari (the god of rice and prosperity, who is the most widely venerated of all), and a host of other kami associated with food-gathering and agricultural activities, such as fishing and the harvest. There is also Hachiman, deity of war, victory, and success (derived from a semi-legendary emperor), whose worship is extremely widespread, and Tenjin (an actual ninth-century court figure) who is the patron of scholarship and learning. There are also regional and family or clan deities (*ujigama*). Kami are not necessarily benevolent; there are also negative or malicious forces known as *oni* (demons) and frightening *obake* (ghosts), all of whom are subject to capricious and human-like behavior to a large extent.[13]

> Shinto maintains that human beings are internally related to *kami* and without this relation people would not be what they are. . . . it is in the inherent nature of *kami* to be interdependent and intimately connected with the world, including human beings. . . . the world is *kami*-filled because the world and *kami* are so interdependent as to be incomplete without one another.[14]

Belief in and veneration of kami is the fundamental requirement of Shinto, although, as mentioned, the Shinto–Buddhist coexistence and mutual interplay through the centuries in Japan has resulted in Buddhist deities and enlightened beings (such as Amida, Kannon, and Jizo) being worshiped as kami and in particular Shinto *kami* being regarded and worshiped as enlightened beings (or *bodhisattvas*) by Buddhists. The system that evolved is known as *shimbutsu-shugo* or *honji-suijaku*. The Buddhist deities were understood to be the original forms (*honji*), and the Shinto kami were incarnations, emanations, or traces of these forms. This complex fusion and assimilation is very well illustrated in art examples discussed later. It has been pointed out that "this ability to grow and change with the times is part of the essential genius of Shinto."[15]

Concurrent with the belief in kami and the importance of venerating, pleasing, and petitioning these elemental forces, Shinto also emphasizes the principle of *wa*. *Wa* can be translated as "benign harmony"—an inherent balance to be maintained in one's personal life and in the world at large. *Wa* involves harmony between humans, kami, and nature and needs to be—indeed can be—fostered by specific ritual actions as well as general ethical attitudes. These include a reverence for nature and the natural world, the maintenance of "purity" (both in personal life and in ritual contexts), and a respect for one's group, family, and ancestors.

Nevertheless, one especially salient aspect of Shinto, and one that has had a great deal of impact on the history of Japan generally and in the modern period particularly, is the relationship of Shinto to Japanese politics. The primary historical/mythological texts of Shinto (notably, the *Kojiki* and *Nibonshoki*, composed in the eighth century) describe the kami who created the earth during the primordial Age of the Gods. The coupling of the divine spirits Izanagi and Izanami resulted in the birth of the sun goddess, Amaterasu (the most important Shinto deity), and ultimately, it was understood that Amaterasu's earthly descendant (her great-great-grandson, the legendary Jimmu Tenno) became Japan's first emperor in the seventh century BCE. Similarly, Amaterasu's brother, Susanoo, gave birth to the legendary great lord of the country, Okuni-nushi, the protector of the imperial family. Thus, the imperial ruling class in Japan has long been seen as having divine lineage, and "since the days of Jimmu Tenno the earthly descendants of Amaterasu have ruled Japan as emperors."[16]

Although veneration of the emperor as a divine being (a descendant of Amaterasu) was a traditional Shinto belief, the close relationship between religion and politics was amplified in Japan especially during the Meiji Restoration of imperial power in 1868 and the development of Shrine Shinto. Eighteenth-century scholars (such as Motoori Norinaga) did a great deal to reestablish and promote the emphasis on the imperial cult and the native or indigenous qualities of Shinto as an especially Japanese (versus foreign or imported) belief system. Belief in the divine lineage and veneration of the emperor had always played a role in Shintoism, but it was during the Meiji Restoration that Shinto-ism became especially closely tied with politics and nationalistic sentiments.[17] When the Emperor Meiji died in 1912, a large shrine in Tokyo was constructed to honor his spirit as kami. The Meiji Shrine is still one of the most-visited of all Shinto shrines. The defeat of Japan in World War II destabilized the political associations of Shinto dramatically, although "State Shinto ideology survives on some level in parts of Japanese society"[18] to the present day, perhaps seen especially at highly politicized monuments such as the Yasukuni Shrine in Tokyo (memorial to the spirits—*kami*—of the war dead).[19]

TRADITIONAL ART AND ARCHITECTURAL FORMS

The art and architecture associated with Shinto have a rich history and have undergone many phases and developments through the centuries. Shinto arts have been significantly influenced by Buddhist as well as Taoist art forms, and thus Shinto art and architecture often bear a great resemblance to the art and architectural forms of the other Asian religions with which it has, for the most part, harmoniously coexisted. There are, however, specific aesthetics and particular forms and styles of art and architecture that can be seen as characteristically Shinto.

Because belief in kami is the fundamental aspect of Shinto, the religious art and architecture of Shinto is concentrated on acknowledging, honoring, and communicating with the kami. This takes place primarily in two contexts: the marking or creation of sacred space and the celebration of religious festivals. In both cases, the aim is to achieve and maintain harmony with the kami.

Sacred Places and Spaces

Kami are believed to reside in nature. Thus, the appreciation and veneration of natural landscape features such as waterfalls, rock formations, forests, mountains, caves, and trees is an essential element in Shintoism. Evidence suggests that the earliest Shinto practices of kami-worship took place outdoors, in nature, with no specific architectural forms associated. This is still reflected today by the fact that Shinto shrines are often located in places of particular natural beauty, and the sacredness of special landscape features (such as trees, mountains, and waterfalls) is often signaled via minimal but highly symbolic means (see Figures 16.3 and 16.4).

The practice of constructing specific buildings in which to honor ancestral spirits dates from the prehistoric period in Japan. The styles of these early house-like "shrines" (wooden buildings constructed in the vernacular style) contributed greatly to the development of later Shinto religious architecture.

Figure 16.3　View of Mount Fuji. Courtesy of Shutterstock.

Figure 16.4 The Wedded Rocks at Futamigaura in Ise Bay. Werner Forman / Art Resource, NY.

The specific religious structures constructed by adherents to the Shinto belief system are commonly termed "shrines" in English translation. However, the inadequacy of this translation has been pointed out by some scholars who have argued that the use of the term "shrine" to describe all Shinto architectural constructions really fails to capture the great variation, diversity, and richness of Shinto forms of architecture.[20] There are many terms in Japanese that are used to describe the diverse types of revered worship-sites in Shintoism—for example, *jinya, yashiro, miya, mori,* and *hokura*—some of which are small-scale and local, and others of which are grand and extensive and deserve to be called "temples" or "temple complexes." Oftentimes, Shinto shrines and Buddhist temples are located in close proximity to each other, so we might call these "Shrine-Temple Multiplexes."[21] The term "shrine" (implying an overall diminutive form of architecture) is not a wholly appropriate translation of the several Japanese words for Shinto religious structures that vary widely. "Different words are used in the Japanese language to refer to places of Shinto worship. The type and status of the worship facility determine the particular word used."[22]

It is estimated that there are currently about 100,000 Shinto shrines (of various types) in Japan. Some of these are large-scale complexes located in beautiful landscape settings, and others are small local shrines found in villages and even commonly on rooftops in crowded urban areas.

Although it is important to acknowledge the challenges with terminology-in-translation and with the use of the word "shrine" to describe a diversity of examples, there are some typical features of Shinto shrines that can be seen in both large- and small-scale examples. Traditionally, the sacred area or precinct is signaled by the presence of a symbolic wooden gate or *torii* (see Figures 16.5 and 16.6). Generally, these gates do not have doors but are open constructions of two columns topped by one or two cross beams—the top beam projecting the widest. Sometimes they are actual gates in a fence enclosure surrounding a shrine; often they are freestanding structures. Although traditionally made of wood, they may be constructed with concrete in the modern day. They are often painted red, one of the colors considered sacred to kami.[23]

Other symbolic markers indicating that one is entering a sacred area include *shimenawa* (thick ropes typically woven from rice straw), cloth or paper hangings (*gohei*), and small votive banners on cloth or paper, inscribed with special prayers or requests, which are often attached to fences or twigs stuck in the ground. In the case of a large shrine complex, a ceremonial pathway may lead the visitor through a carefully tended natural landscape, across a pond or a stream, and to a trough or fountain that is always required for the ceremonial washing of hands and mouth (ritual purification) before proceeding further.

A large shrine complex can include a number of buildings. There is always a *honden*, or sanctuary. This is the most sacred area, access to which is often closed to the public. The *honden* contains a symbolic object known as a *shintai*. These vary in form; they can be human-made or natural objects; mirrors

Figure 16.5　The Akino Miyajima Torii. Courtesy of Shutterstock.

Figure 16.6 Kawahara Keiga (ca. 1786–1860), *Visit to a Shinto Temple*, watercolor. The Art Archive/Rijksmuseum voor Volkenkunde Leiden (Leyden)/Gianni Dagli Orti.

are especially common because of their reflective cleanliness and purity. The *shintai* functions as a type of conduit, facilitating object, or "landing site"[24] that assists the kami's appearance, entrance, and visit to the shrine. Separated from the *honden*, Shinto shrine complexes may also have a main hall (or *haiden*) for worshipers. This structure functions as an enclosed area for prayers and other worship services. Seating is often provided in the *haiden*. Food offerings (for example, carefully presented rice, fruit, and sake) to please the kami are a critical Shinto ritual, and an additional building known as a *heiden* (hall of offerings) may be provided for this. Other buildings and structures associated with Shinto shrine complexes may include music halls, dance platforms or stages, offices, treasuries to house sacred and ritual objects, and shops or stalls from which visitors may purchase amulets and wooden prayer boards on which petitions are written. These small prayer boards are often displayed on special racks.

Traditionally, the buildings found in Shinto shrine complexes are constructed of wood, as Buddhist temples in Japan are, as well. Because Buddhism and Shintoism are so closely connected in Japanese history and art, there are many shared stylistic features in architectural forms. The very earliest Shinto shrines, such as at Ise, reveal an aesthetic that places great emphasis on natural materials and simple, clear construction. Typically, the buildings are plain, rectangular wooden structures with sloping thatched roofs, a roof ridge course often marked by a series of projecting horizontal beams (*katsuogi*), and forked finials (*chigi*) that sprout diagonally upward from the roof at each end of the structure. The basic simplicity of these buildings, their use of natural materials, and their general lack of extraneous decoration reflect the Shinto appreciation for purity, harmony, and directness. Under successive waves of influence from Chinese architectural styles, and in connection with the development of Buddhist art styles, later Shinto architecture exhibits more elements of Chinese design (such as upturned gables) and more elaborate color and decoration. *Torii* remain the characteristic marker of a Shinto space, however, in the same way that pagodas characteristically mark Buddhist spaces or areas.

Religious Festivals

Shinto shrines also provide a focus for highly artistic festivals (*matsuri*) that take place throughout the year.[25] Some Shinto festivals are yearly events overlapping with Buddhist festivals; most are purely local festivals, however, and are painstakingly scheduled by the residents of a village or neighborhood area centered around a shrine.[26] *Matsuri* means "to offer worship,"[27] and the purpose of Shinto *matsuri* is to show devotion to the kami. "During *matsuri*, an extraordinary environment is established in order to capture the attention of the deities and to effect a time of interaction during which the benevolence of the *kami* may be sought for the coming period."[28]

Many forms of Shinto art are produced in conjunction with these festivals, which often involve several days of dances, songs, processions, competitions, games, and activities that are designed to attract and please the kami. These festivals are "mass participatory events . . . [with] throngs of people engaging in celebratory behaviour."[29] The highlight of a Shinto *matsuri* is the procession of the *mikoshi*—a portable wooden shrine that is usually carried on poles (like a litter or ark) by a group of bearers. Depending on the size of the *mikoshi* and the number of people participating, the shrine can be carried by two or four people or as many as one hundred people or more. During the *matsuri*, the kami are invited to temporarily reside in the portable shrine (often via ritual transfer of a sacred object from the permanent shrine), and the procession moves with a jostling, tilting, and shaking motion, believed to give pleasure to the *kami*. Other processional structures, such as decorated wagons with tall wooden wheels (*hikiyama*), boat-shaped floats (*fune*), lanterns (*chochin*), huge multi-storied branches of lanterns (*kanto*), and umbrella-like forms (*kasa*) all play a part in *matsuri*. A notable aspect of *matsuri* is the display and wearing of elaborate and vibrant textiles and costumes. Some of the most impressive, exuberant, and remarkable examples of Japanese textile art are associated with these Shinto festivals. Festivals are frequently illustrated or recorded in art as well.

EXAMPLES

Ise Shrine (ca. 680–Present)

Ise Shrine (Figure 16.7), located on the southeast coast of Japan, is considered to be the most sacred Shinto site and still today serves as a major center for pilgrimage. There are many legends surrounding the foundation of the site that emphasize its importance and direct connections with the sun goddess, Amaterasu Omikami, and the Japanese imperial family. These legends, first recorded in the eighth and early ninth century, explain how the goddess herself chose the site by making her wishes known to the imperial princess in the late first century BCE. Later on, in the late fifth century CE, legends additionally recount that Amaterasu appeared in a dream to the emperor and requested that she be joined by Toyouke no Okami, the goddess of grain, who would provide food for her. Because Amaterasu is understood to be the mythical ancestor of the Japanese imperial family, the shrine complex at Ise has always played an important role in Japanese religion as well as politics.

The shrine complex is very extensive and consists of a number of buildings—the earliest of which were originally constructed by the late seventh century. The complex is divided into two major sections: the Naiku (or Inner Shrine, or Imperial Shrine), devoted to the sun goddess Amaterasu, and the Geku (or Outer Shrine,) dedicated to the grain goddess Toyouke. In addition, there are

Figure 16.7   Ise Shrines, 680–present. Art Resource, NY.

numerous other structures (treasuries, worship halls, ancillary shrines, and administrative buildings) that make up the entire complex. There are about 127 shrines and related structures at Ise today. Additionally and significantly, there is also a series of fences that restrict access to the main sanctuaries to priests only.

The architectural forms of the two major sanctuaries (or *shoden*) at Ise, as well as the majority of other buildings at the site, use construction techniques that appear to reflect native Japanese traditions before the introduction of Buddhist architectural styles. The Ise shrines have thus been lauded as exemplars and prototypes of an essentially Japanese style.[30] They have been "regarded as authentic architectural memorials to a remote past,"[31] and the descriptions and photographic images of Ise have been used to support various aims and claims about the essence of Japan aesthetics and native traditions.[32]

The rectangular sanctuary buildings with their raised, one-room interiors are constructed of poles, beams, and planks of Japanese cypress wood and have distinctive thatched roofs of miscanthus reeds. The buildings have no windows, and their primary function is to serve as sacred spaces to house the powerful spirits of the deities in residence. The sanctuaries of the Naiku and Geku differ slightly, but both have the characteristic forms of beam and plank construction, with projecting ridge beams (*katsuogi*) and forked finials (*chigi*). The exteriors are surrounded by verandahs, and a simple staircase leads up to each building. Although of austere and simple architectural construction, the care and attention to details appear in the metal fittings and plaques found on the exterior of the structures, and especially in the many *suedana*—round ornaments made of painted bronze with flame motifs surrounding them.

An important and somewhat unique tradition at Ise is the periodic rebuilding (*shikinen sengu*) of the main sanctuary structures every 20 years. This has continued, with some periods of significant interruption, to the present day. The complete rebuilding of the sanctuaries is a lengthy and costly undertaking and generally takes about eight years to complete. The structures are rebuilt on empty plots within the two precincts, and when the new sanctuary is complete, the older building is dismantled. Of course all buildings (especially wooden ones) require periodic maintenance, but the complete rebuilding of the Ise shrines (last done in 1993) also serves as a significant and symbolic form of the importance of renewal and purification—values so central to Shinto.

Kasuga Mandara ca. 1300

Kasuga is one of the earliest and most important of Shinto shrines. It was established in the seventh century CE under the patronage of the powerful Fujiwara family and is located in a beautiful park-like setting, inhabited by many deer, at the base of the holy mountain, Mount Mikasa. Closely associated with the nearby Buddhist monastery of Kofukuji, the Kasuga-Kofukuji Shrine-Temple complex was a flourishing art center, specializing—particularly from the 13th century onward—in the production of paintings illustrating the sacred buildings and surrounding natural environment[33] (see Plate 32).

Such "representations of sanctified realms where identification between the human and the sacred occurs"[34] have a lengthy tradition in Buddhist art. Buddhist examples of cosmic diagrams (or *mandalas*) take many forms. Different styles and types developed in India and China and are associated with the rituals and visualization practices of specific Buddhist sects. The traditionally more visionary and geometrically ordered *mandala* formats are found in Japanese Buddhist art too, but in Japan, the tradition of illustrating specific places (such as the important Shinto shrine complex of Kasuga) involves the significant depiction of recognizable landscape and architectural elements. The term *mandara* (versus *mandala*) may be more appropriately used here. This term reflects Japanese usage from the early 11th century onward to describe paintings that often show a specific site, "recognizable sacred precincts on earth," and that depict "relationships among deities who manifest themselves at these numinous places."[35]

Many Kasuga (as well as Kumano—another significant Shinto shrine complex) *mandara* were produced during the medieval period in Japan. These were designed to give devotees an opportunity to admire, pray before, and also take a virtual pilgrimage to the sites. Often these *mandara* were created for branch shrines associated with, but located at some distance from, the preeminent sacred site.

The example of the Kasuga *mandara* illustrated here is a small hanging scroll created of ink and watercolor on silk, plus gold and silver pigments and gold leaf details. It depicts an aerial, or bird's eye view, of the Kasuga shrine complex at the foot of Mount Mikasa, which is shown at the top of the painting. The landscape features and architectural elements are laid out in the painting not with a view toward strict topographical exactitude, but rather to give viewers an overall sense of the experience of visiting the sacred site. One visually enters the *torii* gates (at the bottom of the painting) and progresses upward through the landscape filled with trees, sacred deer, and mist. The deer are a special feature of Kasuga and are frequently depicted in art. It is believed that the Kasuga kami arrived to the site riding on deer and that the deer serve as messengers to the kami. They roam freely at the site today. The path, rendered in gold and silver pigments, meanders through the park until the viewer reaches the shrine buildings themselves. The painting depicts the form and layout of the shrine complex as per its 14th-century date. At that point, the shrine complex had grown significantly and consisted of a variety of different structures. Within the main complex, the visitor/viewer can clearly see four separate shrine buildings (*honden*—with characteristic details such as the forked finials, *chigi*) lined up in a row and surrounded by a roofed corridor with a gate and courtyard. These shrines are for the four major Shinto kami worshiped at this site. One additional or subsidiary shrine for the *wakamiya kami* (the youthful offspring of the main kami, a shrine to whom was added to the complex in the 12th century) is placed to the right of the other shrines.

This view of the shrine complex at Kasuga (Figure 16.8) is visually enticing and informative; however, the viewer's eye is constantly drawn to the top of the painting where an orb filled with deities is shown. These figures, who are depicted in a sphere floating above Mount Mikasa, hover over the site in a way that not only is visually intriguing but that also demonstrates the Buddhist–Shinto interplay in ways that non-visual texts really cannot. There are five Buddhist deities depicted in the orb who are understood to be the *honji* (original forms) of the five Shinto *kami* worshiped at the site. Because the Shinto *kami* worshiped at Kasuga are understood to be *suijaku* (emanations, traces, or incarnations) of various Buddhas, this visual example expresses this perfectly and in a direct manner. Other examples of Kasuga *mandara* similarly show the Buddhist deities in relationship to the Shinto kami with whom they are paired.[36] This *honji suijaku* relationship of original forms and their emanations is a significant aspect of the continued Shinto/Buddhist coordination.

The systematic pairing of all the major *kami* did not occur until the eleventh century. While this unique synthesis seems, in theory, to have placed the Shinto *kami*

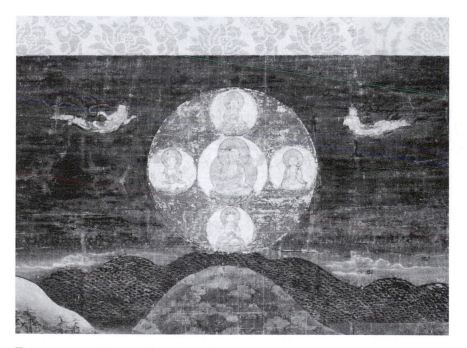

Figure 16.8 Kasuga Shrine *mandara*, ca. 1300, Kamakura period, hanging scroll, detail showing Buddhist deities. The Art Archive / Sylvan Barnet and William Burto Collection.

on a lower plane than the Buddhist deities, in actual practice the development of the *honji suijaku* in no way diminished their status; on the contrary, it vastly enriched the *kami's* radius of religious and cultic connotations.[37]

The *honji suijaku* "interpretation became a religion of its own, which was expressed most clearly in art."[38] In many ways, the visual examples "offer the most compelling examples of the complex syncretism—doctrinal, ritual, visual, and literary—characteristic of the Japanese religion as a whole."[39]

Deified Princess Nakatsu-Hime, Ninth Century

This wooden sculpture (Figure 16.9) is part of a famous triad of images located in the Hachiman shrine of the Yakushi-ji Temple complex in Nara. Three-dimensional figural sculptures for use in shrines, such as this example, began to be produced in Japan probably by the eighth century, and certainly under the influence of Buddhism with its developed traditions of figural arts and wood carving. The worship of Hachiman (deity of war, victory, and success) has a long history in Japan. The origins of the Hachiman cult are partially based on the semi-legendary Emperor Ojin of the third century CE. Hachiman is among the most revered of the kami, evoked for his enormous strength, power, and ability to deal with crises. When the large Buddhist temple complex of the Todai-ji was constructed in Nara in the eighth century, the support of Hachiman was evoked, and he became regarded as the protector and tutelary deity of Todai-ji in 749. Hachiman's rise to prominence and his earliest representations in the visual arts date to this period.[40] Hachiman was, of course, considered to be a major Buddhist *bodhisattva* as well, typical of Shinto–Buddhist synthesis.

In art, Hachiman often appears in the guise of a monk or scholar and is often accompanied by other figures who represent female companions of the Emperor Ojin, such as

Figure 16.9 Wood sculpture of the deified Princess Nakatsu-hime, ninth century. Hachimangu Shrine, Nara, Japan. Werner Forman / Art Resource, NY.

the deified Empress Jingu and the Princess-Goddess Nakatsu-hime. In this example, the Princess-Goddess is seated in a dignified pose and is wearing robes and a hairstyle typical of the imperial court. The bulky, but relatively small, sculpture is carved from a single block of wood and includes painted details of flesh-colored skin, facial features, and garments decorated with green and red details. The clothing and hairstyle are typical of imperial fashion of the ninth century; this reasserts the close connection of Shinto kami with the imperial family and also reflects the important role of female deities in Shinto generally. As a whole the Hachiman triad represents an extremely important early example of the representation of Shinto kami in human form, as well as an early step in the visual and theological merging and overlap of Buddhist and Shinto deities and art styles.

NOTES

1. Ian Reader, *The Simple Guide to Shinto* (Folkestone, England: Global Books, 1998), 33.

2. C. Scott Littleton, *Shinto: Origins, Rituals, Festivals, Spirits, Sacred Places* (New York: Oxford University Press, 2002), 17.

3. Thomas Kasulis, *Shinto: The Way Home* (Honolulu: University of Hawaii Press, 2004), 101.

4. Kasulis, 130.

5. Kasulis, 135.

6. Allan Grapard, "Japan's Ignored Cultural Revolution: The Separation of Shinto and Buddhist Divinities in Meiji ('*Shimbutsu Bunri*') and a Case Study: Tonomine," *History of Religions* 23, no. 3 (1984): 245.

7. Helen Hardacre, *Shinto and the State, 1868–1988* (Princeton, NJ: Princeton University Press, 1989), 3.

8. Littleton, 11.

9. Daniel L. Philippi, trans., *Kojiki* (Princeton, NJ: Princeton University Press, 1969).

10. W. G. Aston, trans., *Nihongi: Chronicles of Japan from the Earliest Times to A.D. 687* (London: Allen and Unwin, 1956; originally published in 1896).

11. Susan Tyler, *The Cult of Kasuga Seen through Its Art* (Ann Arbor: University of Michigan Press, Center for Japanese Studies, 1992), 78.

12. Littleton, 24.

13. "Like the gods of Greek myths, the Japanese *kami* may copulate and procreate, argue, fight, have ambitions, seek to be the most important deity, and occasionally sulk when they do not get their way. They are earthy, and manifest a bawdy humour, enjoy life, get drunk and generally behave in a very humanesque way. They may also exhibit a potential for malevolence and the capacity to be dangerous and harmful to life." Reader, 42.

14. Kasulis, 17.

15. Littleton, 33.

16. Littleton, 30.

17. Helen Hardacre, "Creating State Shinto: The Great Promulgation Campaign and the New Religions," *Journal of Japanese Studies* 12, no. 1 (1986): 29–63.

18. Kasulis, 147.

19. John Nelson, "Social Memory as Ritual Practice: Commemorating Spirits of the Military Dead at Yasukuni Shinto Shrine," *The Journal of Asian Studies* 62, no. 1 (2003): 443–67.

20. Peter Metevelis, "Shinto Shrines or Shinto Temples?" *Asian Folklore Studies* 53, no. 2 (1994): 337–45.

21. Allan Grapard, "Institution, Ritual, and Ideology: The Twenty-Two Shrine-Temple Multiplexes of Heian Japan," *History of Religions* 27, no. 3 (1988): 246–69.

22. Metevelis, 338.

23. Blue (or green), yellow, red, white, and black (or purple) are considered the five sacred colors. This is "a scheme originating in early Indian and Taoist aesthetics, which persists to the present time in cultures throughout Asia." Gloria Granz Gonick, *Matsuri! Japanese Festival Arts* (Los Angeles: University of California at Los Angeles, Fowler Museum of Cultural History, 2002), 46.

24. Allan Grapard, "Flying Mountains and Walkers of Emptiness: Toward a Definition of Sacred Space in Japanese Religions," *History of Religions* 21, no. 3 (February 1982): 197.

25. The bibliography on Matsuri is extensive. An excellent colorful introduction is Hiroyuki Ozawa, *The Great Festivals of Japan: Spectacle and Spirit* (New York: Kodansha America, 1999).

26. C. Scott Littleton, "The Organization and Management of a Tokyo Shinto Shrine Festival," *Ethnology* 25, no. 3 (1986): 195–202.

27. Gonick, 25.

28. Gonick, 25.

29. Reader, 20.

30. Kenzo Tange and Noboru Kawazoe, *Ise: Prototype of Japanese Architecture* (Cambridge, MA: The Massachusetts Institute of Technology Press, 1965).

31. Yasutada Watanabe, *Shinto Art: Ise and Izumo Shrines* (New York: Weatherhill, 1974), 14.

32. Jonathan Reynolds, "Ise Shrine and a Modernist Construction of Japanese Tradition," *The Art Bulletin* 83, no. 2 (2001): 316–41.

33. See Tyler, *The Cult of Kasuga.*

34. Elizabeth ten Grotenhuis, *Japanese Mandalas: Representations of Sacred Geography* (Honolulu: University of Hawaii Press, 1994), 1.

35. Ten Grotenhuis, 143.

36. "In the center of the group sits the historical buddha Sakyamuni, the *honji* of Takemikazuchi of the first Kasuga sanctuary. Above Sakyamuni appears Yakushi, the *honji* of Futsunushi of the second Kasuga sanctuary. To the right of Sakyamuni sits Jizo, the *honji* of Ame no koyane of the third Kasuga sanctuary. To the left of Sayamuni appears the eleven-headed Kannon, the *honji* of Himegami of the fourth Kasuga sanctuary. Just below Sakyamuni sits the bodhisattva Monju, the *honji* of the Kasuga wakamiya." Ten Grotenhuis, 153.

37. Haruki Kageyama and Christine Guth Kanda, *Shinto Arts: Nature, Gods, and Man in Japan* (New York: Japan Society, 1976), 18.

38. Tyler, 75.

39. Ten Grotenhuis, 184.

40. Christine Guth Kanda, "Kaikei's Statue of Hachiman in Todai-ji," *Artibus Asiae* 43, no. 3 (1981–82): 190–208; and Christine Guth Kanda, *Shinzo: Hachiman Imagery and Its Development* (Cambridge, MA: Harvard University Council on East Asian Studies, 1985).

BIBLIOGRAPHY AND FURTHER READING

Alex, William. *Japanese Architecture*. New York: George Braziller, 1963.

Ashkenazi, Michael. *Matsuri: Festivals of a Japanese Town*. Honolulu: University of Hawaii Press, 1993.

Aston, W. G., trans. *Nihongi: Chronicles of Japan from the Earliest Times to A.D. 687*. London: Allen and Unwin, 1956 (originally published in 1896).

Earhart, H. Byron. *Japanese Religion: Unity and Diversity*. Belmont, CA: Wadsworth, 1983.

Encyclopedia of Shinto. http://eos.kokugakuin.ac.jp/modules/xwords/.

Gonick, Gloria Granz. *Matsuri! Japanese Festival Arts*. Los Angeles: University of California at Los Angeles Fowler Museum of Cultural History, 2002.

Grapard, Allan. "Flying Mountains and Walkers of Emptiness: Toward a Definition of Sacred Space in Japanese Religions." *History of Religions* 21, no. 3 (1982): 195–221.

Grapard, Allan. "Institution, Ritual, and Ideology: The Twenty-Two Shrine-Temple Multiplexes of Heian Japan." *History of Religions* 27, no. 3 (1988): 246–69.

Grapard, Allan. "Japan's Ignored Cultural Revolution: The Separation of Shinto and Buddhist Divinities in Meiji ('Shimbutso Bunri') and a Case Study: Tonomine." *History of Religions* 23, no. 3 (1984): 240–65.

Hardacre, Helen. "Creating State Shinto: The Great Promulgation Campaign and the New Religions." *Journal of Japanese Studies* 12, no. 1 (1986): 29–63.

Hardacre, Helen. *Shinto and the State: 1868–1988*. Princeton, NJ: Princeton University Press, 1989.

Harris, Victor, ed. *Shinto: The Sacred Art of Ancient Japan*. London: British Museum, 2001.

Kageyama, Haruki. *The Arts of Shinto*. New York: Weatherhill, 1973.

Kageyama, Haruki, and Christine Guth Kanda. *Shinto Arts: Nature, Gods, and Man in Japan*. New York: Japan Society, 1976.

Kanda, Christine Guth. "Kaikei's Statue of Hachiman at Todai-ji." *Artibus Asiae* 43, no. 3 (1981–82): 190–208.

Kanda, Christine Guth. *Shinzo: Hachiman Imagery and Its Development*. Cambridge, MA: Harvard University Council on East Asian Studies, 1985.

Kasulis, Thomas. *Shinto: The Way Home*. Honolulu: University of Hawaii Press, 2004.

Kuroda Toshio. "Shinto in the History of Japanese Religion." *Journal of Japanese Studies* 7, no. 1 (1981): 1–21.

Littleton, C. Scott. "The Organization and Management of a Tokyo Shinto Shrine Festival." *Ethnology* 25, no. 3 (1986): 195–202.

Littleton, C. Scott. *Shinto: Origins, Rituals, Festivals, Spirits, Sacred Places*. New York: Oxford University Press, 2002.

Metevelis, Peter. "Shinto Shrines or Shinto Temples?" *Asian Folklore Studies* 53, no. 2 (1994): 337–45.

Nelson, John. *Enduring Identities: The Guise of Shinto in Contemporary Japan*. Honolulu: University of Hawaii Press, 2000.

Nelson, John. "Social Memory as Ritual Practice: Commemorating Spirits of the Military Dead at Yasukuni Shinto Shrine." *The Journal of Asian Studies* 62, no. 1 (2003): 443–67.

Nelson, John. *A Year in the Life of a Shinto Shrine*. Seattle: University of Washington Press, 1996.

Ozawa, Hiroyuki. *The Great Festivals of Japan: Spectacle and Spirit*. New York: Kodansha America, 1999.

Paine, Robert Treat, and Alexander Soper. *The Art and Architecture of Japan*. New Haven, CT: Yale University Press, 1992.

Philippi, Daniel L., trans. *Kojiki*. Princeton, NJ: Princeton University Press, 1969.

Picken, Stuart D. B. *Essentials of Shinto: An Analytical Guide to Principal Teachings*. Westport, CT: Greenwood Press, 1994.

Plutschow, Herbert. *Matsuri: The Festivals of Japan*. Richmond, Surrey: Japan Library, 1996.

Reader, Ian. *The Simple Guide to Shinto*. Folkestone, England: Global Books, 1998.

Reynolds, Jonathon. "Ise Shrine and a Modernist Construction of Japanese Tradition." *The Art Bulletin* 58, no. 2 (2001): 316–41.

Sacred Spaces in Shinto. http://www.orias.berkeley.edu/visuals/japan-visuals/shinto.

Sharma, Arvind, ed. *Religion and Women*. Albany: State University of New York Press, 1994.

Tange, Kenzo and Noboru Kawazoe. *Ise: Prototype of Japanese Architecture*. Cambridge, MA: The Massachusetts Institute of Technology Press, 1965.

Ten Grotenhuis, Elizabeth. *Japanese Mandalas: Representations of Sacred Geography*. Honolulu: University of Hawaii Press, 1994.

Tyler, Royall. *The Miracles of the Kasuga Deity*. New York: Columbia University Press, 1990.

Tyler, Susan. *The Cult of Kasuga Seen through Its Art*. Ann Arbor: University of Michigan Press, Center for Japanese Studies, 1992.

Watanabe, Yasutada. *Shinto Art: Ise and Izumo Shrines*. New York: Weatherhill, 1974.

Yusa, Michiko. "Women in Shinto: Images Remembered." In *Religion and Women*, ed. Arvind Sharma, 92–119. Albany: State University of New York Press, 1994.

Conclusion

These volumes opened with a quote from the influential world leader and visionary Mahatma Gandhi (1869–1948) in which he expressed his belief that "a friendly study of the world's religions is a sacred duty."[1] In the same 1926 article, Gandhi, a devout Hindu, went on to say that his interest in and study of the world's religions had enriched his life and perspective in immeasurable ways. This has humbly been the goal of these volumes—not only to provide information about the world's religions but also to promote a respectful and enriching awareness of the diversity of faiths and their visual forms.

Many different forms of religious art have been considered in these volumes, ranging from the small scale to the monumental, from the deliberately ephemeral to the decidedly enduring. Readers will have found that many quite well-known works of religious art and architecture have been described yet again in these volumes. These include several of the most familiar monuments customarily considered to be among the greatest artistic accomplishments of humankind. Any overall survey of the world's religious art necessarily needs to include coverage of the impressive temples of ancient Egypt, the soaring cathedrals of medieval Europe, and the richly decorated monuments of Hindu architecture, for example. Studies of the world's religious art will necessarily also include many examples of painting and sculpture, such as images of holy figures, pictorial scenes representing important historical or mythological events, and numerous other detailed or abbreviated visual symbols developed and used by different faith traditions to teach and inspire. This survey thus discussed many examples of religious imagery and symbolism, from Christian images of Mary and Jesus to the devotional, meditative, and complex imagery employed in Tibetan Buddhist practices.

Conclusion

Much attention was given in this study also to the visible forms of religious expression that do not fall so neatly or comfortably into the categories of architecture, painting, and sculpture—at least in their permanent forms. Readers will thus have encountered, in these volumes, many examples of more temporary forms of religious visual expression, forms of art created for religious purposes but that are designed to serve their powerful functions on a short-term basis. For example, the images and complex traditions of symbols used in Navajo sand paintings, Melanesian *malagan* sculptures, and the many examples of African masking and dance ceremonies all serve to create sacred space and enact religious events in relatively temporary forms as well.

The materials discussed in these volumes have also represented an enormous geographic and chronological range, with selections made from a sweeping range of dates, chosen from around the world. Readers may thus have found a rather dizzying range of materials included, from prehistory to the modern period. Of course, the individual chapters devoted to specific religions of the world have been carefully designed to provide basic historical background information, summaries of the central beliefs of currently practiced religions, information about what is, at least, surmised about the core beliefs of ancient and prehistoric peoples, and introductions to the traditional arts and visual expressions associated with these beliefs. Each chapter might thus be read alone as a self-sufficient unit, and all chapters are equipped with ample suggestions for additional reading.

However, the overall goal of this study has not been to discuss and present the world's religions and their visual manifestations as simply a series of disparate and unrelated phenomena. Sacred art has been described as "the bridge between the material and spiritual worlds . . . inseparable from the particular religion to which it is connected."[2] Accordingly, an understanding of the world's religious art requires knowledge of the unique features of specific faith systems. At the same time, however, all religious art, in all of its celebrated diversity and uniqueness, serves shared purposes. The forms of art may be different indeed, but the creation and use of religious art, generally, serves to unify rather than divide world cultures. It is hoped that attentive readers will find many more connections between the world's religions and their arts than strange or discomforting divergences between them. Careful study and the development of visual sensitivity to diverse faith traditions requires a willingness to see that religious art, in all its forms, serves to provide a crucial and shared entranceway into understanding others and ourselves.

Such understanding is also an ongoing process, continually enlivened by the fact that, for example, new archaeological discoveries are perpetually being made, and new theories about human history and cultures continue to be proposed.[3] Barely a week passes now without the announcement of major and exciting new archaeological finds from around the globe.[4] Many of these ongoing discoveries not only challenge the traditional parameters and chronological dating ranges for the oldest evidence of human activities on earth, but also serve to greatly expand the growing range of material data associated with the world's belief systems, their practices, and their visual expressions.

The religions of the world have continued to grow, evolve, and expand also. Newer forms of artistic expression as well as reinterpretations of older visual traditions continually demonstrate the significance and vitality of the world's religions and their diverse, vibrant, and related forms of art. It is hoped that the wide-ranging examples and modes discussed in these volumes have provided readers with an increased awareness of the diversity as well as the unity in the world's faith traditions and that study of the world religions will, as per Gandhi, continue to be an enriching experience.

NOTES

1. Mahatma Gandhi, *Young India*, September 2, 1926.

2. Seyyed Nasr, *Islamic Art and Spirituality* (Albany: State University of New York Press, 1987), 68.

3. Brian Fagan, ed. *Discovery! Unearthing the New Treasures of Archaeology* (London: Thames and Hudson, 2007).

4. Updates are constantly available on Web sites such as *Science Daily*, http://www.sciencedaily.com, and *Archaeology*, http://www.archaeology.org/.

Selected Bibliography

The Bibliography and Further Reading suggestions found at the conclusion of each chapter include general works as well as specialized studies of specific relevance for the materials covered in the individual chapters. The following list represents a selection of general works of overall interest for the study of the art and architecture of the world's religions.

Print Resources

Adams, Doug, and Diane Apostolos-Cappadona, eds. *Art as Religious Studies*. New York: Crossroad, 1987.

Bowker, John. *The Cambridge Illustrated History of Religions*. Cambridge: Cambridge University Press, 2002.

Brown, Frank. *Good Taste, Bad Taste, and Christian Taste: Aesthetics in Religious Life*. Oxford: Oxford University Press, 2000.

Burenhult, Gören, ed. *Traditional Peoples Today: Continuity and Change in the Modern World*. San Francisco: Harper San Francisco, 1994.

Coleman, Simon, and John Elsner. *Pilgrimage: Past and Present in the World Religions*. Cambridge, MA: Harvard University Press, 1995.

Coogan, Michael, ed. *The Illustrated Guide to World Religions*. New York: Oxford University Press, 2003.

Cotterell, Arthur, and Rachel Storm. *The Ultimate Encyclopedia of Mythology*. London: Hermes House, 1999.

Dikovitskaya, Margaret. *Visual Culture: The Study of the Visual After the Cultural Turn*. Cambridge, MA: The MIT Press, 2005.

Di Leonardo, Micaela, ed. *Gender at the Crossroads of Knowledge: Feminist Anthropology in the Post-Modern Era*. Berkeley: University of California Press, 1991.

Dixon, John. "Art as the Making of the World: Outline of Method in the Criticism of Religion and Art." *Journal of the American Academy of Religion* 51, no. 1 (1983): 15–36.

Dixon, John. "What Makes Religious Art Religious?" *Cross Currents* 43, no. 1 (1993): 5–25.

Edson, Gary. *Masks and Masking: Faces of Tradition and Belief Worldwide*. Jefferson, NC: McFarland, 2005.

Eliade, Mircea. *Symbolism, the Sacred, and the Arts*, ed. Diane Apostolos-Cappadona. New York: Crossroad, 1985.

Elkins, James. *On the Strange Place of Religion in Contemporary Art*. New York: Routledge, 2004.

Elkins, James. *Visual Studies: A Skeptical Introduction*. New York: Routledge, 2003.

Fagan, Brian. *Discovery! Unearthing the New Treasures of Archaeology*. London: Thames and Hudson, 2007.

Fagan, Brian. *From Black Land to Fifth Sun: The Science of Sacred Sites*. Reading, MA: Addison-Wesley, 1998.

Fisher, Mary. *Living Religions*. Upper Saddle River, NJ: Prentice-Hall, 2002.

Freedberg, David. *The Power of Images: Studies in the History and Theory of Response*. Chicago: University of Chicago Press, 1989.

Halifax, John. *Shaman: The Wounded Healer*. London: Thames and Hudson, 1982.

Harpur, James. *The Atlas of Sacred Places: Meeting Points of Heaven and Earth*. New York: Henry Holt, 1994.

Heller, Ena, ed. *Reluctant Partners: Art and Religion in Dialogue*. New York: American Bible Society, 2004.

Jestice, Phyllis, ed. *Holy People of the World: A Cross-Cultural Encyclopedia*, 3 vols. Santa Barbara, CA: ABC-CLIO, 2004.

Johnston, Sarah, ed. *Religions of the Ancient World: A Guide*. Cambridge, MA: Belknap Press, 2004.

Jones, Lindsay. *The Hermeneutics of Sacred Architecture*, 2 vols. Cambridge, MA: Harvard University Press, 2000.

Kleiner, Fred, Christine Mamiya, and Richard Tansey. *Gardner's Art through the Ages*. Fort Worth, TX: Harcourt College Publishers, 2001.

Korp, Maureen. *Sacred Art of the Earth: Ancient and Contemporary Earthworks*. New York: Continuum, 1997.

Littleton, C. Scott, ed. *Eastern Wisdom: An Illustrated Guide to the Religions and Philosophies of the East*. New York: Henry Holt, 1996.

Lundquist, John. *The Temple: Meeting Place of Heaven and Earth*. London: Thames and Hudson, 1993.

Mack, John, ed. *Masks and the Art of Expression*. New York: Harry N. Abrams, 1994.

Mann, A. T. *Sacred Architecture*. Shaftesbury, Dorset: Element Books, 1993.

Mithen, Steven. *The Prehistory of the Mind: A Search for the Origins of Art, Religion, and Science*. London: Thames and Hudson, 1996.

Matthews, John, ed. *The World Atlas of Divination*. Boston, MA: Bulfinch Press, 1992.

Moffett, Marian, Michael Fazio, and Lawrence Wodehouse. *A World History of Architecture*. Boston, MA: McGraw Hill, 2004.

Moore, Albert. *Iconography of Religions: An Introduction*. Philadelphia: Fortress Press, 1977.

Morgan, David. *The Sacred Gaze: Religious Visual Culture in Theory and Practice*. Berkeley: University of California Press, 2005.

Morgan, David. *Visual Piety: A History and Theory of Popular Religious Images*. Berkeley: University of California Press, 1998.

Morgan, David. "Visual Religion." *Religion* 30, no. 1 (2000): 41–53.

Nunley, John, and Cara McCarty. *Masks: Faces of Culture*. New York: Harry N. Abrams, 1999.

Paine, Crispin, ed. *Godly Things: Museums, Objects and Religion*. London: Leicester University Press, 2000.

Pfeiffer, John. *The Creative Explosion: An Inquiry into the Origins of Art and Religion*. Ithaca, NY: Cornell University Press, 1985.

Plate, S. Brent, ed. *Religion, Art and Visual Culture: A Cross-Cultural Reader*. New York: Palgrave, 2002.

Severy, Merle, ed. *Great Religions of the World*. Washington, D.C.: National Geographic Society, 1978.

Sharma, Arvind, ed. *Religion and Women*. Albany: State University of New York Press, 1994.

Sharma, Arvind, and Katherine Young, eds. *Her Voice, Her Faith: Women Speak on World Religions*. Boulder, CO: Westview Press, 2003.

Smith, Huston. *The Illustrated World's Religions*. San Francisco: Harper San Francisco, 1986.

Soltes, Ori. *Our Sacred Signs: How Jewish, Christian, and Muslim Art Draw from the Same Sources*. Boulder, CO: Westview Press, 2005.

Super, John, and Briane Turley. *Religion in World History*. New York: Routledge, 2002.

Wilson, Colin. *The Atlas of Holy Places and Sacred Sites*. New York: DK Publishing, 1996.

Web Resources

There are abundant resources easily accessible on the World Wide Web relevant for all areas of this study. Many major museums have excellent Web sites that include information on various world cultures, time lines of art history, and specific works of art. The following is simply a sampling of some of the resources available.

Archaeology: http://www.archaeology.org
Art History Resources on the Web: http://witcombe.sbc.edu/
The British Museum, London: http://www.britishmuseum.org
Christian Iconography: http://www.aug.edu/augusta/iconography/
Christus Rex: http://www.christusrex.org/
The Internet Sacred Text Archive: http://www.sacred-texts.com/
The Labyrinth: Resources for Medieval Studies: http://labyrinth.georgetown.edu/
The Louvre Museum, Paris: http://www.louvre.fr
Metropolitan Museum of Art, New York: http://www.metmuseum.org/
National Gallery of Art, Washington, D.C.: http://www.nga.gov
Religion On Line: http://www.religion-online.org/
Religious Resources: http://www.religiousresources.org/
Sacred Destinations: http://www.sacred-destinations.com/
Virtual Religion Index: http://www.virtualreligion.net

Index

A'a, 149

Abbas, Shah, 253, 257

Aboriginal cultures, 9–10, 150–53

Abraham, 30, 195, 198, 213, 245–46, 248, 250, 258

Abu Bakr al-Asamm, 246

Adam, 245–46, 248

Adena culture, 132

Aeneid of Virgil, 73

Afterlife, concepts of: in ancient Egypt, 52, 55–58, 60, 66–67; in ancient Greece and Rome, 79; in ancient Mesopotamia, 32; in Christianity, 226; in Mesoamerican cultures, 108; in prehistory, 8, 11. *See also* Death, Immortality, Reincarnation

Ahk, 58

Ahu, 156, 163–64. *See also* Altars

Ahu Tongariki, Easter Island, 164

Akhenaten, 53–54

Akua Ma figurines, 185–86

Al-Aqsa Mosque. *See* Jerusalem, Israel: al-Aqsa Mosque

Alchemy: in African religions, 176; in Taoism, 318, 320, 321, 327

Ali ibn Abi Talib, 246

Allah, 201, 245, 348, 250, 256–58

Altars, examples: in African indigenous religions, 181; in ancient Greece and Rome, 80, 84; in Chinese and Confucian traditions, 330, 342, 349; in Christianity, 228, 233–34; in Judaism, 200, 202; in Native American religious practices, 127, 134; in Oceania, 156; in prehistory, 15, 16, 18; in Vedic and Hindu practices, 278. *See also* Ahu, Sacrifice, Offerings

Amaterasu, 361–62, 368

Ambrose, Saint, 223

Amida Buddha. *See* Amitabha Buddha

Amitabha Buddha, 305, 361

Amulets, 32, 125, 366. *See also* Shamans and shamanism

Amun/Amun-Ra, 62, 65

Analects of Confucius. *See* Confucius, *Analects of*

Anasazi culture, 125

Ancestors and ancestral spirits, veneration of: in African traditions, 175, 179, 186; in Chinese traditions, 338–40, 350; in Mesoamerica, 108–9; in Native American practices, 130–31, 139; in Oceania, 150, 152, 158, 160–61; in prehistory, 5; in Shinto, 358, 362

Angels, 200, 235, 237, 262. *See also* Gabriel, Michael

Anglicans, 234

Animal sacrifice. *See* Sacrifice, animal

Index

About the Author

LESLIE ROSS is Professor and Chair of Art History, Dominican University of California. She is the author of *Artists of the Middle Ages* (Greenwood 2003), *Medieval Art: A Topical Dictionary* (Greenwood 1996), and *Text, Image, Message: Saints in Medieval Manuscript Illustrations* (Greenwood 1994).